Library of
Davidson College

Foundations of Communication
Library Edition

Editors
Roland Posner and Georg Meggle

A. P. Martinich

Communication and Reference

Walter de Gruyter · Berlin · New York
1984

Library of Congress Cataloging in Publication Data

Martinich, Aloysius.
   Communication and reference.

(Foundations of communication)
Bibliography: p.
Includes index.
   1. Languages – Philosophy. 2. Reference (Linguistics)
3. Reference (Philosophy) I. Title. II. Series.
P106.M359   1984   401   84-14283
ISBN 3-11-010067-3 (lib. bdg.)

CIP-Kurztitelaufnahme der Deutschen Bibliothek

Martinich, Aloysius P.:
Communication and reference / A. P. Martinich. – Berlin ; New York : de Gruyter, 1984.
   (Foundations of communication : Library ed.)
ISBN 3-11-010067-3

© Copyright 1984 by Walter de Gruyter & Co., Berlin 30
Printed in Germany
Alle Rechte des Nachdrucks, der photomechanischen Wiedergabe, der Herstellung von Photokopien – auch auszugsweise – vorbehalten.
Satz und Druck: Arthur Collignon GmbH, Berlin
Buchbinder: Lüderitz & Bauer, Berlin

For Avrum Stroll

Preface

The most widely discussed issue in the philosophy of language during the twentieth century is reference: What is it? Under what conditions does it occur? And, given that something is referred to, what determines what object gets referred to? Because the answers to these questions are so varied and contested, the issue of reference deserves to be called the problem of reference. Most attempts to solve this problem have been semantic solutions, that is, solutions cast in terms of the meanings of words or sentences. Bertrand Russell, for example, identified the meaning of a word with its referent.

I believe that such attempted solutions to the basic issues concerning reference must fail because the problem of reference cannot be solved by semantic methods; for reference is not a semantic phenomenon. It is rather a pragmatic phenomenon, one relating to what people do with words and not to what property words have in themselves. Another way to say the same thing is to say that reference is one small part of linguistic communication. Hence to fully understand what reference is one must understand what linguistic communication is and what part reference plays in it. This explains why this book is divided into two parts. The claim that the problem of reference is solvable within a theory of pragmatics or linguistic communication is hollow if it is not clear what such a theory might look like. Thus, Part I: "Communication" gives a general sketch of a theory of linguistic communication, which, because the theory is rather new, is not wholly adequate; nonetheless, it is, I think, on the way to adequacy. Part II: "Reference" presents a solution to the problem of reference within the context of the general theory developed in Part I. It also uses that general theory to refute rival semantic theories and to present alternative explanations for the phenomena discussed there.

There are other reasons for Part I. There is no clear exposition of H. P. Grice's work available to either philosophers or nonphilosophers; and no one seems to have seen how much the work of Grice is of a piece with that of J. L. Austin, John Searle and P. F. Strawson. Part I, then, is the first attempt to present, in a necessarily tentative form, a unified theory of linguistic communication in which Grice's theory of conversation and his theory of non-natural meaning take their place with Austin's and Searle's theory of speech acts.

Part I consists of six chapters. The first of these, *Chapter Two: A General Theory of Linguistic Communication*, describes the most general concepts of conversation: these include specifying the place that conversation has within a general theory of communication and the most general principles regulating the production and interpretation of conversation, "the conversational maxims." *Chapter Three: Speech Acts: Saying and Doing* discusses the most prominent part of linguistic communication, what a speaker says. In this chapter I sketch the theories of Austin and Searle. *Chapter Four: The Total Content of What a Speaker Communicates* explains the different parts that go to make up the content of a linguistically conveyed message. *Chapter Five: Metaphor* applies the theory of conversation developed in the earlier chapters to the concept of metaphor. *Chapter Six: Logical Applications of the Theory of Conversation* discusses two problems in the philosophy of logic: the classification of informal fallacies and the meaning of the logical constants. *Chapter Seven: Utterer's Meaning and Communication* concentrates on the utterer's role in communication in order to describe what communication consists of.

Part II consists of four chapters. *Chapter Eight: Russell on Reference and Descriptions* describes Russell's view that the meaning of a word is the object it directly denotes or refers to and his theory of descriptions. *Chapter Nine: A Speech Act Theory of Referring* describes Strawson's criticisms of Russell's view that reference is a semantic notion and contains an analysis of referring as a pragmatic notion. *Chapter Ten: The Attributive Use and The Speech Act Theory of Referring* argues that Keith Donnellan's distinction between the referential and attributive use is specious and that all the examples that he claims are instances of the attributive use are in fact cases of the referential use. *Chapter Eleven: The Causal and Descriptive Theories of Reference* discusses the views of Donnellan and Saul Kripke on the issue of what determines what objects gets referred to given that reference occurs.

Why is reference so important in the philosophy of language? Although part of its importance is due to the fact that reference is one of the most conspicuous, pervasive and prominent things that speakers do with language, this alone cannot explain why reference has been of paramount importance. For predication and stating, to take just two other things that speakers do with language, are, plausibly, equally conspicuous, pervasive and prominent. What makes reference stand out is the fact that philosophers have believed that it is in virtue of reference that language attaches to the world. And this belief is important because a language-world connection seems fundamental to the possibility of truth; if language is in no way attached to the world, then, it seems, nothing we say could be true about the world; and what philosophical concern is more fundamental than that?

The Introduction is meant to be truly introductory. I try to explain the importance of the philosophy of language and to give my view about the nature of philosophy.

Many people commented on various parts of this book at various stages of its composition. To all of them, my thanks. Two people deserve special mention. John David Stone made extensive stylistic suggestions and contributed several arguments to an early version, of which Chapters One through Three and Seven through Ten survive. Jo Ann Carson, who read the final two drafts pointed out many infelicities and made a number of other helpful remarks.

Part of Chapter Ten, section I, originally appeared as "The Attributive Use of Proper Names," in *Analysis* vol. 37 (1977). I want to thank the editors of the *Philosophical Quarterly* for allowing me to use the material from my article, "A Theory of Conversation and Some Philosophical Problems," *Philosophical Quarterly* vol. 30 (1980), in Chapter Two; and Julius Groos Verlag for allowing me to reprint my article "A Theory for Metaphor," *Journal of Literary Semantics* vol. 13 (1984), in Chapter Five.

Table of Contents

Preface VII

INTRODUCTION

Chapter One: Introduction 3
  I. Why Study Philosophy of Language? 3
  II. Linguistics and the Philosophy of Language 7
  III. The Philosophy of Language and the Philosophy of Communication 9

PART I: COMMUNICATION

Chapter Two: General Conventions Governing Conversation: The Cooperative Principle and Conversational Maxims 17
  I. The Elements of Communication 17
  II. The Two Sides of Communication 18
  III. Conversation 19
  IV. Maxims of Quantity 22
  V. Maxims of Quality 24
  VI. Maxims of Relation 26
  VII. Maxims of Manner 30
  VIII. Interim Summary 31
  IX. Nonfulfillment of Maxims 32
  X. Violating a Maxim 33
  XI. Opting Out of a Maxim 36
  XII. Flouting a Maxim 36
  XIII. Conversational Implicatures 37
  XIV. Moore's Paradox 39

Chapter Three: Speech Acts: Saying and Doing 43
  I. Saying and Meaning 43
  II. Performative Verbs 45
  III. Locutionary, Illocutionary, and Perlocutionary Acts 48
  IV. Analyses of Three Illocutionary Acts 52
  V. Categories of Illocutionary Acts 56

Chapter Four: The Total Content of What a Speaker Linguistically Communicates 63
  I. Grice on the Total Content of What a Speaker Communicates . 63
  II. What a Speaker Expresses and What He Implies 66

III. What a Speaker Expresses or Implies: Force 67
   IV. What a Speaker Indicates by Contrastive Stress 69
    V. What a Speaker Indicates by Tone 70
   VI. What a Speaker Indicates by Tense 71
  VII. What a Speaker Indicates by Adverbial Force-Words 71
 VIII. What a Speaker Indicates by Mood 72
   IX. Other Possible Indicative Elements 76
    X. An Outline of the Total Content of What a Speaker Communicates 76
   XI. The Content of What a Speaker Expresses at the Mad Hatter's Tea Party 77

Chapter Five: Metaphor 79
    I. A Theory for Metaphor 79
   II. Analysis of a Metaphor 81
  III. Metaphor and Other Figures of Speech 85
   IV. Nonstandard Metaphors 86
    V. Generalizing the Theory 89
   VI. Reply to Objections to a Pragmatic Theory of Metaphor 90
  VII. A Comparison with Searle's Theory of Metaphor 92

Chapter Six: Applications to Problems in Logic 95
    I. The Problem of a Taxonomy for Informal Fallacies 95
   II. The Taxonomy 96
  III. Maxims without Fallacies 97
   IV. Maxims with Fallacies 98
    V. The Relation of a Standard Taxonomy to the New One . . . 102
   VI. Violating a Maxim 102
  VII. Formalism and Informalism 103
 VIII. Conjunction and a Maxim of Manner 105
   IX. Conditionals and a Maxim of Relation 107
    X. Disjunction and a Maxim of Quantity 109

Chapter Seven: Utterer's Meaning and Communication 113
    I. Communicative and Non-Communicative Meaning 113
   II. Grice's Analysis of Communicative Meaning 115
  III. Strawson's Critique of Grice's Analysis 118
   IV. Searle's Purported Counterexample 122
    V. Four Notions of Meaning 125
   VI. Utterance Meaning and Timeless Meaning 127

PART II. REFERENCE

Chapter Eight: Reference, Existence and Descriptions 133
    I. The Paradox of Reference and Existence 133
   II. Is Word-Meaning or Sentence-Meaning Primary? 134

        III. A Russellian Referential Semantics 137
        IV. Russell's Theory of Indefinite Descriptions 141
        V. Russell's Theory of Definite Descriptions 143
        VI. Russell's Solution to the Paradox of Reference and Existence 147
Chapter Nine: A Speech Act Theory of Referring 149
        I. Strawson's Critique of Russell 149
        II. Presupposition, Entailment and Implication 151
        III. The Axiom of Existence 153
        IV. Referring: The Speaker and the Hearer 158
        V. An Analysis of Paradigmatic Reference 163
        VI. An Analysis of Successful Reference 166
Chapter Ten: The Attributive Use and The Speech Act Theory of
        Referring 169
        I. A Distinction in Search of a Characterization 169
        II. Purported Examples of the Attributive Use 173
        III. Alternative Analyses of These Examples 177
Chapter Eleven: The Causal and Description Theories of Reference . . 181
        I. Donnellan's Causal Theory of Reference 181
        II. The Description Theory 182
        III. Donnellan's Counterexamples to the Description Theory 183
        IV. Kripke's Causal Theory of Names 186
        V. Fixing the Referent of a Name 188
        VI. The Olympian Description Theory of Reference 189
Bibliography 193
Index 203

Introduction

Chapter One: Introduction

I. Why Study Philosophy of Language?

Why should philosophers (or human beings in their leisurely reflective moments) be interested in thinking about language? There are at least four reasons: First, by thinking about language we might learn something about ourselves, about what it is to be human. Second, certain conceptual puzzles and confusions arise from mistaken beliefs about linguistic structures and functions; we can solve these difficulties, or avoid them entirely, if we understand the nature of language. Third, language may provide clues to the basic structure of reality. Fourth, one might naturally be interested in thinking about language for its own sake. Let's consider each of these reasons for studying language philosophically.

(1) Aristotle proposed a definition of man that is usually translated, "Man is a rational animal." But the sense of the original Greek is really that man is the animal that has a language. No other species, however close biologically, possesses this trait; it is debatable whether any other species *could* possess it.

You might think that Aristotle's definition of man is incorrect, or even that experiments on language acquisition in chimpanzees have scientifically disproved it. The social scientists who have conducted such experiments have concluded that chimpanzees can learn languages; yet most linguists and philosophers, fully aware of the results of the experiments, would reject this conclusion. This seeming dispute between some social scientists on one hand and linguists and philosophers on the other can be resolved by distinguishing two sense of the word 'language'. Social scientists apply this word to any system of symbols, that is, any complex behavioral pattern in which one object, such as a sound, is used to represent another, or to achieve some effect in a non-natural way. In other words, an animal has a language if it has a system of communication. Linguists and philosophers, on the other hand, use the word 'language' in a different (and stronger) sense. They agree with the social scientists in holding that every language is a symbol system, but they require an additional characteristic: In order to qualify as a language, a symbol system must make use of recursive rules that specify both how to construct simple sentences and how to construct structurally more complex sentences from simple ones, thereby generating an infinite number of sentences from a finite vocabulary. Although social scientists say that chimpanzees have language, they agree that the symbol systems that chimpanzees have been taught to use do not have the additional charateristic that the linguists and philosophers require; there are only finitely many sentences in a chimphanzee "language."

Thus the apparent disagreement between social scientists and philosophers is resolved by pointing out that the word 'language' is equivocal, and that each group uses it in a different sense. Many disputes are like this; people often think that they disagree when in fact they are only using words differently. Hence it is important for the two parties in a dispute (or even in an agreement) to be clear about the meanings of the words they use. The meaning of a word is not a trivial matter that can be dismissed as "just a question of semantics"; questions of semantics *must be settled*, since the very intelligibility of the discussion depends upon a common understanding of the words that make it up.

Both philosophers and social scientists often conflate language and communication (naturally enough since they apply 'language' to any system of communication); but even apart from the question whether a system of communication that lacks recursive rules is a language, it is important to distinguish the activity (communication) from the instrument or technique that makes that activity possible (language). We shall see in section III that the philosophical approaches to communication and to language differ in important ways.

(2) By studying language philosophically, we may solve certain conceptual puzzles that arise from mistaken beliefs about linguistic structures. This approach to philosophy was recommended by the twentieth-century philosopher Ludwig Wittgenstein and developed by several schools of his followers. In the following passages from his *Tractatus Locigo-philosophicus*, Wittgenstein states the position with his usual force and concision:

> Language disguises thought. So much so, that from the outward form of the clothing it is impossible to infer the form of the thought beneath it, because the outward form of the clothing is not designed to reveal the form of the body, but for entirely different purposes. . . . Most of the propositions and questions to be found in philosophical works are not false but nonsensical. Consequently, we cannot give any answer to questions of this kind, but can only point out that they are nonsensical. Most of the propositions and questions of philosophers arise from our failures to understand the logic of our language. . . . All philosophy is a critique of language. . . . It was Russell who performed the service of showing that the apparent logical form of a proposition need not be its real one. . . . A philosophical work consists essentially of elucidations. . . . Philosophy does not result in 'philosophical propositions', but rather in the clarification of propositions (Wittgenstein (1922), 4.002, 4.003, 4.0031, 4.112).

Thus Wittgenstein holds that most philosophical issues simply vanish when our preconceived notions about the forms of propositions are corrected. He mentions Russell, whose theory of descriptions was an early paradigm of the kind of "critique of language" Wittgenstein is talking about. (We shall encounter this theory in Chapter Eight.) The same view underlies this passage from Gilbert Ryle's "Systematically Misleading Expressions":

> The gist of what I want to establish is this. There are many expressions which occur in non-philosophical discourse which, though they are perfectly clearly understood by those who use them and those who hear or read them, are nevertheless couched in grammatical or syntactical forms which are in a demonstrable way improper to the states of affairs which they record (or the alleged states of affairs which they profess to record). Such expressions can be reformulated and for philosophy but not for non-philosophical discourse must be reformulated into expressions of which the syntactical form is proper to the facts recorded (or the alleged facts alleged to be recorded) (Ryle (1932), pp. 15–16).

(3) If language sometimes distorts or misrepresents the facts it expresses, one must assume that it sometimes represents them accurately, or at least that it is possible for a language to contain appropriate syntactical forms. In a way, this idea complements the position taken by Ryle in the passage just quoted. Thus, many philosophers and non-philosophers alike hold that language somehow reflects reality. For example, Donald Davidson has argued that

> in sharing a language, in whatever sense this is required for communication, we share a picture of the world that must, in its large features, be true. It follows that in making manifest the large features of our language, we make manifest the large features of reality. One way of pursuing metaphysics is therefore to study the general structures of our language (Davidson (1977), p. 244; see also Strawson (1974), pp. 4, 13–14).

Even if Davidson's brisk argument is not sound, it is nonetheless tempting, and not implausible, to think that if one is unable to study the structure of reality directly, and if one is able to determine the structure of language, then one can simply read off the structure of reality from the structure of language. We find this belief in Plato, who has Socrates tell a charming story about how he got into philosophy and how he came to do philosophy in the way he did. Socrates says, "When I was young . . . I became very keen on this learning which they call 'physical' philosophy [that is, natural science]. It seemed to me a wonderful sort of study, to know the causes of everything, why each thing comes into being and why it perishes and why it exists" (*Phaedo*, 96 A–B). Socrates then explains his failure to find answers to these questions in Anaxagoras' scientific theory. Anaxagoras' bold declaration that all is Mind (with a capital M) appealed to Socrates and raised his hopes; but the consequent theory made little use of this inspiring premise, and Socrates believed that as a result it failed to demonstrate the rational structure of the universe. He continues:

> I decided after this . . . when I had failed in my study of things, that I must beware of experiencing what those who look at and study the sun during an eclipse experience. Some of them are dazzled or blinded if they don't look at its

> reflection in water or something of the sort. That was roughly my idea; I was afraid that my soul might be utterly blinded if I regarded things with the eyes and tried to grasp them with each of the senses. I decided that I should take refuge in language, and study the truth of things by means of it. (*Phaedo*, 99 D – 100 A).

In short, Socrates turned to language because he thought that, since language reflects reality, it would have the same structure; and since he had made no progress in understanding the nature of reality by studying it directly, he might make progress by studying it indirectly through language.

The same idea comes up again and again in the history of philosophy. For instance, John of Salisbury, a twelfth-century thinker, said that "language imitates nature, from which it partly derives its origins. Furthermore, it tends, as far as possible, to conform to nature in all respects" (*Metalogicon* I.14). Philosophical grammarians, guided by this belief, correlated grammatical categories (parts of speech) with metaphysical categories whenever they could:

Grammatical category	*Metaphysical category*
noun	substance
active verb	action (acting)
passive verb	passion (being acted upon)
adjective	quality
adverb	time and place
preposition	relation

Such correspondences were the basis for a whole philosophical school in the fourteenth century; the movement was called "speculative grammar," from the Latin word 'speculum', which means "mirror." The premise was that language is a mirror of reality.

In more recent times this premise has been substantially changed, and in some ways weakened, as a result of the arguments of Immanuel Kant (1724–1804) and his followers. Kant argued persuasively that we have no direct access to reality and that our beliefs about reality are mediated by our innate conceptual scheme (or, in a materialistic version, by the structure of our brains). If this is so, we cannot use language as a guide to reality as it is in itself; but at least we can use it as a guide to our own conceptual scheme, which constitutes the phenomenal world (that is, reality as we perceive it). The most distinguished exponent of the post-Kantian view of language is P. F. Strawson; see his *Individuals* (1959) and *The Bound of Sense* (1964 a). A more recent example is Zeno Vendler's *Res Cogitans* (1972 a). Not everyone, however, was so strongly influenced by Kant. Wittgenstein, for example, who came to philosophy from engineering and cared little for the history of philosophy, said, "To give the essence of a proposition means to give the essence of all description, and thus the essence of the world" (Wittgenstein (1922), 5.4711). It is still possible to maintain that at bottom language and reality are similar in structure.

(4) There is of course nothing to say by way of justification for the claim that one might be interested in thinking about language for its own sake; that is part of what it means to be interested in something for its own sake. This motive, however, should not be ignored, nor its strength underestimated; although idle curiosity is not quite a distinctive characteristic of human beings, it too tells us something about what it is to be human.

II. Linguistics and the Philosophy of Language

The philosophy of language can be broadly defined as the study of the *structure* and *use* of language. There are many linguists (that is, linguistic scientists) who would describe their own work in the same way; linguistics and the philosophy of language overlap, both in theory and in practice. For instance, there are many anthologies that contain papers by philosophers and linguists in roughly equal numbers (Fodor and Katz (1964), Steinberg and Jacobovits (1971), Davidson and Harman (1975), Cole and Morgan (1975), and Cole (1978), among many others). Some journals, such as *Foundations of Language* and *Philosophy and Linguistics*, are designed to serve authors and readers in both groups. At MIT, there is a single department of philosophy and linguistics; and at other institutions there are some professors who have joint appointments in linguistics and philosophy.

What is the basis for this fusion of disciplines? The relation between linguistics and the philosophy of language is in many ways parallel to the relations that other, older sciences had at one time to other branches of philosophy. Unlike Athena, a science does not spring full-grown from the head of Zeus; it develops from an embryonic stage of muddle, confusion, and obscurity. Science arises when much of the muddle, confusion, and obscurity of our concepts about a certain range of phenomena has been dissipated, and it becomes possible to formulate fairly general theses that can be confirmed or refuted experimentally. The muddle, confusion, and obscurity are philosophy.

There are more charitable ways of stating this point. Philosophy is the *struggle to eliminate* muddle, confusion, and obscurity; and, when it is done right, it succeeds. In other words, philosophy is the mother of sciences. Philosophers as different as Bertrand Russell and J. L. Austin have held the same view. In his *Introduction to Mathematical Philosophy*, Bertrand Russell puts it this way:

> Much of what is set forth in the following chapters is not properly to be called "philosophy," though the matters concerned were included in philosophy so long as no satisfactory science of them existed. The nature of infinity and continuity, for example, belonged in former days to philosophy, but belongs now to mathematics. Mathematical philosophy, in the strict sense, cannot, perhaps be

held to include such definite scientific results as have been obtained in this region; the philosophy of mathematics will naturally be expected to deal with questions on the frontier of knowledge, as to which comparative certainty is not yet attained (Russell (1919), p. xi).

It is also worth quoting Austin at some length on the same topic:

Reflecting on the arguments in this lecture, we may well ask ourselves whether they might not be assigned to grammar as to philosophy: and this, I think, is a salutary question to end on. There are constant references in contemporary philosophy, which notoriously is much concerned with language, to a 'logical grammar' and a 'logical syntax' as though these were things distinct from ordinary grammarian's grammar and syntax: and certainly they do seem, whatever exactly they may be, different from traditional grammar. But grammar today is itself in a state of flux; for fifty years or more it has been questioned on all hands and counts whether what Dionysius Thrax once thought was the truth about Greek is the truth and the whole truth about all language and all languages. Do we know, then, that there will prove to be any ultimate boundary between 'logical grammar' and a revised and enlarged *Grammar*? In the history of human inquiry, philosophy has the place of the initial central sun, seminal and tumultuous: from time to time it throws off some portion of itself to take station as a science, a planet, cool and well regulated, progressing steadily towards a distant final state. This happened long ago at the birth of mathematics, and again at the birth of physics: only in the last century we have witnessed the same process once again, slow and at the time almost imperceptible, in the birth of the science of mathematical logic, through the joint labours of philosophers and mathematicians. Is it not possible that the next century may see the birth, through the joint labours of philosophers, grammarians, and numerous other students of language, of a true and comprehensive science of language? Then we shall have rid ourselves of one more part of philosophy (there will still be plenty left) in the only way we ever can get rid of philosophy, by kicking it upstairs. (Austin, (1956a) pp. 231–232).

Philosophy is an odd kind of mother. The mothers of human offspring are human; the mothers of swinish offspring are swinish; but the mother of sciences is not a science. This is where the metaphor breaks down; but it is also consistent with what is often also said about philosophy: that it is either above or below the sciences, but not one of them (Wittgenstein (1922), 4.111).

Typically those who are revered as the founders of sciences were philosophers who made it possible for others to be scientists. Thus Aristotle was one of the founders of biology; Leibniz, independently of Newton, discovered the infinitesimal calculus; Descartes did much of the basic work in analytic geometry, which made it possible to change mathematics from a science confined by the geometrical categories in which virtually all the useful results were phrased into a liberated, mainly algebraic discipline; Adam Smith, one of the founders of economics, was first professor of logic and later professor of moral philosophy at Glasgow; and Franz Brentano, professor of philosophy at Vienna, and William James, professor of philosophy at Harvard, were among the founders of empirical psychology.

Philosophers of language continue this tradition. In *Syntactic Structures,* the revolutionary book which first announced the grammatical theory that currently dominates linguistics, transformational grammar, Noam Chomsky acknowledges the influence of only three people, two of whom are philosophers of language (Nelson Goodman and W. V. Quine). And Chomsky himself is in many respects as much a philosopher as a linguist; Dell Hymes summarized Chomsky's relations to philosophy and linguistics thus:

> In his earlier period, he applied philosophy to linguistics, and the later period he applied linguistics to philosophy. In the first period he brought philosophy of science to bear in a critical way, and mathematical logic in a constructive way, together liberating linguistic practice and setting new goals for it (Hymes (1972), p. 327).

Chomsky is by no means the only linguist who is indebted to philosophers of language, however. It is common practice for linguists to refer to and extend philosophical theories, especially those of J. L. Austin, Donald Davidson, H. P. Grice, and John Searle. One need only consult *Semantic Theory* by Ruth Kempson or *Semantics: Theories of Meaning* by Janet Dean Fodor to see the influence of philosophy on semantic theories in linguistics. And Peter H. Lindsay and Donald A. Norman in *Human Information Processing* virtually reproduce H. P. Grice's work in "Logic and Conversation." Since they do not acknowledge Grice's work in any way, readers may not know the source of the theory. Perhaps ignorance of the origin of doctrines is one reason that philosophical contributions to scientific theories are not better known.

In short, the relation between linguistics and the philosophy of language is that the philosopher clears and levels the ground on which the linguist raises his scientific edifice. It is natural that they should try to coordinate their efforts, and that they should work most closely together in the areas that are most muddled and confused. This book is an essay in the philosophy of language; as we shall see, it is mainly concerned with one of these muddled areas: the conventions governing linguistic communication.

III. The Philosophy of Language and the Philosophy of Communication

As we saw in section I, people often fail to distinguish language and communication. Even linguistics and philosophers of language sometimes use the the words 'language' and 'communication' as if they were synonyms, when in fact they express quite different notions. Consider, for instance, the following remarks:

(1) Language is an interpersonal phenomenon, because communication implies at least two persons or agents exchanging ideas.
(2) Language is not simply a verbal phenomenon, because we communicate with our bodies.

Sentence (1) is false; although communication does imply at least two persons or agents exchanging ideas, and is therefore an interpersonal phenomenon, it does not follow that language is also an interpersonal phenomenon. This would follow only if language were identical with (or a species of) communication. Sentence (2) is false for the same reason. The fact that some communication is non-verbal is irrelevant to the nature of language, since language and communication are not the same.

Language is one *means* of communication; it gives us a way of communicating, but it is not identical with the activity it makes possible. Communication is the transfer of messages or thoughts from one agent to another; it is one use of language among many. Language is also used to clarify one's own thoughts, to express one's emotions (perhaps in a privately written poem, which no one else ever sees or is intended to see), to rehearse one's ideas before giving a speech or a lecture (Chomsky, (1975), pp. 60—61). And language is not the only means of communication (Harman (1968), p. 71); some communication takes place without language. With a glance toward the chair upon which a gun rests, the hero, captured by the villain, lets the heroine know that she should grab it and point it at the villain. By extending his arm out from his side, a hiker indicates to his fellow traveller that he should stop. "Body language," which is not a language in the linguists' and philosophers' sense, is nevertheless a means of communication. Devices like these may or may not be conventional; even if they are, however, they are not the kinds of conventions that count as part of a language, because they are not recursive and do not make it possible to construct infinitely many expressions from a finite vocabulary.

Given this distinction between language and communication, it is possible to divide the philosophy of language into two branches, one concerned with the *structure* of language, the other with its *use*. The first branch, the older and larger of the two, may be permitted to retain the name of "philosophy of language," (now to be understood in a narrower sense); the second may be called "philosophy of linguistic communication."

The philosophy of language in the narrower sense is comprised of syntax and semantics. Syntax is the study of the configurations formed by words in grammatical sentences; the goal of syntax is to specify a finite vocabulary and to formulate recursive rules that generate all the grammatical sentences of a language and no ungrammatical ones. Semantics is the study of the meanings of words and sentences. Here one must be careful to distinguish word-meaning and sentence-meaning from what is sometimes called *speaker-meaning*, the study of which belongs to the philosophy of communication. It is notorious that what a speaker means is not always the same as what his words mean. For instance:

(1) Suppose that Tank McNamara, in one of his prodigious displays of fumblemouth, says, "You can lead a horse to drink, but you can't make him water," when he meant to say, "You can lead a horse to water, but you can't make him drink." A slip of the tongue, a *lapsus linguae*, is a case in which speaker-meaning and sentence-meaning diverge.

(2) In *The Great Dictator*, Charlie Chaplin, playing an oppressed worker who is disgusted with his condition, says disgruntledly, "This is a *fine* country." His remark is overheard by a policeman, who, understanding what Chaplin meant, promptly arrests him. Brought before the magistrate, Charlie defends himself by explaining that all he said was "This is a fine country"; and he is acquitted. What Chaplin meant when he said, "This is a *fine* country," was that the country was awful; the sentence that he uttered, however, means that the country referred to is an excellent one. Speaker-meaning and sentence-meaning diverge in cases of sarcasm.

(3) Jack is afraid that Jill might refuse his direct request to take her to the movies. He says to her, "There's a good double feature at the Roxy," which means that two highly-rated movies are playing at the Roxy Theater; but what *he* means is that he would like to take her to them. In this case, the divergence between speaker-meaning and sentence-meaning is due to indirectness.

(4) Jack says, "Can you reach the salt?" The meaning of his sentence has to do with whether the salt shaker is within the sphere of operations of the arms and hands of the person addressed; *Jack*, however, means to request that Jill pass him the salt. Jack does not say exactly what he means, perhaps in order to be polite.

So here are at least four ways in which speaker-meaning and sentence-meaning can diverge; the reader can easily imagine others. In case (1), the difference is unintentional; but more commonly, as in cases (2) through (4), the speaker makes use of some conventions that go beyond syntax and semantics in order to communicate something that is not to be found in the meanings of the words and sentences that he utters.

The study of speaker-meaning is one of the three main topics in the philosophy of linguistic communication. The second is the study of speech acts, or (as its originator, J. L. Austin, put it) the study of how to do things with words—such things as promising, swearing, christening. The third topic is the study of conversational maxims, the very general rules that are followed in all normal conversations.

What is here called the philosophy of communication is approximately the same as the discipline that was once known as pragmatics. For many years the word 'pragmatics' had a fairly definite meaning; it meant the study of the relations of signs to the persons who used them. This usage was set by Charles Morris in his *Foundations of the Theory of Signs* (1938), p. 84, wherein he also defined "syntactics" (i.e., syntax) as the study of "the formal relations of signs to one another" and semantics as the study of "the relations of signs to the objects to which the signs are applicable. This three-way distinction was widely accepted, at least within analytic philosophy; for instance, Carnap characterizes the three fields in almost precisely the same way:

> If in an investigation explicit reference is made to the speaker, or, to put it in more general terms, to the user of the language, then we assign it to the field of pragmatics. . . . If we abstract from user of the language and analyze only the expressions and their designata, we are in the field of semantics. And if finally, we abstract from the designata also and analyze only the relations between the expression, we are in (logical) syntax (Carnap (1942), p. 9).

More recently, however, a broader intellectual community has taken up the term and applied it indiscriminately to all sorts of linguistic and paralinguistic investigations; occasionally, too, it is confounded with the popular sense of the word 'pragmatic' (which usually describes a person or program that sacrifices long-term benefits to everyone in order to achieve short-term benefits to a few). It seems idle to hope that the term can be restored; it is better to start afresh.

One reason for distinguishing philosophy of language from philosophy of communication is that it gives both parties to a certain territorial dispute their own autonomous realms. Some philosophers, who do what is here called the philosophy of communication, have attempted to outlaw semantics in the philosophy of language. On the other side, some philosophers, who work in the philosophy of language in the narrower sense, have abused those who do the philosophy of communication. Both groups do valuable work and deserve to be protected from the attacks of neighboring disciplines; the only obstacle is the illusion that the two groups are competitors. In fact, however, the phenomena of language and communication are in adjacent, but different, domains. There is little real danger of poaching, since what the philosophers of language are hunting—recursive rules governing the relations of words with one another and their meaning—is of little or no importance to communication. And what the philosophers of communication are hunting—intentions and conventions that are not recursive and concern language *in use*—is of little or no importance to the philosophy of language in the narrower sense. This is not to deny the possibility or the utility of commerce between the two groups; an exchange of ideas and results can only benefit both sides, since there is a close, though perhaps con-

I Introduction

tingent, link between language and communication (cf. Lyons (1977), p. 32). The point is that this exchange is not likely to lead to a community of interests; and there is no reason why it should.

This book is a study in the philosophy of communication, and specifically in the philosophy of linguistic communication (although some of our results will carry over to non-linguistic communication as well). Part I addresses the three issues mentioned earlier as belonging to the philosophy of communication: speaker-meaning, speech acts, and conversational maxims. Part II discusses the speech act that twentieth century philosophers of language have devoted most of their energy to: referring.

Part I: Communication

Chapter Two: General Conventions Governing Conversation: the Cooperative Principle and Conversational Maxims

1. The Elements of Communication

At least three things are needed in an act of communication: a message, a sender, and a receiver. These three suffice for angels and other telepathic communicators, if there are any; human beings, however, cannot communicate with one another except through some medium that carries the message from the sender to the receiver. Despite Marshall McLuhan, we shall not identify the medium with the message.

Information scientists often add further elements to their descriptions of the act of communication, because they are interested in the eventual material construction of artificial instruments of communication or the correction of defects in natural ones. So one might mention the hardware (that is, the physical equipment) that the sender uses to transmit the message and the receiver to pick it up, the channel along which the message is sent, and the interference ("noise") that obstructs the process. Because philosophers do not have such practical worries, they seldom have to take such things into account.

For a philosophical treatment of communication in general, then, we need to consider four elements: message, sender, receiver, and medium. Different philosophers have proposed different technical terminologies for these elements. Here we use 'thought' for the message, 'utterer' for the sender, 'interpreter' for the receiver, and 'utterance' for the particular item that the utterer selects from among those available in the medium to be the vehicle of his act of communication. (The term 'thought' is taken from Frege; 'utterer' and 'utterance', from Grice.)

Since we shall be dealing primarily with linguistic communication, it is natural to think of this terminology as applying to cases in which language is the medium and the utterances in question are linguistic utterances. It would be a mistake, however, to construe it as applying *only* to such cases. 'Utterer' is not a synonym for 'speaker'; 'utterance' is not synonymous with 'linguistic utterance'. An utterer is *any* communicator; a speaker is a communicator who uses language as his medium of communication. Similarly, an utterance need not be a linguistic item. It need not even be conventional; any gesture invented for the occasion of communication might convey meaning and hence be an utterance. But even if an utterance is a conventional sign, forming part of a system of conventional signs, it is not necessarily linguistic; as we saw in Chapter One, not all symbol systems are languages. (It has been claimed that all utterances are in some sense representations. We prefer to use the term 'utterance' noncommittally.)

In refusing to restrict the word 'utterance' to linguistic items, we are following Grice, who introduces the term this way:

> I use the term 'utter' (together with 'utterance') in an artificially wide sense, to cover any case of doing x or producing x by the performance of which U [the utterer] meant that so-and-so. The performance in question need not be a linguistic or even a conventionalized performance. A specificatory replacement of the dummy 'x' will in some cases be a characterization of a deed, in others a characterization of a product (e.g. a sound) (Grice (1968), p. 55).

In another article ("Utterer's Meaning and Intentions"), he says:

> I would like, if I can, to treat meaning something by the utterance of a sentence as being only a special case of meaning something by an utterance (in my extended sense of utterance), and to treat a conventional correlation between a sentence and a specific response as providing only one of the ways in which an utterance may be correlated with a response (Grice (1969), p. 161).

The "extended sense of utterance" that Grice alludes to is explained earlier in the article: "I use the terms 'uttering' and 'utterance' in an artificially extended way, to apply to any act or performance which is or might be a candidate for nonnatural meaning" (Grice (1969), p. 151).

The main justification for our decision to follow Grice's use of these terms is that we shall in large part follow Grice's treatment of communication, and it will be easier to expound his views if we adopt his terminology. Moreover, since some of his critics have confused 'utterer' with 'speaker' and 'utterance' with 'sentence' in precisely the way that the passages just quoted were intended to prevent, it is important to stick with the terminology simply to drive home the point about it.

Finally, Grice's extension of the sense of 'utter' is by no means as artificial as his modest remarks suggest. If we lean a bit on etymology, we shall see that an utterer is one who makes something outer, and language is just one way of "outering" what is inner, namely, the thought. Grice's terminology preserves the generality of this root meaning.

II. The Two Sides of Communication

There are two sides to an act of communication, the utterer's side and the interpreter's side. Ideally, the two sides understand the utterance in the same way, that is, the utterer means precisely what the interpreter understands him to mean. But this ideal is not always achieved; there are several ways in which a particular act can fall short of the ideal.

Let us call the meaning that the interpreter ascribes to the utterer the *interpreter's meaning*. Now in some cases there is no interpreter's meaning, either because the interpreter does not recognize that the utterer intended his action to be meaningful or because, although he recognizes this intention, he cannot figure out what the utterance is supposed to mean. In such a case, no act of communication takes place, even though an utterance is produced and the utterer means something by it. The existence of the utterer's meaning is not enough to guarantee communication; unlike meaning, communication requires some uptake by the interpreter (see Austin (1955), pp. 116–117).

Secondly, there are cases in which the interpreter does ascribe some meaning to the utterer, so that there is an interpreter's meaning, but it is not the same as the utterer's meaning; the interpreter *mis*understands. Again, in such a case, an act of communication does *not* take place. Where the utterer's meaning and the interpreter's meaning diverge nothing is communicated. For the interpreter cannot receive (as a meaning) what the utterer has not sent.

Thirdly, there are ideal cases in which the utterer's meaning and the interpreter's meaning are the same; these are successful and non-defective cases of communication.

Finally, there are cases in which the utterance has a conventional meaning that does not jibe with the utterer's meaning. However, so long as the interpreter understands what the utterer meant, the act counts as a successful, albeit defective, communication.

In all of these cases, the utterer does intend to communicate something by his act; otherwise there would be no utterer's meaning with which to compare the interpreter's meaning. No communication is unintentional. It is true that a person can sometimes correctly judge the thoughts and motives that underlie someone's actions from various physiological signs — "From his tic, I knew that he was lying" —; but such judgments are not *communicated* by the utterer even though they are in some sense derived from the utterer.

To summarize: an act of communication takes place only when an utterer means something by what he utters and and an interpreter correctly understands what he means by it. The act of communication is defective if the conventional meaning of the utterance diverges from the utterer's meaning.

III. *Conversation*

We shall apply the term 'conversation' to any communication in which language is the medium. This is, of course, an extension of the ordinary sense of the word, which is usually restricted to communicative episodes in which persons repeatedly interchange the roles of utterer and interpreter. Thus monologues, speeches, and filibusters are not ordinarily thought of as conversations; yet, since they are instances of linguistic communication, they will be included under that heading here. So will the utterance of a person who greets another with a brisk "hello" and receives no answer. (These are, however, limiting cases.)

The theory of conversation presented below is based on the work of H. P. Grice's William James Lectures at Harvard (1967). Some of the ideas go back to the 1957 paper "Meaning," in which Grice outlined the utterer's side of a theory of communication; but inasmuch as the development there is not specifically directed to *linguistic* communication, it cannot be described as a theory of conversation (though critics have sometimes mistaken it for one, failing to recognize that conversation is only one species of communication).

The keystone of conversation is what Grice calls the "Cooperative Principle." He introduces this notion as follows:

> Our talk exchanges do not normally consist of a succession of disconnected remarks, and would not be rational if they did. They are characteristically, to some degree at least, cooperative efforts; and each participant recognizes in them, to some extent, a common purpose or set of purposes, or at least a mutually accepted direction. This purpose or direction may be fixed from the start (e.g. by an initial proposal of a question for discussion), or may evolve during the exchange; it may be fairly definite, or it may be so indefinite as to leave very considerable latitude to the participants (as in a causal conversation). But at each stance, SOME possible conversational moves would be excluded as conversationally unsuitable. We might then formulate a rough general principle which participants will be expected (*ceteris paribus*) to observe, namely: Make your conversational contribution such as is required, at the stage at which it occurs, by the accepted purpose or direction of the talk exchange in which you are engaged. One might label this the COOPERATIVE PRINCIPLE (Grice (1975), p. 45).

The idea, then, is that a conversation has a purpose or goal that is shared by the participants and is achieved in a stepwise fashion that leads Grice to say that conversation has a direction. The fact that conversation is directed to some end also implies that it is *organized* or *structured* in certain ways, rather than being totally random. Since the purpose of a given conversation is shared, it is rational for the participants to cooperate. Thus, the sum and substance of the Cooperative Principle might be put this way: Do whatever is necessary to achieve the purpose of your talk; don't do anything that will frustrate that purpose.

Although at each stage of a conversation the full weight of the Cooperative Principle is on the speaker, because he has the leading role, it imposes certain obligations on the hearer as well. There is, for example, the general requirement that a hearer try to understand what the speaker means, even if he has to ignore the literal meaning of the words that the speaker utters. This requirement, which obviously follows from the Cooperative Principle, explains why defective utterances so often succeed in communicating the speaker's meaning to the hearer. Despite grammatical errors ("One of the trees are blooming"), solecisms ("The cat laid down on the sofa"), mispronunciations ("This course was not reverent [relevant] to me"), and misdescriptions ("Margaret Thatcher is the president of England"), the hearer generally succeeds in interpreting the speaker's utterances correctly. So deep and perversive is this principle that hearers are often oblivious to the defects of utterances; they make the necessary adjustments without conscious effort (or perhaps they simply hear what they expect to hear rather than what is actually being uttered; this very often works, precisely because the purpose that the participants in a conversation share generates a common set of expectations).

The Cooperative Principle is revealing and important, but because of its generality it is not terribly informative. In order to understand the structure of conversation, we need to know what specific rules the participants observe. Grice mentions a number of rules of this sort, which he calls "Conversational Maxims" and sets out in four groups: There are maxims of quantity, maxims of quality, maxims of relation, and maxims of manner. (The term 'maxim' is borrowed from Immanuel Kant's theory of morals; the grouping of the maxims into categories of Quantity, Quality, Relation, and Manner is an adaptation, or perhaps a parody, of Kant's division of the concepts of pure reason in his *Critique of Pure Reason*. Needless to say, the value of the distinction is entirely stylistic and mnemonic; it bears no theoretical weight whatever.) Here is Grice's list of maxims.

Quantity
A1. Make your contribution as informative as required (for the current purposes of the exchange)
A2. Do not make your contribution more informative than is required.

Quality
B. Try to make your contribution one that is true.
B1. Do not say what you believe to be false.
B2. Do not say that for which you lack adequate evidence.

Relation
C. Be relevant.

Manner
D. Be perspicuous.
D1. Avoid obscurity of expression.
D2. Avoid ambiguity.
D3. Be brief (avoid unnecessary prolixity).
D4. Be orderly.

(Grice (1975), p. 46).

The next four sections contain explanation and critical discussion of these maxims.

IV. Maxims of Quantity

As an illustration of the maxims of quantity, consider the following situation. Professor Wisdom is the college advisor of student Precocious, and on one occasion he needs to know whether Precocious has accumulated credit enough to be counted as a senior (perhaps because there are some courses that only seniors can take). He calls the registrar's office, explains the situation, and asks, "How is Precocious classified?" The clerk goes to the records, and after some time returns to the telephone and replies, "Precocious has a total of eighty-eight hours of credit and is classified as a senior." The clerk (let's call her Ledger) has told Wisdom precisely what he needs to know; she followed the maxims of quantity, making her contribution neither more nor less informative than was required. It is true that Ledger could have answered Wisdom's question without telling him precisely how many hours of credit Precocious has; a flatly literal answer to the question "How is Precious classified?" would simply be "Precocious is classified as a senior." But Ledger presumably knows that Wisdom would not have been calling the registrar's office unless there was some uncertainty about Precocious's total number of credits; and Ledger may also have learned by experience that professors are seldom satisfied with the flat assertions of clerks, and that a statistic takes the edge off their dissatisfaction. Although the sentence-meaning of "How is Precocious classified?" does not involve credits at all, the utterer's meaning includes an implicit request for the total number of credits.

Contrast this case with one in which the maxims of quantity are not fulfilled. Suppose, in the same situation, that the registrar's clerk is not Ledger but the considerably less competent Edger. When Wisdom poses his question, Edger searches the records and eventually comes back and replies, "Precocious is classified as an undergraduate." This contravenes maxim A1, "Make your contribution as informative as required (for the current purposes of the exchange)." Or perhaps Edger replies, "Well I have Precocious' record in front of me, and it looks like she has fifteen hours from fall of '79 and seventeen hours from spring of '80, and fifteen hours again from fall of '80 and fourteen from spring of '81, and then she took summer courses in summer of '81 and got six hours there, and twelve in fall of '81 — no — she took a withdrawal for three of those hours, so that's nine in fall of '81, and twelve more in spring of '82, so she's got, let's see, five and seven make twelve, and five, hmmm, eight and carry your three, eighty-eight hours, and you need eighty-seven to be classified as a senior, so she's a senior and one credit-hour over." This contravenes among others, Maxim 2, "Do not make your contribution more informative than is required." Or, as Voltaire said, "The secret of being a bore is to tell everything."

In either of these cases, Wisdom, at least is likely to feel that something has gone wrong with the conversation, though the problem is more serious

II The Cooperative Principle and Conversational Maxims

in the first case. This feeling is correct; Edger is not cooperating with Wisdom by not telling him what he needs to know. Too much information is not as bad as too little; but in either case one has the sense that the requisite community of purpose has not been achieved.

It is possible, incidentally, for both maxims of quantity to be contravened simultaneously. We can imagine Edger rattling off the number of credits Precocious received in each semester of her college career, and then stopping without giving the total or explaining Precocious' classification. In that case, Edger is providing both too much information and too little.

The fact that a violation of maxim A1 is worse than a violation of A2 might lead one to suspect that A2 is not really a Conversational Maxim at all. Grice himself raises (and answers) two specific objections against A2.

The first of these objections is that being overinformative "is not a transgression of the Cooperative Principle but merely a waste of time" (Grice (1975), p. 46). Hence, if the Conversational Maxims are supposed to be specifications of the Cooperative Principle, A2 is not a Conversational Maxim. One reply to this objection is that contributing something that is admittedly "a waste of time" is itself a violation of the Cooperative Principle, since by definition wasting time tends to frustrate the purpose of the conversation. Grice refutes the objection somewhat differently, saying that "overinformativeness may be confusing in that it is liable to raise side issues; and there may also be an indirect effect, in that the hearers may be misled as a result of thinking that there is some particular POINT in the provision of the excess of information" (Grice (1975), p. 46). Such distractions also tend to obstruct the progress of the conversation towards its goal, and hence they do contravene the Cooperative Principle.

The second objection is that A2 is superfluous, given C, the Maxim of Relation. If a speaker's contribution is relevant, then he will not provide more information than is necessary; and if he does, then the information provided is not relevant. But this claim is simply false. In the example given earlier, in which Edger goes on and on about the number of hours Precocious took each semester, everything he says is *relevant* to the question of Precocious's classification; the problem is simply that Professor Wisdom does not need to know, nor does he *want* to know, everything that is relevant. Thus, there is such a thing as relevant information that is not needed, and to include such information in a conversation is to violate maxim A2, not maxim C.

What makes this point a little hard to see is the fact that maxim C is vague. "Be relevant" sounds okay, but what is it that one is supposed to be relevant to? It is arguable that the long-winded answer that Edger gives, though it is relevant to the question that was put to him, is not relevant to the interests of the person who asked that question. This is a problem that we shall have to face in section VI; meanwhile, it makes sense to retain the relatively straightforward A2, especially since it is a natural complement to

A1. If there is a conversational requirement for a speaker to make his contribution strong enough, it seems natural also to require that it not be too strong. We might then combine A1 and A2 to form a Supermaxim of Quantity:

> A. Contribute as much as, but not more than, is required (for the current purposes of the exchange).

V. Maxims of Quality

Grice's Maxims of Quality are too narrowly formulated. Recall that they are as follows:

> B1. Do not say what you believe to be false.
> B2. Do not say that for which you lack adequate evidence.

One difficulty is that they deal only with what is said and not with what is implied. Yet we need an explanation of the speaker's conversational violation in such scenarios as this one: Suppose that Mr. Allworthy, who is the officer of a bank, is being considered for the position of bank president, and that in order to thwart the appointment, Mr. Envious goes before the directors who are to make the decision and says, "It is possible that Allworthy will be arrested for embezzlement." Now, what Envious says is true, since he has no guarantee that Allworthy will not be arrested, and hence his arrest is *possible* (though the possibility may charitably be described as remote); so Envious's assertion conforms to maxim B1. Moreover, he has evidence that is adequate to support his claim, since he knows that Allworthy is a bank officer, and that is a sufficient reason to believe it *possible* for him to be arrested for embezzlement; thus Envious's assertion conforms to maxim B2 as well. And yet Envious has violated the Cooperative Principle by deceiving the directors (or at least trying to deceive them); he has falsely implied that Allworthy is a crook and that he, Envious, has evidence to that effect. In order to explain Envious's conversational violation, it is necessary to broaden B1 and B2 as follows:

> B1'. Do not say or imply what you believe to be false.
> B2'. Do not say or imply that for which you lack adequate evidence.

In other words, the Maxims of Quality forbid deception, whether it is explicit (in what is said) or implicit (in what is implied).

Even B1' and B2', however, are too narrow; indeed, they are so radically defective that they need to be scrapped completely, or at least demoted from their exalted position. The basic problem is that like Grice's Supermaxim of Quality:

> B. Try to make your contribution one that is true.

they apply only to those speech acts in which the speaker tries to say how the world is, that is, to statements, assertions, and the like (the general word for speech acts of this kind is "constative"). Perhaps B can survive as a supermaxim and B1' and B2' as maxims of constatives, but for conversation in general B1' and B2' are at best minimaxims, and B a super-minimaxim. We need to formulate our maxims so that they cover the entire spectrum of speech acts, since conversation (that is, linguistic communication) includes them all.

That the Maxims of Quality need to be broadened is clear; how to broaden them is not. Nevertheless, we have some clues. The notion of quality suggests that the maxims have something to do with excellence, with satisfying a criterion or measuring up to a high standard; and this links up with something Grice says about quality when he discusses the notion as it applies to one's contribution to *any* rational cooperative activity: He says that one's contribution should be "genuine and not spurious." Now, there is, so to speak, a semantic cluster of words that ensphere the notion we are interested in: 'genuine', 'sincere', 'authenic', 'reliable', and 'true' in a broader sense that applies to friends, spouses, or (allegedly) Americans rather than to statements. All these words come close, but none is quite right as a substitute for 'true' in the Supermaxim of Quality: 'genuine' is perhaps the best of the lot, but "Try to make your contribution one that is genuine" is too broad, and, more importantly, too vague. We shall have to rewrite the maxims in order to make clear exactly what sort of character the contribution is supposed to have.

We want to enjoin from dissembling. Someone who is familiar with the classics of existentialism might suggest that their notions of authenticity and good faith are what we are seeking; but this is an illusion. The sense of 'authentic' that Sartre thinks justifies him in his canonization of the notorious thief and liar, Jean Genet, as a saint of authenticity, is precisely what we want to reject; we want a bourgeois authenticity, one that celebrates sincerity and condemns deviousness and impersonation. After all, we are trying to state the conventions that are normally followed in conversation; we can hardly make defiance of conventions a virtue without undermining the whole project.

What kind of genuineness or authenticity does a person who makes true statements have that a person who deliberately makes false ones lacks? Well, one thing about the maker of true statements is that his speech acts are not defective, whereas those of the liar *are* defective. And this is a characteristic that generalizes easily. In the case of a promise, say, we feel that the Maxims of Quality should require the maker of the promise to intend to do what is promised; and unless he does intend to keep his promise, his act of promising is defective. Similarly, in the case of a command, the Maxims of Quality should require that the person who issues the command want the hearer (or hearers) to do as he says; once again, his speech act is defective unless this is so. We can say, therefore, that the kind of genuineness that the Maxims of Quality demand is a willingness to perform only non-defective speech acts. The Supermaxim of Quality, accordingly, is:

> B″. Do not participate in any speech act unless you believe that the conditions for its successful and non-defective performance are satisfied.

More specific maxims can be derived from this one by considering what conditions must be satisfied in order for particular speech acts to be performed successfully and without defect: Do not make promises that you do not intend to keep; do not inaugurate the President-elect of the United States if you are not legally entitled to do so; and, of course, do not make statements unless you believe, and have some reason to believe, that they are true.

It is noteworthy that the Supermaxim of Quality applies to hearers as well as to speakers. For in many cases a speech act in which the speaker has brought off his part flawlessly can be rendered defective by the hearer. For example, the Supermaxim of Quality usually requires the hearer to make an effort to understand what the speaker means, whatever words he may utter; and in some cases the hearer must have a certain status: Only the duly elected presidential candidate may be inaugurated, for instance. Similarly, one might formulate a Maxim of Quantity: "Do not read more into what is said than is intended." People who are easily offended contravene this maxim; Groucho Marx became a classic comedian by flouting it.

VI. Maxims of Relation

We saw in section IV that Grice's Maxim of Relation, "Be relevant," is too vague. It needs to be supplementend with more specific maxims. Let us consider the sorts of relevance that the Cooperative Principle requires of our conversational contributions, that is, the sorts of relevance that they must have if the purpose of the conversation is to be achieved.

In the first place, the participants in a conversation cannot achieve their purpose if they lose track of the direction of the conversation and cannot see how it is moving towards its goal. The Cooperative Principle therefore imposes on all parties an obligation to keep track of the conversation and to make clear to one another how their own contributions fit in. This obligation can be stated either affirmatively or negatively, as an obligation to make the direction of the conversation clear or as an obligation not to obscure it; perhaps the best formulation of the maxim will include both the affirmative and the negative obligation:

> C1. Make your contribution one that indicates, or at least does not conceal, the direction in which the conversation is moving.

In the simplest case, a conversation has a beginning, a middle, and an end, and moves continuously from beginning to end in a single direction. There is a sense in which the beginning and the end of a conversation are more critical than the intermediate portions; as a result, we have many explicit conventions (for example, 'Hello', 'Once upon a time', 'Goodbye', 'The End') for beginning and ending conversations; and even when we do not use such formulas, we frequently indicate explicitly what we are doing, saying, for example, "I want to begin today's lecture with a discussion of maxim C1," or "In conclusion, . . ." Such devices may be called *starters* and *stoppers*. They provide us with a repertoire of ways of conforming to maxim C1.

Perhaps it is a little difficult to see why stoppers are needed. How do they make it any more probable that the goal of the discourse will be achieved? It seems that they come into play only *after* this goal has been achieved. The answer is that it is not enough for the interlocutors to have arrived at their goal; they need to *know* that they have arrived. The analogy of a trip may help to make this point clear: If you're driving from Chicago to Cleveland, and you wind up in Cleveland, but you don't realize that you're in Cleveland, you have not yet achieved your goal; the trip is not really over until you *do* realize that you're in Cleveland. Similarly, arriving at the goal of a conversation is not the same as achieving it.

In the middle of a conversation, on the other hand, no explicit markers are needed as long as the conversation continues to flow smoothly in one direction. Consider the following dialogue:

H: Hello, how are you today?
S: Not too well. I feel pretty punk.
H: What seems to be the problem?
S: My throat is sore and I ache all over.
H: Sounds like the flu.
S: I saw my doctor today; he says it's whatever is going around.

Notice that after H's starter, the discourse proceeds without any mention of how the speaker's contribution ties in with the earlier ones. For example, S does not need to explain how his visit with the doctor is relevant to H's judgement that S has the flu and his own earlier report of a sore throat and achiness. The general rule is that a conversational contribution that simply continues the motion of the conversation, without changing its direction, does not have to contain any explicit indication of this fact; we assume that the hearer can keep track of the direction of the conversation without any help from the speaker in such cases.

However, speakers do not always want to keep the conversation moving in the same direction. There are a variety of ways of changing it. One can refuse to accept someone else's contribution, either by outright rejection ("You're a liar," "That's not true") or by demurrer ("I'm not convinced," "Are you sure about that?"). One can change the direction of the discourse ("Let's consider a different possibility"), stop its advance either temporarily ("Wait a minute — let's examine this more closely") or permanently ("I'd rather not talk about it"), or retrace the path ("Let's go back to the point where . . ."). Ordinarily we explicitly indicate any such radical change in the motion of the conversation, as C1 requires, so that all the participants are able to follow it, as the Cooperative Principle requires.

In the second place, the participants in a conversation cannot achieve their common purpose, even if they all see the general direction in which the conversation is moving, unless they can also perceive the relationship between what each speaker says and the broader conversational context. If there is no such link, or if the participants in the conversation generally do not perceive it, then what the speaker says contributes nothing to the achievement of the conversational goal, even if it succeeds in keeping the conversation moving. Accordingly, the second Maxim of Relation is:

> C2. Express yourself in terms that will enable your hearer to tie your contribution into the conversational context.

This maxim actually imposes two requirements. One is topical: Your contribution should be about the same thing that the conversation you are contributing to is about, or at least about something that bears some obvious relation to what the conversation is about. For instance, in the short dialogue between H and S above, the general topic of S's health holds the discourse together, and each contribution after the initial exchange concerns this topic. In "Identifying Reference and Truth Values" (1964b), P. F. Strawson deals with this aspect of C2 as follows:

> Statements, or the pieces of discourse to which they belong, have subjects, not only in the relatively precise senses of logic and grammar, but in a vaguer sense with which I shall associate the words 'topic' and 'about' . . . For stating is not a gratuitous and random human activity. We do not, except in social desperation, direct isolated and unconnected pieces of information at each other, but on the contrary intend in general to give or add information about what is a matter of standing or current interest or concern. There is a great variety of possible types of answer to the question what the topic of a statement is, what a statement is 'about' — about baldness, about what great men are bald, about which countries have bald rulers, about France, about the king, etc. — and not every answer excludes every other in a given case. This platitude we might dignify with the title, the Principle of Relevance (Strawson (1964b), p. 92).

(Of course, what Strawson says here about statements applies to all speech acts, that is, to conversation generally.) The fact that a given utterance is about many different things makes it easier to tie one's conversational contributions to what has been said already and leads to the possibility of moving gradually from one topic to another without any radical break or disruption in the flow of the conversation.

II The Cooperative Principle and Conversational Maxims

The other requirement is rhetorical: One should adjust what one says to reflect the beliefs and attitudes of one's hearers and the circumstances in which the conversation takes place; these things are also part of the conversational context. Again we find an anticipation of this idea in Strawson's work, under the title "The Principle of the Presumption of Knowledge," which is that when a speaker produces an utterance with communicative intention, the speaker typically presumes that the audience knows certain empirical facts relevant to the particular point expressed in the utterance. (It seems more plausible to relate Strawson's principles to Grice's Maxims of Relation than to connect the former with the Maxims of Quantity, as Ruth Kempson does in Kempson (1975), p. 142, n. 1, and p. 166.)

Strawson's version, however, has two defects. First, it is too strong; the speaker need not presume that the audience *knows* the propositions in question, but only that they believe them (or even, in some cases, that they would like to believe them). Second, in Strawson's original presentation the Principle of the Presumption of Knowledge is brought in only in connection with the speech act of referring; this is unnecessarily parochial.

The kind of rhetorical adjustment that a speaker makes in order to conform to maxim C2 is not stylistic, and is not covered by the Maxims of Manner. Consider, for example, the following exchange:

H: I think White was the one jilted, not Black. Who do you think it was?
S: I think that the one with more hair was jilted.

Unless S is aware that H believes either that White has more hair than Black or that Black has more hair than White, he is violating maxim C2; S gives H no way of tying S's contribution into the conversational context. It is clear that he cannot rectify the situation by changing the *style* of his remark, making it, say, briefer or more orderly; he must identify the one he thinks was jilted in a way that H can understand. A hearer can be well acquainted with an object and yet lack the information necessary to understand references to the object; in such cases the hearer will not understand what the speaker means.

Incidentally, even if S knows that H believes that Black has more hair than White, he may still be violating C2; for, given what S and H are talking about and how they are talking about it, it is not clear that one party's having more hair than the other has any topical relation to the rest of the conversation.

The beliefs that a speaker takes advantage of under maxim C2 are not always shared by all the participants at the beginning of the conversation; usually, in fact, new shared beliefs emerge in the course of a discussion. For instance, when a credible authority advances a plausible thesis, it generally becomes an object of belief to his hearers. In some cases the speaker "invokes" a thesis that his hearer is supposed to believe by simply asserting it;

but since it would be tedious to introduce predicatively each new point that one wants to discuss, speakers sometimes use descriptions referentially, thereby "convoking" the appropriate beliefs. A random example: "The Treaty of Cateau-Cambrésis between France and Spain was signed the following day, April 3, 1559" (O'Connell (1974), p. 35). The author clearly does not presume that the reader already knows about this treaty; yet he never flatly asserts that any such treaty existed. (The only previous hint is a brief mention of "substantive discussions at Cateau-Cambrésis.") However, the phrase "The Treaty of Cateau-Cambrésis between France and Spain" convokes the belief expressed by the assertion that there was such a treaty. (Cf. Strawson (1961), p. 60, note 1 and p. 64).

As a generic term to cover both invoking and convoking, I propose the coinage 'advoking', which preserves the Latin root (*vocare*) and is sufficiently different from 'advocating' to forestall confusion. The rhetorical requirement imposed by maxim C2 can therefore be stated thus: Advoke only beliefs that the other participants in the conversation share (or can be brought to share). Of course, this does not mean that the speaker is supposed to assert only propositions that his hearers believe or can be brought to believe; it means that only through such propositions can the speaker tie his utterance into the conversational context.

VII. Maxims of Manner

Whereas there was good reason to adopt a Maxim of Quality (in section V) that embodied the bourgeois virtues of sincerity and authenticity, the problem with the Maxims of Manner that Grice proposed is that they are rather *too* bourgeois. As the reader will recall, they are:

D. Be perspicuous.
D1. Avoid obscurity of expression.
D2. Avoid ambiguity.
D3. Be brief (avoid unnecessary prolixity).
D4. Be orderly.

It is possible to quibble with the formation of some of these maxims (for instance, the opposite of 'prolix' is not 'brief' but 'concise'), but Grice has done a remarkable job in compressing into fifteen words a stylistic ideal that many composition teachers seem unable to impart to their students in a full semester: that of a crisp, limpid, functional style that gets the message across with a minimum of fuss and bother. It is an attractive ideal, and if everyone would master such a style at an early age, a blessed era of peace and prosperity would quickly ensue. Nonetheless, this style is not equally suited to all occasions; there are times when perspicuity is, if not out of place, at least of secondary importance, and there are some speech acts which require a certain measure of obscurity, ambiguity, prolixity, or disorderliness. Grice's Maxims of Manner are directed to constatives; but suppose one wants to make, not a statement, but a pun. How then should one avoid ambiguity? Or suppose one is writing a poem. Of course, it is generally recognized that obscurity for obscurity's sake is an aesthetic defect, especially when it is carried to an extreme; but unless the poet approaches his subject with a certain creative obliqueness, he is really just an essayist who uses eccentric line divisions. We do not want maxim D 1 to oblige the poet to abandon his art in the name of clarity.

The Cooperative Principle directs us to make our conversational contributions such as are required by the accepted purpose of the conversation. The point is that perspicuity does not serve every purpose; and when it does not, Grice's maxims are inapplicable. The Supermaxim of Manner should rather be something like:

> D'. Make your contribution in the manner best suited to the speech act you intend to perform and to the purpose of the conversation in which you are participating.

More specifically, the speaker should adapt the style of his utterance to the conditions under which the conversation takes place (it is a mistake to talk the same way in a barroom and in a cathedral), to the age, social standing, and intellectual level of his hearers, and so on, since by doing so he makes it more likely that the common purpose will be achieved.

There is little point in going into more detail. The particular adaptations one makes and the kinds of advantage that accompany various stylistic techniques belong to rhetoric rather than to the philosophy of communication; no issues of theoretical importance emerge. In what follows we shall introduce Maxims of Manner appropriate to various kinds of speech acts on an *ad hoc* basis, as special cases of D'.

VIII. Interim Summary

From the discussion of Conversational Maxims in sections III through VII, we can recover the following Maxims of Quantity, Quality, Relation, and Manner:

> A 1. Contribute as much as is required (for the current purposes of the exchange).
>
> A 2. Do not contribute more than is required for the purpose of the exchange.
>
> B''. Do not participate in any speech act unless you believe that the conditions for its successful and nondefective performance are satisfied.

C. Be relevant; more specifically,
   C1. Make your contribution one that indicates, or at least does not conceal, the direction in which the conversation is moving; and
   C2. Express yourself in terms that will enable your hearer to tie your contribution into the conversational context.
D'. Make your contribution in the manner best suited to the speech act you intend to perform and to the purpose of the conversation in which you are participating.
   D1. Avoid obscurity of expression.
   D2. Avoid ambiguity.
   D3. Be concise.
   D4. Be orderly.

IX. Nonfulfillment of Maxims

Although speakers normally observe the Cooperative Principle and the Conversational Maxims, they do not always do so. This should not be surprising, since it is of the essence of a convention that it need not be observed; and, since human beings are fallible, it follows that they are sometimes not observed. If there were nothing more to be said about the nonfulfillment of maxims, the topic would be uninteresting. What makes it interesting is that not all of the cases in which the maxims are not observed are due to human fallibility; sometimes a speaker (or a hearer) *deliberately* contravenes a maxim. What is even more surprising is that he does not necessarily thwart communication; a speaker's apt contravention of a maxim can be the medium of a message.

Grice distinguishes four different ways in which a maxim can go unfulfilled: violating, flouting, opting out and being faced with a clash of maxims (Grice, (1975), p. 49). Violating a maxim is quietly and unostentatiously not fulfilling one. Opting out of a maxim is openly choosing not to fulfill a maxim that is in effect. Being faced with a clash of maxims is not fulfilling some maxim because two or more maxims come into conflict. For example, a person who is asked to explain briefly Einstein's theory of relativity may be faced with a clash of the maxims "Be brief" and "Do not say that which is false," among others. A moment's reflection should reveal that Grice is mistaken in thinking that being faced with a clash is a way of not fulfilling a maxim. Rather, it is a cause or reason for not fulfilling one. A person who is faced with a clash can choose not to fulfill a maxim either by violating one, flouting one or opting out of one. So, the person charged with explaining Einstein's theory can resolve the clash by either violating a maxim of quality by slightly misrepresenting the theory; or flout a maxim of quantity by saying only, "$E = mc^2$," or opt out of a maxim of manner by saying, "There is no brief explanation." Or, to quote H. H. Munro: "A little inaccuracy sometimes saves a ton of explanation." Grice himself might have noticed this disparity, for it is implicit in his characterization of one of his own examples: "an example in which a maxim is violated, but its violation *is to be explained by* the supposition of a *clash* with another maxim" (Grice, (1957), p. 51). This quotation is fully italicized in the original; I have retained some italics for emphasis. Again, in explaining how to flout a maxim, he remarks, "On the assumption that the speaker is able to fulfill the maxim and to do so without violating another maxim (because of a clash) . . ." (Grice (1975), p. 49).

Although excluding "being faced with a clash of maxims" from the ways of not fulfilling a maxim reduces Grice's original number to three, there is a fourth way that he does not mention. A person can *suspend* a maxim. This way of not fulfilling a maxim should be contrasted with opting out of a maxim just as violating a maxim contrasts with flouting one. When a person opts out of a maxim, that maxim remains operative; but when a person suspends a maxim, that maxim becomes inoperative. Institutions that allow filibustering suspend the maxims "Be brief" and "Be relevant." The Congress of the United States also in effect suspends the first maxim of quality, "Do not say that which is false" in that no congressman can be charged with criminal activity for anything he says on the floor of Congress. Further, consider two similar legal systems. According to our actual system, a defendent is protected against forced self-incrimination; he has the right to remain silent. However, once a defendant chooses to take the witness stand, he must answer all questions put to him fully and truthfully. A defendant who lies under oath is subject to punishment for perjury. In short, in our system, the first maxim of quality is never suspended. Now consider a slightly different system, one that would allow a defendant to take the witness stand in his own behalf but would exempt him from charges of perjury. In other words, the first maxim of quality would be suspended.

In the next three sections, we shall take up a number of examples of the other three ways in which a maxim can go unfulfilled. Although any of the Conversational Maxims can go unfulfilled in any of the three ways, we shall not go through all the possible combinations; instead, we shall concentrate on examples in which maxims are violated, dealing more briefly with opting out and flouting.

X. *Violating a Maxim*

The first thing to notice is that 'violating a maxim' is not synonymous with 'not fulfilling a maxim'; maxims can go unfulfilled without being violated. This confusion is surprisingly common (see Carr (1978), pp. 93, 94); even Grice succumbs to it occasionally, as in the following passage:

Examples in which an implicature is achieved by real, as distinct from apparent, violation of the maxim of Relation are perhaps rare, but the following seems to be a good candidate. At a genteel tea party, A says *Mrs X is an old bag*. There is a moment of appalled silence, and then B says *The weather has been quite delightful this summer, hasn't it?* B has blatantly refused to make what HE says relevant to A's preceding remark. He thereby implicates that A's remark should not be discussed and, perhaps more specifically, that A has committed a social gaffe (Grice (1975), p. 54).

Since by definition a violation of a maxim must be quiet and unobtrusive, Grice's example, in which B "blatantly" did not observe the Maxim of Relevance, cannot be an example of *violating* a maxim. It is an example of another kind of non-observance: flouting. The same confusion appears in his characterizations of "Group A" and "Group B" on p. 51 of Grice (1975).

Now let's consider some cases in which maxims are genuinely violated.

1. Suppose that Mr. Rolls, a tax assessor, asks Mr. Taxed, "Do you have a goat?" If Taxed has four goats but answers "Yes," without letting on that he in fact could supply more information about the number of his goats (in other words, if he answers quietly and without ostentation), then Taxed violates the maxim "Make your contribution as informative as is required (for the current purposes of the exchange)." One might think that Taxed has not violated this Maxim of Quantity, but rather a Maxim of Quality: "Try to make your contribution one that is true." But in fact Taxed has spoken truly in answering that he has a goat. (If, however, Taxed had said, "I have one and only one goat," then he would have been saying something that he (presumably) knew to be false; and this would be a violation of the Maxim of Quality just cited.)

It must be admitted that Taxed *is* violating a Maxim of Quality that we developed in section V: "Do not say or imply what you believe to be false." Although he does not *say* that he has only one goat, there is a sense in which he *implies* that he has only one goat. However, this implication arises only because Rolls assumes that Taxed is doing his best to fulfill the Maxim of Quantity; it is not an implication in the strictly logical sense. Hence, the fundamental violation is against the Maxim of Quantity.

Incidentally, one should not think that every violation of a Maxim of Quantity (or, indeed, of any maxim) is self-serving, malevolent, or surreptitious; the only requirement is that it be quiet and unobtrusive. Often one violates a maxim with the best of motives, and it is well advised to do so. In this connection one might mention the principle of the asceticism of truth. Truth should not be used as a stick with which to beat people over the head. So, for example, if one is asked, "Tell me honestly: What do you think of my hat (my body, my philosophical ability)?", it is probably better to violate at least the Maxim of Quantity than to observe it too strictly.

2. As an example of violating the other Maxim of Quantity for constatives, "Do not make your contribution more informative than is required," we can go back to the case discussed near the beginning of section IV, in which the registrar's clerk Edger answers Professor Wisdom's question with a rambling account of a student's scholastic progress. Originally we supposed that Edger was simply not very competent and contravened the maxim unintentionally; but we might alternatively suppose that Edger is a former student of Wisdom's who sat through many boring and repetitive lectures in Wisdom's course and is now taking his revenge. His failure to observe the maxim is now both deliberate and unobtrusive: it is a violation.

3. Any lie is a violation of the maxim "Try to make your contribution one that is true." However, it should be noted once again that violations need not be either surreptritious or malevolent. Teachers know that it is often pedagogically sound to contravene the Maxims of Quality quietly and unobstrusively, since students are often led to the truth more quickly and surely by first being brought to understand an idea that is simpler but false. And theologians, it is said, should lecture *sola fide, sola gratia* at the podium, but preach good works from the pulpit. To be sure, such professional exemptions are occasionally abused by lazy teachers and heretical or hypocritical theologians; but at any rate the exemptions show that untruths are not always malicious.

4. We have a general word for persons who violate the Supermaxim of Quality in cases where the speech act is of great moment and requires some special status of the participant; they are imposters. A person who enters into a second marriage before disengaging himself from the first is an imposter, in this sense; an unauthorized person who steps in for the priest or minister an the ceremony of marriage is another.

5. A violation of maxim C1, "Make your contribution one that indicates, or at least does not conceal, the direction in which the conversation is moving," involving what we called in section VI a starter, is found at the beginning of D. Z. Philip's paper "Philosophy and Commitment" (1979). The first words of the paper are "This essay begins with a rather lengthy quotation from Kierkegaard." The quotation referred to, however, does not appear immediately; it follows almost a page of explanation of the passage from which the quotation is drawn.

6. A violation involving a stopper occurs in Tony Richardson's film version of *Tom Jones*. Near the end of the film Tom Jones is hanged and the words "The End" appear on the screen; then the film is (apparently) run backwards past the hanging scene and then forwards to a new ending, in which Jones is saved from the gallows.

7. Prideful boasts often involve violations of maxim C2, "Express yourself in terms that will enable your hearer to tie your contribution into the conversational context," especially as it relates to advoking the hearer's existing beliefs. Suppose that Professor Turk has won a prestigious grant

and wants to impress his hearer with this fact, without saying flat out that he won it. He might instead approach the subject by saying, "It's a shame that my Socrates Foundation grant doesn't begin until September; I'm anxious to start work on my project."

8. For a variety of violations of the four constative Maxims of Manner, the reader is invited to peruse a randomly selected passage from Hegel's *Phenomenology of Spirit*.

XI. Opting Out of a Maxim

There are all sorts of reasons for opting out of a maxim. Sometimes one is faced with a clash of maxims and chooses simply to drop one; sometimes one is not in a position to say what the maxim requires, or is obliged to say something that the maxim forbids; and so on.

1 (opting out of a Maxim of Quantity). Suppose that Mrs. A is writing to a friend of the family who lives in France and discovers that she has misplaced the friend's address. She asks Mr. A, "What is Pierre Duplessis's address?" Mr. A does not know. He is faced with a clash between the Maxim of Quantity, "Make your contribution as informative as required," and the Maxim of Quality, "Do not say that for which you lack adequate evidence." He opts out of the Maxim of Quantity, replying, "I don't remember, dear."

2 (opting out of a Maxim of Quality). The obvious cases are ones in which we explicitly adopt a pretense: Let's pretend that I'm the Pope and you are the general secretary of the Polish Communist Party.

3 (opting out of a Maxim of Relation). Suppose that Mrs. B, who has been talking about her plans for the evening, interrupts herself to say, "Before I forget, Jones wants you to return his call tonight." She has opted out of the maxim that requires a topical relation among a speaker's contributions to a conversation.

4 (opting out of a Maxim of Manner). Replying to the request, "Explain Einstein's theory of special relativity to me without bringing in all those obscure technicalities," one might well say, "What you ask is impossible.

XII. Flouting a Maxim

To flout a maxim is to contravene it deliberately and openly — "blatantly," as Grice puts it. Now, since the maxims are supposed to be nothing more than elaborations of the Cooperative Principle, one might wonder why anyone would ever want to contravene a maxim and let the other participants in the conversation know that one is contravening it. Sometimes, of course, one gets caught up in a conversation in which he does not want to cooperate with the other participants, because he does not accept the purpose or direction of the conversation, or dislikes the other participants, or simply wishes that he were somewhere else. The more interesting case, however, is where one does want to cooperate with the other participants and to advance the conversation towards its goal, and finds that the best way to do this is to flout a maxim. Situations of this sort arise because maxims are not universal laws. They summarize the *normal* or *regular* standards for conversational contributions, but on occasion one can make an *exceptional* contribution to the conversation by going against them.

For example, suppose that a teacher has been asked to comment on the philosophical ability of one of her students, and she replies, "Well, he has beautiful handwriting." She is flouting maxim C2, since her comment is topically irrelevant to the request; there is no way for the hearer to tie it into the conversational context. However, although the hearer may be taken somewhat aback for an instant, it requires no great sensitivity to realize that the teacher is broadly hinting that the student has no philosophical ability to speak of. The purpose of the conversation is served, since unless the hearer is unusually inattentive or dense, he finds out what he wanted to know; although a maxim is contravened, the Cooperative Principle is not. The speaker has actually exploited the maxim, flouting it in order to communicate a specific thought.

XIII. Conversational Implicatures

Grice invented the term 'conversational implicature' for communications in which maxims are exploited in one way or another. His general notion can be defined as follows:

A speaker S who says, or makes as if to say, that p, has conversationally implicated that q to a hearer H iff
1. H justifiably assumes that S is observing the Cooperative Principle;
2. H's assumption that S is adhering to the Cooperative Principle and S's saying, or making as if to say, that p together entail that S thinks that q (though neither entails this separately); and
3. S thinks, and expects H to realize that S thinks, that H can realize that the entailment described in 2 holds.

It is implicit in this characterization that conversational implicatures involve computation. This term 'computation', chosen in deference to Thomas Hobbes, is intended to suggest that some process or procedure for calculating what other participants in a conversation are likely to think is necessary in order to arrive at an implicature; in other words, conversational implicatures cannot be inferred from what is said alone, or with the help of semantic postulates. The speaker's intention to observe the Cooperative Principle must form part of the basis for the inference. So, for example, someone who asserts that John loves Mary and Mary loves Sam does not conversationally implicate that John loves Mary, precisely because the assertion itself logically entails that John loves Mary, regardless of the speaker's intention to observe the Cooperative Principle. Similarly, someone who asserts that Jerome is a bachelor does not thereby conversationally implicate that Jerome is unmarried; that is a conventional linguistic implication, justified by the semantic conventions of the speaker's language, not a conversational implicature.

Here is Grice's description of a computation:

> A general pattern for the working out of a conversational implicature might be given as follows: 'He has said that p; there is no reason to suppose that he is not observing the maxims, or at least the CP [Cooperative Principle]; he could not be doing this unless he thought that q; he knows (and knows that I know that he knows) that I can see that the supposition that he thinks that q IS required; he has done nothing to stop me thinking that q; he intends me to think, or at least is willing to allow me to think, that q; and so he has implicated that q' (Grice (1975), pp. 49–50).

Because conversational implications are not derived from the speaker's words alone, but depend also upon the hearer's awareness of the speaker's intentions, it is possible to cancel or annul them by clarifying one's intentions. For example, opting out of a maxim is an explicit way of cancelling any conversational implicature that would depend on that maxim. When the President's press secretary announces, "The President is either in Moscow or in Peking," he conversationally implicates that there is some uncertainty about where the President is; if he adds, "But I'm not at liberty to say which," no such conclusion can be drawn. It seemed at first that if the press secretary knew which capital the President was in, he would have conformed to the constative Maxims of Quantity by naming only that city rather than presenting alternatives, since "The President is in Moscow," say, is more informative than "The President is either in Moscow or in Peking." By adding that he knows more than he can tell the press, however, the secretary opts out of these Maxims of Quantity.

It is evident from this example, incidentally, that not all conversational implicatures involve flouting a maxim. Indeed, conversational implicatures arise even when all the maxims are followed. What they have in common is that the speaker *exploits* a maxim in order to communicate something that he does not simply say.

Sometimes a speaker can block a conversational implicature by appending a disavowal ("I'm hot, tired, and anxious, but really I'm not at all cranky"). Sometimes, however, more is required — perhaps an explanation of why the implicature does not hold. Two of Grice's examples illustrate this point. The first is the example given above in which a teacher is asked about her student's philosophical ability and replies, "Well, he has beautiful handwriting." Suppose now that the teacher does not want to leave the impression that her student is not good at philosophy. She might attempt to get this across by adding, "I do not mean to suggest that he is not good at philosophy." This may or may not work; the danger is that the hearer will be confused by the apparent incoherence of the teacher's comments. In order to cancel the implicature completely, the teacher must explain more fully: "Excuse me; I was just remembering how surprised I was the first time I noticed his handwriting, because in my experience the best philosophers usually have terrible handwriting, and yet this student, who is excellent at philosophy, happens to write very well." And now the teacher can go on with her evaluation. Alternatively, we can imagine a Platonistic explanation: "He has beautiful handwriting. But I am not suggesting that he is not good at philosophy. On the contrary, I believe that anyone who participates in any part of beauty thereby manifests a love of wisdom which is philosophy in the truest sense of the word." In this case there is still the possibility of an elaborate satire; but if the hearer is convinced that the speaker is sincere, he will at any rate not draw the disparaging conclusion that seemed at first to be implicated.

The charge of incoherence has been lodged against another scenario offered by Grice (Platts (1979), p. 77). Grice claims that someone who says "She is poor but honest" can cancel the implied contrast between poverty and honesty by a disavowal: "Though of course I do not mean to imply that there is any contrast between poverty and honesty." One might well balk at such a remark, which sounds incoherent. As it stands, the disavowal does indeed ring hollow. But this is not decisive. Here again our reluctance to accept the cancellation is due to a failure of imagination; it is possible to find ways of reconciling apparent contradiction. Suppose that the sentence is uttered about Scarlett O'Hara (who has met with reverses of fortune not described in *Gone With the Wind*). The speaker might continue: "I don't mean to imply that there is in general a contrast between poverty and honesty; it is just that she had vowed to lie, cheat, and steal if she were ever poor again."

XIV. Moore's Paradox

G. E. Moore once pointed out that although it is not contradictory to say "p, and I don't believe that p" — indeed, such an assertion will always be true for some value of p, provided that the speaker does not believe every true proposition — it is nonetheless a very odd thing to say (Moore (1942), 540–543). It seems as though the speaker is being inconsistent in some subtle way that is not wholly contained in the words that he utters.

The theory of conversational implicature offers an explanation for the oddity of the utterance in question. When a speaker S asserts that p, he conversationally implicates that he believes that p. For, supposing that S has asserted that p and that the hearer has no reason to think that S is not observing the Cooperative Principle, the hearer is entitled to conclude that S

believes that *p* is true; otherwise, *S* would be contravening the Maxim of Quality that prohibits assertions that are not believed. And *S* knows (and knows that the hearer knows) that the hearer can draw this conclusion, and so forth. In short, it is apparent to everyone that if *S* asserts that *p*, and is observing the Maxim of Quality, then *S* believes that *p*.

Now let us return to the assertion that constitutes the paradox: "*p*, and I don't believe that *p*." What is the speaker trying to say here? Ordinarily we (as hearers) would assume that he is conforming to the Maxim of Quality with respect to both halves of his assertion. But this leads to the conclusion that he doesn't know what he believes, since if he is observing the Maxim of Quality with respect to the first part of the assertion, he believes that *p*, while if he is observing the Maxim of Quality with respect to the second half of his assertion, he believes that he *doesn't* believe that *p*. It seems very unlikely that the speaker is mistaken about his own beliefs, so we are driven to the conclusion that the speaker is not conforming to the Maxim of Quality. But why not? The oddity lies in the fact that there is no motive for the speaker's apparent flouting of the maxim.

In fact, it is possible to take away some of the oddity of the speaker's assertion by supplying such a motive. For instance, we can imagine Galileo before the inquisitors who obliged him to recant, saying, "I hereby abjure and reject my former belief that the earth moves about the sun and rotates on its axis." And then, *sotto voce*: "But it does move, all the same." We know why Galileo contravened the Maxim of Quality; he was forced to. In this context, his assertions, though still out of the ordinary, are understandable. Again, a philosopher who has just explained Moore's paradox to his class might jokingly say, "Now you all understand perfectly what Moore was saying in this passage. But I don't really believe that." He opts out of the Maxim of Quality temporarily in order to make the joke.

This solution depends on the thesis that when a speaker asserts that *p*, he conversationally implicates that he believes that *p*. Surprisingly, Grice himself rejects this thesis:

> On my account, it will not be true that when I say that *p*, I conversationally implicate that I believe that *p*. . . . For to suppose that I believe that *p* (or 'rather' think of myself as believing that *p*) is just to suppose that I am observing the first maxim of Quality on this occasion (Grice (1978), p. 114).

The idea is that the hearer's inference that the speaker believes that *p* is based entirely on his assumption that the speaker is observing the Cooperative Principle and more specifically, the Maxim of Quality, not at all on the speaker's saying that *p*; the content of the utterance, according to Grice, has nothing to do with the conclusion that the speaker believes that *p*. So the second condition in the definition of 'conversational implicature' is not satisfied.

But this is clearly incorrect. If Grice were right, it would be possible for the hearer to infer that the speaker believes that p even if he could not hear what the speaker was saying, provided that he recognized that the speaker was intending to observe the Cooperative Principle — which is absurd.

Although there is no need to say more in refutation of Grice's view, it is illuminating to speculate about the source of his error. It may have less to do with his theory of conversational implicature than with his ideas about the indicative mood. In "Utterer's Meaning, Sentence-Meaning, and Word-Meaning," Grice presents the view that the indicative mood "corresponds to believing" (Grice (1968) p. 59), so that whenever someone expresses a proposition indicatively, he thereby expresses his belief in that proposition. On this theory, the hearer of an utterance can infer that the speaker believes what the utterance expresses without knowing what the content of the utterance is, provided that he recognizes that the main verb is in the indicative mood. This still will not do as a reason for denying that when S asserts that p, he conversationally implicates that he believes that p, since the hearer still cannot reach the conclusion that S believes that p without knowing the content of S's utterance; but it is now possible to see how the confusion might arise: Grice is thinking that *some* conclusion about what S believes can be drawn simply from the *form* of his utterance, together with the usual assumption that S is observing the Cooperative Principle.

However, Grice's treatment of the indicative mood is also incorrect. To provide only one counterexample: When someone asks a question by uttering an indicative sentence with a rising inflection at the end (for instance, "That's a *cat*?"), it cannot be the function of the indicative mood to signify the speaker's belief in the proposition. Moreover, this account of the indicative mood entails that a person who asserts a sentence of the form "I believe that p" is both asserting that he believes that p and, in virtue of the sentence's indicative mood, expressing the belief that he believes that p. But surely this second supposed expression of a belief is otiose and not in fact part of what the speaker has signified.

Chapter Three: Speech Acts: Saying and Doing

I. Saying and Meaning

The Cooperative Principle and the Conversational Maxims constitute a framework within which individual contributions to discourse are made. To make a conversational contribution is to perform a speech act; for instance, making a statement is a speech act, and so is asking a question, or issuing a demand, or telling a joke. A theory of speech acts is a theory of what it is to *say* something; what 'say' means in this context is one of the things that we shall explore in this chapter.

It is clear, in the first place, that there is an important difference between what a speaker says and what he means. We encountered this distinction briefly in the first two chapters; it is now time to deal with it in some detail. We may begin with one of Alice's misadventures in Wonderland:

> The Hatter opened his eyes very wide on hearing this; but all he *said* was "Why is a raven like a writing-desk?"
> "Come, we shall have some fun now!" thought Alice. "I'm glad they've begun asking riddles — I believe I can guess that," she added aloud.
> "Do you mean that you think you can find out the answer to it?" said the March Hare.
> "Exactly so," said Alice.
> "Then you should say what you mean," the March Hare went on.
> "I do," Alice hastily replied; "at least — at least I mean what I say — that's the same thing, you know."
> "Not the same thing a bit!" said the Hatter. "Why, you might just as well say that 'I see what I eat' is the same thing as 'I eat what I see'!"
> "You might just as well say," added the March Hare, "that 'I like what I get' is the same thing as 'I get what I like'!"
> "You might just as well say," added the Dormouse, which seemed to be talking in its sleep, "that 'I breathe when I sleep' is the same thing as 'I sleep when I breathe'!"
> "It *is* the same thing with you," said the Hatter, and here the conversation dropped (Lewis Carroll, *Alice's Adventures in Wonderland*, Chapter 7).

It is not immediately obvious how much of this conversation is mere quibbling and how much of it contains an element of truth. Let's work through it. The Mad Hatter produces his pointless riddle, and Alice says, "I believe I can guess that." The March Hare asks, "Do you mean that you think you can find the answer to it?" Alice's affirmative answer is correct; this is part of what she meant, although she did not say it in so many words. The

March Hare unfairly exploits this fact when he replies, "Then you should say what you mean." The reason that this reply is unfair is that, as we shall see, it is neither desirable nor possible for a speaker to say everything that he means; certainly a speaker has no *obligation* to do so, as the March Hare's remark implies if it is taken literally.

But there is more to the March Hare's remark than its literal meaning. By saying what he does, the Hare conversationally implicates that Alice is saying something that she does not mean; he is, in effect, accusing her of insincerity. This implicature arises because Alice assumes that the March Hare is observing the Maxim of Relation, and hence would not have made this remark unless he believed that there was a disparity between what Alice had said and what she really meant. Alice is flustered by this accusation, and replies hastily in order to refute it. Unfortunately, the phrasing of the March Hare's remark makes it difficult for her to do this, and she incautiously equates saying what one means with meaning what one says. One way to rebuff an accusation of insincerity is to retort "I mean everything I say"; but as the inhabitants of Wonderland go on to point out (with their usual rudeness), this is quite different from "I say everything I mean."

What *did* Alice mean when she said "I believe I can guess that"? Among other things, she meant that she was willing to make a guess, that her guess would be a proposed answer to the Mad Hatter's riddle rather than some other question, that she believed that her guess would be correct, and that she did not already know the answer to the riddle. Although Alice did not say any of these things, she meant them by implication. Some of the things she implied are conversational implicatures; others depend on the semantic conventions that govern the meanings of her words; still others are wholly non-conventional. At any rate, it is clear that Alice cannot be reasonably expected to say everything that she means.

There are, of course, scenarios that illustrate the distinction between saying and meaning more straightforwardly. Consider the following exchange:

> A: You seem to have extremely limited powers of reasoning; solutions to the simplest and most trivial problems burden you as a mountain would burden an ant, when they do not elude you completely.
> B: You're saying that I'm an idiot.
> A: I didn't say that.
> B (after a bewildered pause): Well, you implied it.

A and B are sensitive to the distinction between saying and implying. A is correct in maintaining that he did not *say* that B is an idiot; B is correct in maintaining that A quite clearly implied it.

The concluding episode of the Gospel of John provides another example of the difference between meaning something by saying it and meaning something by implying it. The scene is the shore of the Sea of Tiberias.

During one of his strolls with his apostles after his resurrection, Jesus foretells the manner of Peter's death. This makes Peter curious about how "the disciple whom Jesus loved" (namely John) would die. So Peter asks, "But, Lord, what about him?" Jesus answers, "If it should be my will that he wait until I come, what is it to you? Follow me." The author of the gospel then remarks: "That saying of Jesus became current in the brotherhood, and was taken to *mean* that the disciple would not die. But in fact Jesus did not *say* that he would not die; he only *said* that if it should be his will that John wait until he comes, what is it to Peter?" (John 21:22−23; italics added).

In all of these cases, what the speaker means is different from what he says. Sometimes, as in Alice's case, the speaker means what he says and more besides; in other cases, the speaker's meaning does not include the meaning of the sentence he utters (as in the Tank McNamara example back in section III of Chapter One) and may even be contrary to it (as in the Charlie Chaplin example in the same section). The question arises: Is it *ever* the case that a speaker says exactly what he means and no more? It would seem that this is impossible. For in the course of spelling out the implications of even the shortest and least significant remark, the speaker would inevitably imply more and more, and if he tried to articulate these implications as well, he would imply still more, *ad infinitum*. It is logically possible that the implications would eventually begin to repeat, so that instead of getting new implications all the time the speaker would eventually reach a point where his statements of the earlier implications would imply only other earlier implications. However, it seems that this abstract possibility does not occur in real or plausibly imagined cases.

Whether or not it is possible for a speaker to say exactly what he means, it is certainly not desirable. Conversationalists who explicitly draw attention to what they imply tend to be gassy and tedious; it is a habit that impedes communication rather than facilitating it.

II. Performative Verbs

The fact that we mean more than we say indicates that the proponent of a theory of communication cannot explain what happens in a conversation by looking only at the utterances of the participants; he also needs to understand the non-semantic conventions and institutions within which the conversation takes place. Speech-act theory is one avenue to such understanding.

The originator of speech-act theory, J. L. Austin, has written that his ideas on the subject began to take shape in 1939, and that he first made use of them in an article entitled "Other Minds," which appeared in 1946. He also delivered lectures at Oxford under the title "Words and Deeds" each year between 1952 and 1954. The first public presentation of his tentative theory of speech acts was his William James Lectures at Harvard in 1955.

These lectures, published posthumously in 1962 as *How to Do Things with Words*, are also the most developed expression of his views. Two other oral presentations were likewise published posthumously: "Performative Utterances," a talk broadcast by the BBC in 1956, and "Performatif-Constatif," a paper that Austin presented at an Anglo-French Conference at Royaumont in 1958.

Speech-act theory began as a reaction to an account of meaning propounded by a school of philosophers known as logical positivists. (At one time, Austin himself may have been sympathetic to logical positivism; see Ayer (1977), pp. 151–152.) The logical positivists held that only two kinds of sentences are meaningful: truths of pure logic and mathematics, which can be established deductively, and sentences expressing empirically testable propositions, which can be confirmed or refuted experimentally. Ethical and aesthetic judgements, metaphysical and religious doctrines, poetry and political propaganda were all dismissed as cognitively meaningless, or at best as expressions of emotion or desire, having no cognitive content. (There are some notable exceptions to this general description of the stand of the logical positivists; see, for instance, Charles Stevenson (1944) and (1963).) In general, the idea was that only by deduction or by application of the scientific method can the truth or falsity of a sentence be determined to everyone's satisfaction, and if there is no satisfactory way of determining whether a sentence is true or false, it must be nonsensical.

Austin undertook to refute this view by showing that there are "perfectly straightforward utterances, with ordinary verbs in the first person singular present indicative active" (Austin (1956b), p. 235), which are meaningful without being true or false at all. His first four examples are these:

> I do [sc. take this woman to be my lawful wedded wife].
> I name this ship the *Queen Elizabeth*.
> I give and bequeath my watch to my brother.
> I bet you sixpence it will rain tomorrow (Austin (1955), p. 5).

These sentences are used in what Austin calls "performative utterances" and contrast with statements of fact. When someone says, "I give and bequeath my watch to my brother," under appropriate circumstances, he is not stating a fact about himself, saying something that might be true and might be false; he *is giving and bequeathing* his watch to his brother. Similarly, the person who says, "I name this ship the *Queen Elizabeth*," is not making a remark about what she is doing; she is *doing* it.

Thus Austin tentatively divides sentences into those that are used for "merely *saying* something," which he calls "constatives," and those that are used for "*doing* something," which he calls "performatives" (Austin (1956b), p. 235). This distinction, however, is somewhat misleading, as Austin quickly realized. A constative sentence is used for stating a fact, and to state a fact is to "*do* something". It is true that getting married or christening a ship is a more momentous action, but that does not mean that mere fact-stating is not an action at all. To quote Austin:

> We see that stating something is performing an act just as much as is giving an order or giving a warning; ... this seems to mean that in its original form our distinction between the performative and the statement is considerably weakened, and indeed breaks down (Austin (1956b), p. 251).

Constative sentences thus become one category of performative sentences.

However, there is something special about the examples of performativity cited above: They contain what came to be called "performative verbs," which explicitly mark the performance of the speech-act they express. Whereas a typical constative utterance does not have the word 'state' or 'assert' in it, 'I name this ship the *Queen Elizabeth*' contains the word 'name', which explicitly marks the act of naming.

The intuitive idea here is that the mere utterance of certain verbs in the first person singular present indicative active seems to make something so or to constitute the performance of the act expressed; so for instance it seems that in saying "I promise," I promise, and in saying "I swear," I swear, and so on. Austin, and many others after him, tried to construct criteria of performativity. So far all such attempts have met with various degrees of failure; but there are three rules of thumb, derived from Austin's work, that yield approximately correct results. Zeno Vendler calls these rules of thumb the "to say" formula, the "in saying" formula, and the "hereby" formula (Vendler (1972a), p. 8). Let's see how they work by trying them out on a typical performative verb, 'promise', and a typical non-performative verb, 'run':

The "to say" formula
To say (in the appropriate circumstance) "I *promise* to pay you $5" is to promise to pay somebody $5. (Right.)
To say (in the appropriate circumstances) "I *run* two miles every morning" is to run two miles every morning. (Wrong.)

The "in saying" formula
In saying that he *promised* to pay Jerome $5, he promised to pay Jerome $5. (Right.)
In saying that he *ran* two miles every morning, he ran two miles every morning. (Wrong.)

The "hereby" formula
I hereby *promise* to pay you $5. (This makes sense.)
I hereby *run* two miles every morning. (This does not make sense.)

By inventing analogous sentences for other verbs and seeing whether they are true and coherent, or false or nonsensical, one can classify those verbs as performative and non-performative, respectively.

What performative verbs have in common is that they express actions of a certain kind, namely, intentional communicative actions. It is important, therefore, not to confuse performative verbs with verbs that express states of any sort, especially mental states, such as 'know', 'believe', 'hope', 'fear', 'intend', or with verbs that express actions that have nothing to do with communication, such as 'scheme' and 'imagine'. Among the verbs that are classified as perfomatives by the rules of thumb given above are these:

affirm	define	propose
apologize	deny	question
appraise	grade	rate
ask	guarantee	rank
assert	inquire	request
censure	judge	rule
claim	order	state
classify	pardon	suggest
command	pledge	swear
concede	praise	testify
congratulate	predict	thank
declare	promise	vow

How many performative verbs are there in English? Austin cagily estimates that they number between 10^3 and 10^4.

III. Locutionary, Illocutionary and Perlocutionary Acts

Having renounced the performative/constative distinction, Austin makes a fresh start on the analysis of speech acts, the analysis of "the total situation in which the utterance is issued (Austin (1955), p. 52). He begins by asking "how many senses there are in which to say something is to do something" (Austin (1955), p. 94). He distinguishes three broad types of acts connected with saying something, and the first of these again into three:

1. locutionary act
    a. the phonetic act
    b. the phatic act
    c. the rhetic act
2. illocutionary act
3. perlocutionary act

Although initially it is easy to confuse locutionary and illocutionary acts, and illocutionary and perlocutionary acts, with a little attention, errors will be minimized. Let's first separate perlocutionary acts. While locutionary and illocutionary acts are two broad kinds of saying, perlocutionary acts are *not* a kind of saying at all. Intuitively, a perlocutionary act is an act per-

III Speech Acts: Saying and Doing   49

formed *by* saying something, or as a consequence of saying something, and not *in* saying something. Persuading, angering, inciting, comforting and inspiring are often perlocutionary acts; but they would never begin an answer to the question "What did he say?" Perlocutionary acts, in contrast with locutionary and illocutionary acts, which are governed by conventions, are not conventional but natural acts (Austin (1955), p. 121). Persuading, angering, inciting, etc., cause physiological changes in the audience, either in their states or behavior; conventional acts do not.

Let's now separate locutionary and illocutionary acts. They are kinds of saying, but importantly different kinds of saying. The verb "to say" is dangerously equivocal and Searle has shown that Austin succumbed to the equivocation (see Searle (1968)). If someone asks a question of the form,

What did x say?

he might be asking for either (i) a report of the exact words uttered, that is, a report of the locutionary act performed, or (ii) a report of the speech act or illocutionary act performed. If the first question is being asked, then a correct answer takes the form of

x said, "..."

That is, the correct way to report a locutionary act is by means of direct quotation. Thus, in answering the question, "What did he say?" when this is a request for a report of the locutionary act, one might answer

He said, "Shoot her."

or

He said, "You can't do that."

One can similarly report, without grammatical violation, what someone said in this sense, when what was said was in a foreign language:

He said, "Kennst du das Land, wo die Zitronen blühen?"

or

He said, "Gallia est omnis divisa in tres partes."

If the second question is being asked, then a correct answer sometimes (but only sometimes, as will be shown below) takes the form of

x said that ...

That is, the verb "to say" is followed by indirect quotation. Thus, one might answer a request for what someone said, in this latter sense, as follows:

He said that I was to shoot her

or

He said that I was not permitted to do that.

One can also mix direct quotation with indirect quotation to report someone's illocutionary act. If someone says, "John became ill" and means it, what he said can be reported as

> He said that "John became ill."

But care must be taken. One cannot indiscriminately use direct quotation in indirect discourse. If someone says, "Kennst du das Land wo die Zitronen blühen?", it is gibberish to report

> He said that "Kennst du das Land wo die Zitronen blühen?"

And if someone says "I am ill," it is false to report

> He said that "I am ill."

One can use direct quotation within indirect discourse only if the speaker's original language is translated into the reporter's language and if no adjustments are needed for the pronouns used and the tense of the verb. If someone says "Ego incido in morbum" it is acceptable to report

> He said that he became "ill."

Another difference between the sense of "to say" in (i) and (ii) is that a speaker might say something which could be correctly reported to answer (i) without saying anything that could be correctly reported as the answer to question (ii), e.g. an actor rehearsing his lines.

In order to disambiguate the question, "What did *x* say?" and the cognate wh-nominal, "what he said," I shall write them, when they concern the illocutionary act performed, as

> What did *x* say-that?

and

> what he said-that.

Before making some additional points about saying-that, let me complete my discussion of a locutionary act. Within the locutionary act, Austin distinguishes three different aspects, which are themselves acts: the phonetic, phatic and rhetic act, which he explicates as follows: "The phonetic act is merely the act of uttering certain noises. The phatic act is the uttering of certain vocables or words, i.e. noises of certain types, belonging to and as belonging to, a certain vocabulary, conforming to and as conforming to a certain grammar. The rhetic act is the performance of an act of using those vocables with a certain more-or-less definite sense and reference" (Austin (1955), p. 95). As Austin explains these notions, brute animals are capable of and perform phonetic acts, but not phatic or rhetic acts, since brutes lacking language do not utter certain noises "as belonging to, a certain vocabulary . . . and as conforming to a certain grammar" (Austin (1955),

III Speech Acts: Saying and Doing

p. 95). Parrots utter certain noises belonging to a language but not *as* belonging to one.

Let's now focus our attention on illocutionary acts and begin by returning to the notion of saying-that. An answer to the question

What did x say-that?

might take any one of the following forms:

(1) x asserted that ...
(2) x bet that ...
(3) x promised to ...
(4) x asked whether ...

or some other. As (1)–(4) indicate, a complete answer to the question typically consists of two parts: the main verb of the report specifies the illocutionary force of the speech act and the clause of indirect discourse specifies its propositional content. For mnemonic purposes, one can think of the portmanteau verb "say-that" as representing these two parts: first, "say" representing some performative verb or verb phrase of saying and second, "-that" representing some clause of indirect discourse. On the one hand, the same propositional content can be advanced with various different forces:

(1) I assert that Socrates is wise.
(2) I order you, Socrates, to be wise.
(3) I ask whether Socrates is wise.
(4) I swear that Socrates is wise.

Each of these sentences would *ceteris paribus* be used to express the same propositional content. In each is a reference to Socrates and a predication of wisdom. Following Searle, we shall call this part of an illocutionary act its propositional content. Each of these sentences is different in expressing, in virtue of the performative verb, a different illocutionary force: asserting, ordering, asking and swearing.

On the other hand, different propositions can be advanced with the same force:

(5) I claim Mondale will be elected.
(6) I claim Kennedy will be elected.
(7) I claim Reagan will be elected.
(8) I claim Dole will be elected.

Searle has devised some representational devises for illocutionary acts. Assertive force is represented by a turnstile; interrogative force by a question mark and imperative force by an exclamation mark; others could be devised. The propositional content is represented by a lower case italicized letter from the latter part of the Roman alphabet. Thus, (1)–(4) might be represented:

(R1) ⊢ (p)
(R2) ! (p)
(R3) ? (p)
(R4) X (p)

One can express what Searle has done in regard to Austin's distinctions. Searle has transferred the rhetic act from the locutionary act into the illocutionary act, and thus espouses the following distinction:

1. Locutionary act
    (a) Phonetic act
    (b) Phatic act
2. Illocutionary act
    (1) Force
    (2) Content (rhetic act)
3. Perlocutionary act

IV. Analyses of Three Illocutionary Acts

A paradigmatic case of an illocutionary act is a promise, performed, for example, by saying, "I promise I will go to the party." How can we give a precise and explicit analysis of this kind of illucutionary act? First, we have to distinguish between those acts of promising that are both successful and nondefective from those that are successful but defective. Since successful and nondefective cases are the clearest ones, let's begin with such an analysis of promising.

A speaker S successfully and nondefectively promises that p in the utterance of a sentence T in the presence of an audience A if and only if:
1. S expresses that p in the utterance of T;
2. In expressing that p, S predicates a future act X of S;
3. A would prefer S's doing X to his not doing X;
4. It is not obvious to both S and A that A would do X in the normal course of events;
5. S intends to do X;
6. S recognizes that the utterance of T puts him under an obligation to do X;
7. S intends that A intends that A will understand that S recognizes that the utterance of T will place him under an obligation to do X, and he intends that A will recognize his intention in virtue of A's knowledge of the meaning of T;
8. A recognizes that conditions 1–7 obtain.

The basic pattern of this analysis is due to Searle (1969), pp. 57–61. One condition I have omitted is his first, which reads, "Normal input and output conditions obtain." Both the speaker and his audience must be competent speakers of the language and not suffering from any long or short term disabilities that would affect their communication; and the environment must not interfere with their abilities, e.g., rock music cannot be played loudly at the time. Because this condition is common to every paradigmatic speech act, I have not included it in the analysis of this particular speech act.

I have also added a condition, condition 8, because I do not believe that a promise has been made unless there is audience uptake; that is, unless the audience recognizes that the speaker tried to promise. This view is controversial, and I will not argue for it here. (An analog of this problem will arise in Chapter Nine: A Speech Act Theory of Referring.) Let's now consider successful but defective promising. People expect promises to be sincere; that is, they expect someone who promises to satisfy condition (5): S intends to do X. However, even if the speaker does not intend to do what he says he will do, he nonetheless promises, albeit defectively, and is still under an obligation to do what he has promised. (Crossing one's fingers does not nullify a promise either.) Contrast the failure of condition 5 to obtain with the failure of some one of the other conditions. Suppose that condition 3 does not obtain; that the audience would prefer that the speaker not do what he says. Here we may have a case of a threat, not a promise, even if the speaker says something like "I promise I will fail you." There are two ways to treat a case like this. We can either hold that "promise" is equivocal and in one sense means "threaten" or "warn"; or one can hold that the speaker who says "I promise I will fail you" only makes-as-if to perform a promise and in fact conversationally implies a threat or warning in virtue of the context and his seriousness of purpose as expressed by the word "promise." Condition 4 is like condition 5 and not like condition 3. To promise to do what it is obvious that one would do in the normal course of events is an odd but genuine case of a promise. For, if a person says he promises to do such a thing and does not do it, he is criticizable for failing to live up to an obligation that he, perhaps needlessly, put himself under. All the other conditions are necessary for a successful act of promising, which we can specify as follows:

> A speaker S successfully promises that p in the utterance of a sentence T in the presence of an audience A if and only if:
> 1. S expresses that p in the utterance of T;
> 2. In expressing that p, S predicates a future act X S;
> 3. A would prefer S's doing X to his not doing X, S *believes that* A would prefer his doing X to his not doing X;
> 6. S recognizes that the utterance of T puts him under an obligation to do X;

7. S intends that A will understand that S recognizes that the utterance of T will place him under an obligation to do X, and he intends that A will recognize his intention in virtue of A's knowledge of the meaning of T;
8. A recognizes that conditions 1–7 obtain.

In order to provide more samples of speech act analyses from which we can draw some generalizations, I will present two additional analyses, one of apologizing and one of forgiving, largely without comment. These anaylses do not, however, indicate the full range of speech acts that might be analysed. (See Martinich (1975) and Martinich (1980) for some indication of the range.) For it is the pattern of speech act analyses and not the details of specific speech acts that is important for us. Ethics, not the philosophy of language, is the correct place to argue about the details of such concepts as promising, forgiving and apologizing.

Forgiving

A speaker S successfully and nondefectively forgives an audience A in the utterance of a sentence T if and only if:
1. S expresses that p;
2. In expressing that p, S predicates a past action I of A;
3. I injured S;
4. A caused I;
5. A intended his causing of I to injure S;
6. S does not harbor bad feelings towards A for I;
7. S understands that the utterance of T counts as releasing A from all the future bad consequences of I, and as expressing that he does not harbor bad feelings towards A for I;
8. S intends that A will understand that conditions 1–7 obtain.
9. A recognizes that conditions 1–8 obtain.

Apologizing

A speaker S successfully and nondefectively apologizes to an audience A for an act I with an utterance of a sentence T if and only if;
1. S expresses that p;
2. In expressing that p, S predicates a past action I of S;
3. I injured A;
5. S intend his causing of I to injure A;
6. S is sorry for doing I;
7. S understands that the utterance of T counts as an expression of sorrow for causing I;
8. S intends that A will understand that conditions 1–7 obtain in virtue of the meaning of T.
9. A recognizes that conditions 1–8 obtain.

III Speech Acts: Saying and Doing   55

There are certain general features of the speech act analyses given so far that should be mentioned. One is that speech act analysis at one level is nothing more than traditional conceptual analysis, or at least has the same goals. A speech act analysis of promising is a conceptual analysis of promising; a speech act analysis of apologizing is a conceptual analysis of apologizing. What speech act analysis can bring out is the inescapably linguistic character of many of our actions. (Caveat: You should notice that there are two different acts of forgiveness: one that is essentially linguistic, and one that is not, the forgiveness that resides in the heart.) Not all concepts are linguistic; for example, speech act analysis does not advance the analysis of such traditional notions as belief, knowledge, truth or goodness. (Actually, some philosophers think that goodness is pretty closely bound up with a speech act (see Hare (1952)). Also, the conditions are collectible into categories. Five categories can be distinguished on the basis of the few speech acts analysed here.

First, there are propositional content conditions, which specify who or what is being talked about and what is being said about that object; in short, the propositional content conditions specify the references and predications that must be made for a certain speech act. Conditions 1 and 2 of promising, forgiving and apologizing express propositional content conditions. Notice that each of these acts must express a proposition, in contrast with an act of greeting ("hello"), which need not. Also notice that each of these acts can be compared and contrasted on the basis of these conditions. Promising and apologizing are similar in that both require that the predication be made of the speaker. But forgiving and apologizing are similar in that both require that the act predicated be an act that occurred in the past.

Second, there are preparatory conditions, which specify things that must be the case before the utterance of the sentence can begin. Condition 3 of promising and conditions 3–5 of both forgiving and apologizing express such conditions. Notice how forgiving and apologizing can be contrasted in virtue of these conditions. For example, as condition 3 indicates, in forgiving, the audience is the cause of the injury while in apologizing the speaker is the cause of the injury.

Third, there are sincerity conditions, which specify a certain state of mind or feeling that the speaker must have in performing his action. Condition 5 of promising and condition 6 of both forgiving and apologizing express the kind of state of mind or feeling that is required.

Fourth, there is the essential condition, which specifies the point or purpose of the act. Condition 7 of promising and condition 8 of forgiving and apologizing express the essential condition.

Fifth there is an audience uptake condition, which expresses what the hearer has to do in order for the speech act to be successful. For the speech acts we have been considering, the hearer need do no more than understand what the situation is. For other speech acts, another speech act, a speech act sequel is required. For example, in order to get married, it is not enough for one of the parties to perform his part; the other one must do the same in order for either to have effect. And if either has effect, then both do.

V. Categories of Illocutionary Acts

Is there any plausible and satisfying way of categorizing performative verbs? More to the point, are there basic categories or types of illocutionary speech acts? Most speech-act theorists think so, and several classifications have been suggested. In this section we shall deal with the proposals of Austin, Vendler, and Searle.

The earliest proposal of this kind was Austin's. He tentatively distinguished the following five categories:

> The first, verdictives, are typified by the giving of a verdict, as the name implies, by a jury, arbitrator, or umpire. . . . It is essentially giving a finding as to something — fact, or value — which is for different reasons hard to be certain about. [For example, acquitting, convicting, grading, assessing, and ranking are all verdictive acts.]
> The second, exercitives, are the exercising of powers, rights, or influence. Examples are appointing, voting, ordering, urging, advising, warning, &c.
> The third, commissives, are typified by promising or otherwise undertaking; they *commit* you to doing something, but include also declararions or announcements, which are not promises, and also rather vague things which we may call espousals, as for example, siding with. They have obvious connexions with verdictives and exercitives.
> The fourth, behabitives, are a very miscellaneous group, and have to do with attitudes and *social behaviour*. Examples are apologizing, congratulating, commending, condoling, cursing, and challenging.
> The fifth, expositives, . . . make plain how our utterances fit into the course of an argument or conversation, how we are using words, or, in general, are expository. Examples are 'I reply', 'I argue', 'I concede', 'I illustrate', 'I assume', 'I postulate' (Austin (1955), pp. 150–151; italics in original).

Although it constituted an excellent start, this set of categories is inadequate. The worst problem seems to be that there is "non consistent principle of classification" (Searle (1975c), p. 354); as a result, some illocutionary acts belong to more than one category. For example, many of Austin's behabitive illocutionary acts, such as commending and congratulating, call for verdicts just as much as the verdictives that he lists.

Recognizing the source of the problem, Zeno Vendler attempted to rectify it by taking syntactic differences among the verbs that express illocutionary acts as the principle of categorization. He pointed out, for example, that expositive verbs can be followed by *that*-clauses:

> I state that . . .
> I declare that . . .

III Speech Acts: Saying and Doing

while Austin's verdictives favor a nonpropositional structure, often involving the construction known as "double accusative" or "double direct object":

I call it murder.
I rank him second.
I classify the piece as a novel.

Commissives favor the infinitive construction:

I promise to pay on time.
I vow to be chaste.

as do exercitives:

I order you to proceed.
I advise you to remain silent.

But commissives and exercitives differ in that the (unexpressed) subject of the infinitive phrase that follows a commissive verb is 'I'; after an exercitive verb, it is 'you'. Using these and similar syntactic characteristics, Vendler distinguishes a total of seven categories: Austin's five plus separate categories of operatives (appointing, condemning, surrendering) and interrogatives (asking, questioning).

Vendler is proud of the similarity between his results and Austin's, for it was his intention to "vindicate Austin's own intuition in the grouping of illocutionary forces" (Vendler (1972a), p. 12). Unfortunately, precisely because his results match up well with Austin's, the categories he proposes are subject to the same criticisms as Austin's: They are neither mutually exclusive nor jointly exhaustive (there is no natural place in either man's scheme for the illocutionary act that an umpire performs when he says, "Out!" or for the one that the president of the International Olympic Committee performs when he says, "I declare these games open").

One might wonder why Vendler's categorization fails in spite of the fact that, unlike Austin, he provided a consistent principle of categorization. One explanation is that Vendler attended to the wrong feature of language. The syntactic features of verbs that express illocutionary acts are at best indirect reflections of the nature of the acts themselves; the semantic and pragmatic features of such verbs are bound to be more relevant.

This is the insight behind Searle's attempt to categorize illocutionary acts. He mentions "twelve significant dimensions of variation in which illocutionary acts differ from one another" (Searle (1975c), p. 345), which we may conveniently state as questions to be answered by the would-be classifier:

1. *What is the point (or purpose) of the act?* The illocutionary point of statements, assertions, asseverations, and remarks is to represent how

things are. The illocutionary point of commands and requests is to get the hearer to do something. The illocutionary point of oaths, promises, and vows is to impose an obligation on oneself. And so on. It is important not to confuse the illocutionary point either with the act itself (speech acts are seldom performed for their own sake) or with its perlocutionary effects.

2. *How are the words the speaker utters to be fitted to the world?* There are four possible answers to this question. (A) In some speech acts, the speaker tries to get the world to match his words. For instance, one issues a command or makes a request, such as "Please open the door," in order to get someone to make the propositional content of one's utterance true — in this case, by opening the door. Again, a promise is an arrangement by which the speaker undertakes to make the propositional content of his own utterance true by acting in such a way that the world comes to fit it. (B) In other cases, the idea is to get the words to fit the world. Statements and assertions are the paradigm cases of this. When one states or asserts that p, one's utterance purports to represent the world as it is. (C) The performance of speech acts of certain sorts actually creates facts that the utterances *ipso facto* fit. When the president of the International Olympic Committee declares that the Olympic Games are open, they are open; when the president of the United States declares a national holiday, the day in question is indeed a national holiday. (D) There are some speech acts that are not supposed to have any relationship to the world. Entertaining a proposition, or raising it as a possibility, has this characteristic; in raising some proposition as a possibility, we do not commit ourselves to its truth or to its falsity, past, present, or future.

In a few cases answers (B) and (C) can be combined. For example, when a jury says, "We find the defendant guilty," or when an umpire shouts, "Safe," the defendant is (legally) guilty and the player safe; the statement makes it so. So answer (C) is in order. But at the same time neither a jury nor an umpire can say just anything, regardless of the pre-existing facts; or, more precisely, they are not *supposed* to say just anything, but rather to attend to and base their declarations on those facts as they perceive them. Their speech acts will be defective unless they conform to the pre-existing facts; so in a way answer (B) is appropriate too.

Juries and umpires try to get their verdicts in line with the world; but even when they fail, their declarations are binding and create new facts: the defendant is (legally) guilty, the player is safe. These are institutional facts, that is, they derive their existence from social institutions and can only be understood in the context of such institutions. Sometimes the institution provides a way in which the facts can be changed, as the verdicts of juries can be reversed on appeal; other institutional facts, such as the pronouncements of umpires, are "irreformable of themselves" and cannot be overturned by higher authority. It is sometimes argued that all facts are institutional; but I shall not assume this.

3. *What psychological state is expressed?* A person who states or asserts something expresses his belief that it is the case. A person who apologizes expresses his regret for something he has done. A person who makes a promise or a vow expresses his intention to keep it.

4. *How strongly is the illocutionary point presented?* The difference between suggesting that something be done and insisting that it be done is one of strength.

5. *What does the utterance indicate about the status or position of the speaker and the hearer?* An act of sentencing requires a judge as speaker and a defendant as hearer. A command requires someone who is at least nominally superior as speaker and someone who is at least nominally subordinate as hearer. By extension, there are speech acts that can *only* be performed by collections of individuals; for instance, only nations can declare wars.

6. *How is the utterance related to the interests of the speaker and the hearer?* The difference between a promise and a warning is that in a promise the hearer wants (or is assumed to want) the propositional content to become true, while in a warning he wants (or is assumed to want) it not to become true.

7. *How is the utterance related to the rest of the discourse in which it occurs?* This question is particularly relevant to speech acts carried out in observation of maxim C1 (of section VI of Chapter Two), "Make your contribution one that indicates . . . the direction in which the conversation is moving." The class includes starters ("Hello"), stoppers ("The end"), and a variety of direction-signals for use in the middle of a conversation ("I now turn to . . ."). There are also more general expositives that define the character of a stretch of discourse ("I argue . . .", "I reply . . .", "I object . . ."). Acts of this sort have been called "master speech acts" (Fotion (1971)).

8. *Are there any constraints on propositional content?* The propositional content of an act of reporting must concern the past, not the future; in an act of predicting, the reverse is true.

9. *It is possible to perform this act without language?* Some illocutionary acts are by definition speech acts; others can be performed without the help of language, at least in exeptional circumstances. For example, arguing can only be accomplished with the help of a language (otherwise it turns into fighting); on the other hand, in some societies a couple can get married by jumping over a broomstick as well as by making a verbal commitment or going through a verbal ritual.

10. *Does this act require any extra-linguistic institutions and conventions for its performance?* The distinction here is between institutional speech acts (such as excommunicating, bidding in bridge, and declaring war) on one hand and non-institutional speech acts (such as stating and inquiring) on the other. One might also distinguish between speech acts that

must be performed in conjunction with other actions and speech acts that can be performed independently; in the first class are included such acts as baptizing someone (which requires the speaker either to immerse the hearer or to pour or sprinkle water on his head) and calling a runner out (which requires the speaker to sweep his fist, thumb extended, back past his ear).

11. *Can the verb that expresses this act be used as a performative?* Searle, at least, maintains that boasting and threatening are illocutionary acts even though the verbs 'boast' and 'threaten' fail the "hereby" test (see section II). Perhaps it would be more accurate to call acts that cannot be marked with an explicit performative "circumlocutionary." Insinuating is another example of the same sort.

12. *In what manner is the act performed?* Here Searle's example is the difference between announcing and confiding, which might plausibly be said to have the same illocutionary point but which are performed in different ways.

Obviously, some of these dimensions of difference are more important than others, and when Searle comes to set up his categories, he deals mainly with the first three. He recognizes five categories:

Representatives
Purpose? To say how something is.
Direction of fit? (B), word to world.
State expressed? Belief.

Directives
Purpose? To get the hearer to do something.
Direction of fit? (A), world to word.
State expressed? Desire (to have the hearer act in the specified way).
Propositional content? Future.

Commissives
Purpose? To impose an obligation on the speaker.
Direction of fit? (A), world to word.
State expressed? Intention to act.
Propositional content? Future action by speaker.

Expressives
Purpose? To express some attitude.
Direction of fit? (D), no fit required.
State expressed? Varies.

Declarations
Purpose? To create a fact.
Direction of fit? (C), fact creating.
State expressed? Usually none; sometimes belief.

This table follows Searle's account of the five groups; in certain details it seems to be mistaken. The entire category of expressives is problematical. It is not at all neat; it contains such diverse acts as congratulating, apologizing, condemning, and forgiving, which hardly seem enough alike to be placed together.

Another objection that can be raised against Searle's classification is that it does not comfortably house a number of illocutionary acts, especially the "master speech acts" mentioned under question 7 above. However, Searle's twelve dimensions of variation provide a useful framework for distinguishing illocutionary acts, which is a step in the right direction; as in biology, no taxonomy is likely to succeed unless it is preceded by and based on detailed observation and description.

Chapter Four:
The Total Content of What a Speaker Communicates

I. Grice on the Total Content of What a Speaker Communicates

In the previous chapter, we discussed various senses of saying something and have at least implicitly distinguished two ways of linguistically communicating something: by saying it and by implying it. This distinction alone, however, does not have much theoretical significance because it is neither characterized nor part of any more systematic classification of the total content of what is linguistically communicated. Characterizing different parts of the total content of what is linguistically communicated is very difficult and, at this stage of the theory of conversation, it should not be demanded. However, if the distinctions that are intuitively drawn are illuminating and solve philosophical problems, then they are fruitful, and this fruitfulness should spur on the efforts to characterize them.

One of the merits of H. P. Grice's work on conversation is that he has gone a long way towards identifying the elements of what is linguistically communicated. In this chapter, I begin by sketching Grice's view; I then criticize, revise and extend his theory.

Grice divides the total content of what a speaker communicates into what the speaker says and what he implies (Grice (1975), pp. 43–45; and Grice (1978)). What the speaker says is closely tied to the actual words uttered and includes all the references and predications made. Thus, a person who utters

(1) John is a bachelor

and means it, typically has said-that John is a bachelor since he has typically referred to John and has predicated bachelorhood of him. Intuitively, it might seem that what is said should be reported by making use of the very words uttered, whenever possible. This is not always possible. If the speaker says, "I am standing here," the egocentric elements must be changed such that a correct report of what was said becomes: He said that he was standing in his office (or wherever).

Grice's treatment of saying-that raises many questions. For example, does a person who utters (2) say the same thing as one who utters (3)?

(2) Thomas Jefferson was the best president of the United States.
(3) The wealthiest slave-owning president was the best president of the United States.

Grice does not answer this question and I will not treat it since I think that how we answer this question is largely a matter of decision. The best answer is the one that provides the simplest explanation of the phenomenon and accords best with other features of the general theory of conversation. There are other difficult questions. Let's bring back the tangle-tongued Tank McNamara. Suppose that Tank sets out to say that the vice-president of the United States is ambitious, but actually produces the sentence, "The president of the United States is vicious." We may imagine that the reporter *R* who hears him say this is well aware of Tank's linguistic propensities and somehow manages to figure out that he meant to say that the vice-president of the United States is ambitious. The question is: How does *R* report what Tank has said? There are at least three attractive possibilities:

> (i) He didn't say anything, because his words didn't accurately reflect his intentions.
> (ii) He said that the vice-president of the United States is ambitious, because his audience managed to reconstruct that proposition as the speaker-meaning of the utterance.
> (iii) He said that the president of the United States is vicious, because, as Grice puts it, what is said should be "closely related to the conventional meaning of the words (the sentence) he [the speaker] has uttered" (Grice (1975), p. 44).

There is a way of incorporating the intuitions behind all three of these possibilities into a single account. Let us say that a speaker *S* says something if, and only if, what *S* means is consonant with the sentence-meaning of his utterance. Moreover, given that *S* says something, *what* he says is determined by the relation between his words and what they express in the context of utterance. Thus, although the sentence, "This table of mine is blue" will express different things in different contexts, once the context (which includes the speaker and hearer, their beliefs, the time and place of utterance, and the immediately preceding stretch of discourse) is specified, it will be possible to determine what the speaker is using that sentence to say. In the Tank McNamara example, this account leads us to conclude that (i) Tank did not *say-that* anything, although (ii) he *meant to say* that the vice-president of the United States is ambitious, and (iii) he made-as-if to say that the president of the United States is vicious.

Another issue raised by the notion of what a speaker says is this: Should the force of an utterance — its assertive, interrogative, promisory, etc. force — count as part of what is said or not? Also, what part of an utterance conveys the force of an utterance? Both of these questions will be answered in the next section.

In addition to what is said, a speaker implies various things. Grice distinguishes two kinds of implication: conventional and nonconventional. Thus, a speaker who utters

> (4) John is a womanizer

IV The Total Content of What a Speaker Communicates 65

and means it has, in normal circumstances, not said but implied both

(5) John has sexual intercourse with many woman.

and

(6) John is a scoundrel.

Grice calls the implication holding between (4) and (5) conventional implication and the implication holding between (4) and (6) nonconventional implication. As Grice makes clear, what lies behind this terminology is the idea that conventional implication occurs in virtue of the conventions or rules governing the use of the words uttered, that is, in virtue of the meanings of the words uttered (Grice (1968), p. 1). Thus, in uttering

(1) John is a bachelor

the speaker conventionally implies that John is unmarried. The terms "conventional" and "nonconventional" are, however, misleading because they suggest that only conventional implications are governed by conventions, and that is false. A better terminology, I think, is "linguistic" and "nonlinguistic." Linguistic implication, then, is implication in virtue of the meaning or conventions governing the use of the words uttered. Nonlinguistic implication is implication that does not occur in virtue of the conventions governing the use of the words uttered.

This distinguishes linguistic from nonlinguistic implication. It does not, however, define either. Consider

(7) John is a happy bachelor

and

(8) John is happy.

Sentence (7) entails (8); however, in saying (7) the speaker in part says (8). Since we want saying and implying (in our sense) to be mutually exclusive terms, we have to stipulate that what is implied is not part of what is said. Taking what a speaker says as basic, we can define linguistic and nonlinguistic implication rather simply. Saying that p linguistically implies that q just in case (a) saying that p entails that q in virtue of the words uttered, and (b) that q is not part of what is said. Saying that p nonlinguistically implies that q just in case saying that p implies that q and does not linguistically imply that q.

The most prominent kind of nonlinguistic implication, conversational implication, which was discussed in Chapter Two, depends upon conversational maxims. There are also social maxims and maxims of politeness. Little serious work has been done on these; however, some of them will have to incorporate the ideas expressed in these tentative maxims: "Do not say or do what will embarrass the audience;" "Do not say or do what will offend the audience;" and "Do not say or do something in a manner that will embarrass or offend the audience." In addition, there are what might be called "histrionic" conventions, involving tone of voice, facial expression, stance, gait, hand movements, and the like. Behavior instantiating these conventions can be as blunt as an obscene gesture or as subtle as a faintly ironical inflection. Finally, there are possibly a variety of moral and aesthetic maxims that also regulate our communication.

This ends my sketch of Grice's way of distinguishing the various elements of what a speaker linguistically communicates. In the rest of this chapter, I want to discuss various revisions and extensions of his distinctions. Section II sketches a refined version of the elements of what a speaker communicates. Section III discusses illocutionary force as an element of what a speaker says. Sections IV–IX discuss various elements of what a speaker indicates.

II. What a Speaker Expresses and What he Implies

As helpful as Grice's way of distinguishing the total content of what a speaker linguistically communicates is, it is not detailed or complicated enough. To begin, we should be suspicious of the initial distinction between what the speaker says and what he implies. The terms of this contrast, while mutually exclusive, do not seem to be exhaustive. What is implicit contrasts with what is explicit or *expressed*. What a speaker says is just one, albeit the more explicit and prominent, of the two ways in which a person might express something. The other is what I shall call "indicating."

The distinction between saying and indicating something is observed in ordinary language although ordinary speakers are not reflectively aware of it. A person who says, "Jones is an Englishman; he is, therefore, brave," has not said that being brave is a consequence of being an Englishman, but he did indicate it (cf. Grice (1975), pp. 44–45). Indicating differs from saying in explicitness; indicating is less explicit than saying. All elements of saying are conveyed by phrases or individual words or the roots of individual words. The two most prominent parts of saying something are the reference of a subject expression and the property expressed by the predicate. Being conveyed by a word or the root of a word is, however, a necessary, not a sufficient condition for being an element of what is said. Later, I will suggest that some words, more precisely, some adverbial words and phrases, express indicative elements. Indicative elements are typically syntactic particles or prefixes or suffixes of words. What is implied must, of course, be implicit, it cannot be realized in any syntactic marking. That is, a necessary condition for some thing being implied is that it is not syntactically marked. Conversely, every element of what is expressed is usually syntactically marked either by a word or phrase or by a grammatical particle.

Thus, the initial division of what a speaker linguistically communicates should look like this:

IV The Total Content of What a Speaker Communicates   67

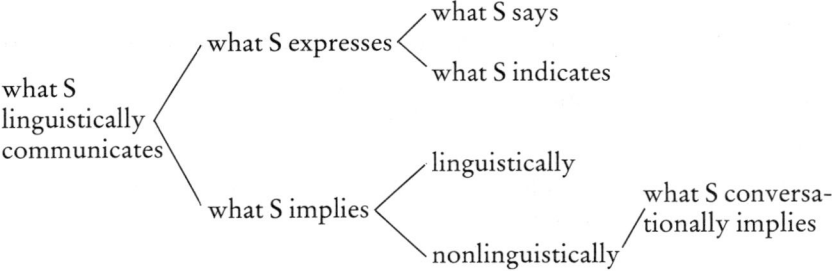

III. What a Speaker Expresses or Implies: Force

Reference and predication are elements of what is said. What about the force of a speech act? On my view, the force is sometimes an element of what is said, sometimes indicated (see section VII) and sometimes (usually) implied. The principal and paradigmatic way of expressing force is by the use of a verb expressing an illocutionary act in performative form, that is, first person present, nonprogressive, tense, indicative mood; when the force is expressed in this way, it is part of what is said. (Interrogative sentences possibly indicate their force in virtue of word order. Force can also be indicated by an adverbial word or phrase; see section VII)

Suppose Jones says

(9a) I promise that Mary is safe.
(10a) I ask whether Mary is safe.
(11a) I bet that Mary is safe.

Then (9)–(11) are correct reports of what he said:

(9) Jones promised that Mary was safe.
(10) Jones asked whether Mary was safe.
(11) Jones bet that Mary safe.

In short, a complete report of what a speaker said in paradigmatic cases consists of two parts: the force of his speech act and the proposition he expressed. Since most sentences do not contain a verb in performative form, most sentences do not *express* any force at all.

When "say" serves as the main verb of a report of what someone said, it can often be treated as a dummy force-verb, marking the spot where a verb representing the force of a speech act would have gone had it had one. It is similar in function to "someone" in the sentence, "Someone hit me." The verb "say" is highly equivocal and its sense, as used in reports of what a speaker says, should not be confused with "state" or "assert." Consider three brief talk exchanges that take place between Smith and Jones on a farm:

(A)
Smith: You're a country boy. Can you predict what the bull is about to do?
Jones: The bull is about to charge.

(B)
Smith: Let's bet five dollars on what that bull is going to do. You can choose the issue.
Jones: The bull is about to charge.

(C)
Smith: You're a city boy. Can you guess what that bull is going to do?
Jones: The bull is about to charge.

In no case did Jones state or assert that the bull is about to charge, if for no other reason than that Jones lacked the evidence necessary for a statement. Further, in no case did Jones say or even indicate (in my technical sense) that he either was predicting, betting or guessing. For there is no syntactic marker expressive of such acts. In each of these exchanges, Jones has said the same thing: that the bull is about to charge. Moreover, in each case, Jones expressed the same proposition, in Searle's sense (Searle (1969), pp. 29–33) and this proposition is force neutral.

My view that force is usually implied should be understood in contrast with another of Searle's views. Searle claims that "no sentence is completely force neutral." He goes on to claim that "Every sentence has some illocutionary force potential if only of a very broad kind, built into its meaning" (Searle (1968), 412). When a sentence does not contain an illocutionary force verb in performative form, then the force of the sentence, according to Searle, is expressed by the mood of the verb. The indicative mood expresses generic assertive force; the imperative mood expresses generic directive force. This is the view I am opposing. I hold that neither the indicative mood nor the imperative mood conveys any force.

To hold that Jones *said* the same thing in each exchange is not to hold that Jones communicated the same thing. In (A) Jones communicated a prediction; in (B) he communicated a bet; in (C) he communicated a guess. He communicated these different forces, not expressly, but by implication; more precisely, by conversational implication. Given the context of (A), for example, Jones has said that the bull is about to charge. Since he is observing the conversational maxims, in particular, the maxim of relation, it is appropriate for him to communicate a prediction about the bull's imminent behavior, and what he has said satisfied the propositional content condition for such a prediction; Jones has not given Smith any reason to think that he is not following the conversational rules; therefore, Jones is conversationally implying that he is communicating the force of a prediction.

IV The Total Content of What a Speaker Communicates

My treatment of standard sentences without a performative verb is an extension of Searle's view about indirect speech acts (Searle (1979a), pp. 30–57). An indirect speech act is the (indirect) performance of one speech act in virtue of the (direct) performance of some other speech act. For example, a person can request that someone pass the salt by asking the question, "Can you pass the salt?" For Searle, every speech act requires the direct performance of some illocutionary act. My view, in contrast, is that often the force of a speech act is indirectly conveyed. One merit of my view is that it simplifies the account of many indirect speech acts. For example, if Jones attempts to get Smith off his foot indirectly by saying, "You are standing on my foot," then, according to Searle, Jones is performing two illocutionary acts. Jones directly states that Smith is standing on Jones's foot and Jones indirectly requests that Smith get off Jones's foot. It seems otiose to have the speaker communicating two illocutionary act forces and to have the same proposition communicated twice. On my view, Jones has expressed just one illocutionary act: he has directly expressed the proposition that Smith is standing on Jone's foot and he has indirectly communicated the force of a request.

Because a speaker who expresses a proposition without a force typically communicates some force or other by conversational implication in saying what he does, I hold that the speaker performs an illocutionary act. In saying, "The bull is about to charge" in (A), the speaker performs the illocutionary act of predicting. In saying the same thing in (B), the speaker performs the illocutionary act of betting. In saying the same thing in (C), the speaker performs the illocutionary act of guessing. This way of treating illocutionary acts is consonant with Austin's. Recall that Austin distinguished between the act of expressing a proposition – to use his terminology, the rhetic act – and the illocutionary act (Austin (1955), pp. 94–101). The rhetic or propositional act is part of the complete locutionary act, that is, the complete act of saying something. The illocutionary act, when the force is not expressed, is not part of the locutionary act and is not constituted by the words uttered, although it is performed in the utterance of those words. That is also the view I am espousing here. Often the illocutionary act that is performed is determined by the kind of force that is conversationally implied.

IV. What a Speaker Indicates by Contrastive Stress

One of the clearest cases of an indicative element involves contrastive stress. Fred Dretske has illustrated the phenomenon clearly in this passage:

> I have three friends who are variously misinformed about one of my recent transactions. The first wants to know why I gave my typewriter to Clyde. I set him straight by telling him that I did not *give* my typewriter to Clyde:

(1) I *sold* my typewriter to Clyde.
Somewhat later my second friend gives it to be understood that he thinks I sold my typewriter to Alex. In correcting him I say,
(2) I sold my typewriter *to Clyde*.
Still later the third asks me why I sold my adding machine to Clyde and, once again, I find myself saying,
(3) I sold *my typewriter* to Clyde.
How shall we describe the difference? (Dretske (1972), 411).

On my view the differences between (1)–(3) are differences in what the speaker has indicated. Further, these differences have the consequence that there is a difference in what the speaker expressed. Using Searle's sense of "proposition," I hold that the same proposition is being expressed: in each case, the same reference and predication are made, namely, a reference to the speaker and the predication of himself that he sold his typewriter to Clyde. None of the utterances makes a statement although the force of a statement is conversationally implied. Since the propositions expressed are the same, I hold that the meaning of what is said is the same although what the speaker meant in saying it is different in each case since the speaker meant more than what he said. The differences between (1)–(3) are principally pragmatic; they differ in what they communicate, and this difference is not due to any difference in the meaning of the words uttered. The difference is not, however, merely pragmatic, since the difference in the content of what is communicated is due to the phonetically different stresses of each sentence. And these phonological differences also affect the meaning of the sentence.

V. What a Speaker Indicates by Tone

There is something other than a difference in the cognitive content between the word pairs: slut and daughter of joy; nigger and black; kike and Jew. A person who says that Jones is a slut (nigger, kike) expresses his disdain for Jones. He does not say that he disdains Jones but he does indicate it in virtue of the tone of the words he chooses.

The concept of tone is one that Frege recognized as having a place in language, but was also one that he did not know how to accommodate. Neither tone nor force are parts of what Frege calls a "thought" (Frege (1918), p. 22). A thought is something "for which the question of truth arises" (Frege (1918), p. 20). It corresponds roughly, but only roughly, to what Searle means by a proposition since for Frege an imperative sentence does not express a thought; nor do sentences that express desires or requests. Frege variously explicates the tone of a sentence as "mood, fragrance, [or] illumination in a poem" (Frege (1918), p. 23.) If we identify what Frege meant by "the thought" with a proposition, then it is natural to assign the tone of the words uttered to what is indicated, and we have solved the problem of locating tone within a theory of what gets linguistically communicated.

VI. What a Speaker Indicates by Tense

Following Grice, I hold that what a speaker says includes the reference of the subject expression and the principal predication. Certain temporal and spatial references should also be included in the notion of what is said. If someone utters "John first exhibited these traits in Chicago, Illinois in 1979" and means it, then the references to Chicago, Illinois and the year 1979 also form part of what is said. Verb tense, however, is more difficult to deal with. It does not seem to me to express an element of what is said. A person who says, "John went to the store," indicates that John's going to the store occurred in the past, but does not say so. When a speaker says, "I am standing," he normally indicates, in our technical sense, the present time. When a speaker says, "I was standing," or "I stood," he typically indicates the past. Contrast, "I will stand," with "I will stand tomorrow." Both sentences indicate future time; the latter sentence also, however, says something more, specifically that the future time at issue is tomorrow.

It is important to emphasize here that the distinction between saying and indicating is a technical one. Further, what is indicated forms part of the truth-conditions of a speech act. Thus, although "John stands tall" and "John stood tall" say the same thing, in the technical sense of "say" relevant here, they express different things and have different truth-conditions because of the differences in what they indicate in virtue of the different tenses. Finally, the utterances of the two sentences "say" different things in the sense that they constitute different phatic acts.

VII. What a Speaker Indicates by Adverbial Force-Words

A speaker who uttered sentences (12) and (13) would seem to express the same proposition:

(12) I conclude that Jones is happy.
(13) Therefore, Jones is happy.

The expressive content of (12) and (13) is the same; both sentences express that the speaker draws the conclusion that Jones is happy. They differ, however, in part of what they say and indicate. Sentence (12) says that the speaker concludes that Jones is happy. Sentence (13) does not say that the speaker draws this conclusion, but it does indicate it; obviously, it is the word "therefore" in virtue of which this is indicated. And, instead of "therefore," we might have used "consequently" or "hence" to indicate what "I conclude" says. A strictly analogous treatment applies to "further" ("moreover"/"additionally") on the one hand and "I add" on the other. A similar treatment can be given to some prepositional phrases and infinitive phrases: In conclusion/I conclude; To begin/I begin.

One might wonder why I want to treat sentential adverbs such as "therefore" and "further" as representing indicative elements rather than as representing elements of what is said, since performative verbs represent elements of what is said. My answer is that, while adverbial phrases are not less explicit than other parts of speech for some purposes, it seems to be the case that they are less explicit than and are sometimes grammatically derived from performatives, when they express the force of the speech act. Force adverbs and adverbial phrases expressing force are standardly derived from performatives in generative grammars. This diminished explicitness is captured by treating an element that expresses force adverbially as an indicative element.

VIII. What a Speaker Indicates by Mood

The most controversial indicative element to discuss is that of mood. Whatever it is that the mood of a verb expresses, it does so by indicating, not saying.

Traditional grammars distinguish three moods in English: indicative, imperative and subjunctive. It is arguable that the imperative mood is not genuinely a mood. Although Chomsky's transformational grammar is currently out of vogue, it typically treated the imperative mood as the result of a transformational deletion rule. An imperative sentence like "Go to the store" can be treated as a remnant of a sentence like "I order (request) you to *go to the store*" (Bach (1974), p. 22). If we accept this, then the imperative mood poses no problem. The subjunctive mood is more mysterious. It indicates some nonfactive staus, but what more precisely can be said about it is dubious. Most contemporary theoretical grammars say little or nothing about it (e.g., Akmajian *et al.* (1979)). In any case, it is clear that the subjunctive mood does not express the force of an utterance.

This leaves the indicative mood. My view is that the indicative mood expresses that a propositional tie or a quasi-propositional tie holds between the verb and its subject (Strawson (1959), pp. 167–173). It turns what otherwise would be a sequence of words expressing no thought or proposition into a sentence that does.

This treatment of the indicative mood is directly opposed to the standard treatment of mood, and the large issue to be considered in this section concerns why I think the standard view is mistaken. According to the standard view, of which Grice (1968) and Hare (1952), are distinguished proponents, it is the mood of the verb that expresses the force of a speech act. According to Grice, the function of the indicative mood is assertive; it expresses that the speaker believes the proposition expressed. For example, a person who says, "I am happy," expresses in virtue of the indicative mood of "am" that he believes that he is happy. I think the standard view is incorrect and I want to present nine arguments against it. Nine may seem like a large number, especially when one good argument ought to be enough. However, since the standard view is deep-seated, wide-spread and intuitively plausible, it is unlikely that one argument, even one very good argument, is likely to dislodge it from the minds of philosophers. Further, several of the arguments I will adduce deal with interesting features of speech.

Most of my objections will be directed against Grice's treatment of the indicative mood since that is the linchpin of the view. I begin with some brief and familiar arguments. First, the indicative mood is sometimes used in conditionals without expressing belief: In the sentence, "If Bill is in New York, then he is on vacation," the speaker is not asserting that Bill is on vacation even though the verb in "He is on vacation" is in the indicative mood. Since "is" is not functioning to express assertive force in the antecedent, it is dubious that it is expressing assertive force in the consequent (Jespersen (1924), p. 316). Second, the indicative mood, as I recently mentioned, is used in interrogative sentences, and, in such cases, it is not expressing the belief of the speaker. Third, if the indicative mood expresses belief, then every indicative sentence, even those in mathematics and science, are not merely expressions of the beliefs of the speakers but express that they are expressions of such beliefs. But this is implausible; mathematics and scientists scrupulously keep their personal beliefs out of their professional propositions.

Fourth, if the standard view of the indicative mood were correct, then the most familiar entailments would no longer hold. Since "Alice believes that if whales live in the ocean, then mammals live in the ocean," does not entail "Alice believes that if mammals do not live in the ocean, then whales do not live in the ocean," the rule of transposition, to take one example, would no longer hold if the indicative mood expresses the belief of the speaker.

The fifth argument is that if the mood of a verb expressed the force of the speech act, then the expressive content of most sentences would be redundant. Consider again the sentence, "I am happy." On the Gricean view, "I am happy," expresses what "I believe that I am happy" says. Further, the sentence, "I believe that I am happy" expresses what "I believe that I believe that I am happy" says. Clearly, on the Gricean view, "I believe" in "I believe I am happy" is expressively redundant. And this again is implausible.

One way to reply to my objection is to account for the redundancy. A defender of Grice might hold that sentences of the form, "I believe that p" are uttered normally when it is necessary to emphasize that the speaker does in fact believe a certain proposition, and repetition, or redundancy, if you insist, is a way of emphasizing something. This reply is not persuasive because the Gricean has so far given us no reason to think that "I believe" provides emphasis by repetition and not simply by providing the hitherto unexpressed guarantee of the speaker.

A seventh argument against the Gricean view is that if the indicative mood expresses belief then such expressions stack up in intolerable numbers in sentences of any complexity. Since the sentence, "It is not the case that it is raining when the sun is out" contains three verbs in the indicative mood, the sentence contains three expressions of belief. In other words, it expresses what the following sentence says: I believe that it is not the case that I believe that it is raining when I believe that the sun is shining.

Verbs in the indicative mood in opaque contexts present an eighth problem. Consider the sentence:

(14) John claimed that Bill reported that it is not the case that it is raining.

It contains four verbs in the indicative mood. "Claimed" is perhaps not a problem. What about the others? What does "Bill reported" express in (14)? Does it express "Bill believes that Bill reported" or "I believe that Bill reported" or "John believes that Bill reported"? The first of these possibilities is the most attractive. The indicative mood in this case expresses the belief of the subject of "reported" and not the belief of the person uttering the sentence, nor the person who made the claim about Bill's report. And the same holds for the remaining verbs. Thus, on Grice's view, sentence (14) expresses what sentence (15) says:

(15) I believe that John claimed that Bill believed that Bill reported that Bill believed that it was not the case that Bill believed that it was raining.

A defender of Grice might respond that only the main verb in the indicative mood expresses belief. None of the others do; in particular, the force of a mood is neutralized when it occurs in opaque constructions. This eliminates the stacked and intolerably numerous expressions of belief.

What is wrong with this defense is that it changes the Gricean view about mood from a claim about the mood of a verb to a claim about its first occurrence. That is, it is no longer the mood of the verb that expresses the belief, but its first occurrence, all other occurrences of that mood either doing nothing or doing something else that remains to be specified. This is obviously not a very attractive treatment of mood. It would be better if there were a view that assigned the same function to all occurrences of a mood. My view that the indicative mood expresses a kind of propositional tie does this.

An eighth argument against the proposition that the mood of a verb expresses the force of a speech act is this: Consider the sentence

(16) The bull is about to charge.

IV The Total Content of What a Speaker Communicates   75

Depending upon the circumstances of its utterance, a person might communicate

(a) a statement;
(b) a warning;
(c) a conjecture;
(d) a question;
(e) a bet.

If the speaker and hearer are safely situated behind some fence and the speaker, an experienced rancher, says it, then he conversationally implies a stating force. If the hearer is vulnerable to and ignorant of an impending attack by the bull, then the speaker conversationally implies a warning force. If the speaker and hearer are city dwellers speculating on the imminent behavior of the bull, then the speaker conversationally implies a conjectural force. If it were the mood that expressed force, then, since sentence (16) is in the indicative mood, the indicative mood would seem to express at least five different forces. Again, I think this view of force is implausible. If the indicative mood is five ways equivocal, it would be worse than inefficient at expressing force. The only way to disambiguate (16) would be to investigate features of the context; but, if it is features of the context that determine what force the indicative mood represents, then the mood of the verb is superfluous. Rather than being equivocal, sentence (16) is indeterminate with regard to force. Whether a speaker communicates a statement, prediction, etc., by uttering (16), is determined by features of the speech context other than any single syntactic element of the sentence. Rather, in every circumstance of its utterance, sentence (16) expresses a proposition only. It expresses the proposition that the bull is about to charge. For Searle, propositions do not contain a force although a force can be tacked onto them. My view, as I explained in section III, is that no force is expressed by uttering sentence (16). Further, whatever else the circumstance of its utterance, whoever utters (16) and means it expresses the same thing, namely, the proposition that the bull is about to charge (so long as the references are fixed). Whatever force the speaker communicates he communicates by conversational implication.

The ninth argument showing that indicative mood does not have the function of expressing the belief of the speaker can be seen by considering the actual operation of the indicative in English. Consider this passage:

> How can Reagan's attitude towards the rich and the poor be summarized? Everyone who is rich deserves his wealth. Everyone who is poor deserves his misery. I want to argue that these attitudes are both pernicious and not true to the facts.

While the second and third sentences are in the indicative mood, it is clear that the author has not committed himself to their truth; just the contrary is true. The author is putting forth the second and third sentences as part of his exposition of the view that he will eventually argue against. My way of treating such sentences is simply to claim that they express propositions only and that they express no force themselves. The force that is actually communicated, when there is one, varies from context to context and is conversationally implied. In the present case, no actual force is even conversationally implied although the context makes clear that if Reagan were to express these propositions, he would conversationally imply that they have the force of statements.

IX. Other Possible Indicative Elements

Highly inflected languages have a richer network of indicative signs than English. In Latin, the genitive case typically indicates possession; the dative case typically indicates the kind of directedness characteristic of the indirect object. Analogous remarks can be made for Latin verbs and other parts of speech. It is difficult to say what an indicative element of some language expresses, and perhaps impossible if the metalanguage does not have the resources to say what that element expresses, but, like the object language itself, can only indicate it.

There are probably other indicative elements that I have not discussed. The surface grammatical position of the subject might represent an indicative element of topic or focus. This might explain the pragmatic difference between active and passive sentences: "Mary hit Bill" vs. "Bill was hit by Mary." It is worth exploring whether there are additional indicative elements; however, whether there are or are not does not affect a central claim of this chapter, namely, that there are such elements and that they are part of what a speaker expresses, but does not say.

X. An Outline of the Total Content of What a Speaker Communicates

    I. What a speaker expresses
       A. What a speaker says
          1. Force
          2. Proposition
             a. Reference
                (1) subjective
                (2) temporal
                (3) spatial
             b. Predication
       B. What a speaker indicates
          1. By contrastive stress
          2. By tone
          3. By tense

            4. By adverbial force-words
            5. By word order
            6. By case endings
    II. What a speaker implies
        A. Linguistcally
        B. Nonlinguistically
            1. In virtue of conversational maxims
            2. In virtue of histrionic maxims
            3. In virtue of politeness maxims
            4. In virtue of social maxims
            5. In virtue of moral maxims
            6. In virtue of aesthetic maxims

XI. The Content of What a Speaker Expresses at the Mad Hatter's Tea Party

Many of the notions introduced in the course of this chapter are illustrated and put to use as we analyse another passage from the tea-party chapter of *Alice's Adventures in Wonderland*:

> "Take some more tea," the March Hare said to Alice, very earnestly.
> "I've had nothing yet," Alice replied in an offended tone: "so I can't take more."
> "You mean you can't take *less*," said the Hatter: "it's very easy to take *more* than nothing."
> "Nobody asked *your* opinion," said Alice.

Like much of Carroll's humor, this passage trades on the distinction between what is expressed and what is implied. (Since "say" is more familiar than "express" in this context, though technically less correct, I will use "say" for "express" in this context; there will no substantial loss of precision in doing so.)

Consider, for instance, what the March Hare communicates when he says, "Take some more tea." What he says is quite normal; he is inviting Alice to have more tea (or perhaps, in virtue of this "earnest" tone, *urging* her to do so); in other words, to drink a quantity of tea over and above what she has already drunk. In virtue of the linguistic conventions of English, the Hare implies that Alice is able to take and drink some tea over and above what she has already drunk. This is true, since at this point Alice has had none at all, and she can certainly drink a non-zero quantity of tea. However, in virtue of the conversational maxims, and in particular the Maxim of Quantity, "Do not contribute more than is required," the Hare also implies that Alice has previously had some tea, which is false. To see this, notice that the Hare could have said, "Take some tea" rather than "Take some more tea;" if he had said, "Take some tea," he would have implied that Alice was able to take and drink some tea, but not that she was able to take and drink some tea over and above what she had already drunk. This additional implication is what is out of order in the Hare's remark; he is contributing more than is required.

Alice, who is not so dull as to miss a conversational implicature, detects the inappropriateness of the March Hare's invitation and protests against this last implication ("I've had nothing yet"). Unfortunately, she follows this up with a rejection of the particular word that seems to her to be the cause of the trouble ("I can't take more"). She is, in effect, denying that she can accept the invitation to take more tea, presumably because she thinks that having had some tea is a necessary condition for accepting the invitation or perhaps even for issuing it. The trap here is that the Hare's implication that Alice has had some tea is only a conversational implicature, and hence can be cancelled. Hence it is not a necessary condition either of issuing the invitation or of accepting it. The invitation is indeed defective, by our standards, because the March Hare does conversationally implicate something that is false, with no apparent excuse; but it is not unsuccessful – the illocutionary act of inviting (or urging) has been performed. Alice's rejection of the March Hare's invitation suggests to the Hatter that she thinks that some necessary condition of issuing the invitation was not satisfied, some condition having to do with the word "more". We saw above that the Hare's invitation semantically or linguistically implies that Alice can drink a quantity of tea over and above what she has already drunk; this implication, since it is a fixture of the language, *is* such a condition. However, as the Hatter, with devious presence of mind, proceeds to point out, *this* condition is satisfied. The Hatter's remark stymies Alice, who did not have the benefit of having learned Grice's theory of communication. Having lost control of her share in the conversation, she applies a stopper ("Nobody asked your opinion").

Imprecise as it is, this analysis may nevertheless seem too complicated for such a short exchange. In the first place, however, one of the reasons why language is such a useful instrument is that it gets a lot of things done very efficiently. In any real conversation, the words the participants utter are merely the surface that simultaneously outlines and conceals the underlying substance of communication and meaning. Second, as Wittgenstein pointed out, humor is especially deep; because of the elements of surprise and unconventionality, it typically requires a more elaborate analysis. Indeed, what we have said here about seven lines of Carroll's book is really much too hasty and superficial; a more accurate analysis would be much longer. But it would be heartless, in a way, to go into such great detail. Philosophical analysis takes the laughter out of humor.

Chapter Five: Metaphor

I. A Theory for Metaphor

A good theory, whether it be a scientific or a philosophical theory, is one that can be used to solve a lot of intellectual problems. The more problems of varying sorts that a theory solves the more powerful that theory is. Judging by this measure, we will find our revised version of Grice's theory of conversation to be a very good one. At the end of Chapter Two, the theory was used to solve Moore's paradox. The next two chapters are devoted solely to using the theory to solve some additional problems; and it will be used again and again to solve various problems connected with the problem of referring.

A lot of interesting work has been done recently on the concept of a metaphor, and any adequate theory of metaphor will have to take account of much of this work, accommodating what is true and explaining where this recent work goes wrong. (Typically, this work errs either by overgeneralizing or by mistaking an essential but subordinate feature of metaphor for the whole or the most central feature.) However, as interesting as much of this work is, it lacks something essential to an adequate theory of metaphor, namely, a place within a more general theory of language or language use. The reason metaphor needs to be placed within a more general theory is that metaphor itself is a logically derivative phenomenon and, derivative, in particular, from some aspect of language use. In this chapter, I will place metaphor within such a theory, namely, Grice's theory of conversation. By extending his theory to account for metaphor, I am holding in effect that metaphor is pragmatically and not semantically based. Although there is a sense in which the sentence used metaphorically has a metaphorical meaning, this meaning is itself a consequence of the mechanisms that give rise to the metaphor and are not what makes the metaphor possible. In Grice's terminology, the metaphorical meaning of an utterance is an instance of utterance occasion meaning and not (applied) timeless utterance meaning. (These terms are explained in Chapter Seven.)

One of the most difficult and important issues for a theory of metaphor to get right concerns the question of whether a person who utters a sentence metaphorically says-that anything or only makes-as-if-to-say something. On the one hand, it is correct to hold that a speaker who utters a sentence metaphorically, for example, "My love is a red rose," is not asserting that his love is a red rose. For, if he were, then he would be saying something false, and, surely, a person who utters a metaphor typically is not speaking falsely, *pace* Plato. A person who speaks metaphorically aims at the truth. To hold that a person who speaks metaphorically is speaking falsely is a kind of philistinism. These considerations incline one to say that a person who speaks metaphorically does not say-that anything but only makes-as-if-to-say something. On the other hand, a metaphor can contain its literal reference or its literal predication (though not both). Suppose the parents of an ebullient young woman are disturbed by her reckless social life. Her Dutch uncle might say to them, "I will clip the wings of that butterfly" and refer to himself while also speaking metaphorically. Or he might say, "The butterfly will be home by 10:00 p. m." and predicate being home by 10:00 p. m. It is also important to recognize that some metaphorical utterances have their literal illocutionary forces. The Dutch uncle might say, "I promise that I will clip that butterfly's wings," and thereby make a promise. Since a metaphorical utterance can have its literal illocutionary force, and its literal reference or predication, one is inclined to think that a person who speaks metaphorically is saying what would normally be said by a sentence. I think the truth lies in between these two extreme positions. A person who speaks metaphorically does succeed in performing some of the subacts that together constitute a complete act of saying-that, namely, reference, predication and illocutionary force. However, a person who speaks metaphorically does not say-that what he would normally be taken to have said-that if he were speaking literally; further, he does not represent himself as saying-that such and such, but only makes-as-if-to-say it by flouting a maxim of quality.

It is very important to distinguish what a speaker says (or makes-as-if-to-say) from what he communicates in some other way. Merrie Bergmann has conflated these elements and has consequently come up with a defective theory of metaphor. She holds that metaphors are typically used successfully to make true assertions (Bergmann (1982), 225–245). The falsity of her view is evidenced by typical metaphors: Mary is a butterfly; The Middle East is a time bomb. If someone were actually asserting these sentences, he would be asserting respectively that Mary is a butterfly and that the Middle East is a time bomb. Both assertions are patently false. What is not false is what a speaker might be implying by uttering the sentences in question metaphorically. Bergmann holds that what the speaker communicates by such utterances are assertions; but she is mistaken. For what a person asserts must be explicit and determined by the rules governing the use of the words uttered; but what a person, speaking metaphorically, means by the sentence in question is not explicit in the utterance, but implicit, and is not governed by the rules for the use of those words. What the speaker communicates, he communicates by some kind of implication.

If we accept Grice's formulation of the maxims of quality, then a central thesis about metaphors can be stated simply and in nontechnical language (cf. Bergmann (1982), 234): Every metaphor either is (or is thought to be) literally false or is supposed to be false. This disjunction reflects a genuine division of two types of metaphor. Let's call metaphors that are literally false *standard* metaphors; and those that are supposed to be false *nonstandard* metaphors. By "supposed," I do not mean that the metaphor is intended to be false but that the metaphor is *treated as if* or *entertained as if* it were false in order to consider the consequences, as when, in a *reductio ad absurdum* argument, the proposition to be proved is *supposed* to be false in order to show that the consequences of such a supposition are absurd. Most of this article will be devoted to standard cases of metaphor because the nonstandard cases are derivative, rare and merely an unavoidable complication to the theory. Until further notice, then, by "metaphor" I will mean "standard metaphor."

Every metaphorical proposition is false. Every metaphor flouts the *first* maxim of quality. This is not to say or imply that the point of a metaphor (what the speaker intends to communicate) is false. On the contrary, the point of a metaphor is typically true. Further, the point of a metaphor is conversationally implied in virtue of the fact that the speaker *flouts* the first maxim of quality. This is not to say or imply that any metaphorical proposition is a lie. Indeed, no metaphor *can* be a lie. It can be inapt or inept, imaginative or dull, cheery or morbid or any number of other things. But no metaphor is a lie. The reason is that every lie, by definition, must be unostentatious; it violates the first maxim of quality. A metaphor, in contrast, flouts the maxim. A hearer relies upon the open and ostentatious falsity of the utterance as one important clue that the speaker is speaking metaphorically.

II. Analysis of a Metaphor

Let's now see how the foregoing applies to the analysis of a particular metaphor. Suppose someone writes the sentence, "My love is a red rose," in the context of a poem, singing the praises of his lover. The audience reads the sentence and tries to interpret it. If the audience takes the poet to be saying-that his love is a red rose, then the audience must take the poet to be uttering a patent falsehood, and not fulfilling the maxim of quality, "Do not say that which is false." But the audience knows that the poet cannot be intending to utter a patent falsehood, because a falsehood would make sense in the context only if it were disguised, and the audience is justified in believing that the poet is observing the conversational maxims. Consequently, the audience infers that the poet is not saying-that his love is a red rose, but only making-as-if-to-say that she is. Once the audience has determined that the speaker is only making-as-if-to-say something, it is then able to begin calculating the actual content of what the speaker has signified. Since the poet is signifying by implication, he must believe that the audience is able to work out the implication. For this reason, the features of the rose that are exploited will be those that the audience is as likely to know as the poet. They will be held mutually, or, as we might say, commonly. Max Black saw this point, more or less clearly, and made it part of his theory of metaphor. He calls such features "related commonplaces" (Black (1954), 41; see also Black (1979), pp. 28–29). Typically, metaphors do exploit "related commonplaces." (Jones is a dog (gorilla); my love is a red rose (a doll)). Yet, it is also true that some metaphors do not trade on commonplaces, such as "The fog came in on tiny cat's feet." Such metaphors are, however, exceptional, the work of poets or poetic spirits. Such metaphors force the audience to explore the concepts introduced by the metaphor in order to come up with terms that, working in conjunction with the metaphor, will yield the meaning the poet intends, the metaphorical truth. Nonetheless, even in such "creative" metaphors it must be possible for the audience to determine which properties of the metaphorical term the speaker is thinking of and which the speaker thinks that the audience will think that the speaker thinks the audience will think of. And these features we call salient. What features these will be cannot be specified in advance of extensive knowledge of the context: who the speakers are, what their mutual beliefs are; what has been said earlier in the conversation, etc.

Not all salient properties are meant by the speaker; there are too many of them. Thus the set of salient properties must be further reduced. There are two further principles that limit the properties the speaker intends to be operative in the metaphor. One concerns a conversational requirement. Since the speaker has flouted a maxim of quality, he is exploiting that maxim and thereby conversationally implying something. The pattern of inference involved in calculating what the speaker conversationally implies typically involves the maxim of relation: Be relevant. In order to interpret what the poet means, it is necessary to understand his utterance as relevant to the context. The poet is comparing his lover to a rose and hence, given that his comparison is apt, only those salient properties will be considered that are relevant to the poet's attitude towards his love.

The other principle that limits the salient properties is this: the properties intended are only those that contribute to a true conclusion. One plausible statement of the salient features of a rose, relevant to the context of utterance and leading to a true conclusion, is that a red rose is beautiful, or sweet-smelling, or highly-valued ... Putting the poet's sentence and the statement of salience together and drawing an obvious inference, we construct the following argument:

My love is a red rose.
A red rose is beautiful, or sweet-smelling, or highly-valued ...
Therefore, my love is beautiful, or sweet-smelling or highly-valued, ...

There are at least four things to notice about this argument as it relates generally to the analysis of metaphors. First, the conclusion is presumably true. People who use metaphors aim at the truth, even in those cases in which they fall wide or short of the mark. The premise expressing the salient features of the rose, the major premise, is also true and typically such premises will be true, though not always. Some metaphors can trade on false but commonly held beliefs or false beliefs mutually held by speaker and audience, even when they alone hold the false beliefs; other metaphors can trade on myths or folklore that the community knows to be false. Take for example the folklore that elephants have infallible memories. Someone might exploit this folkloric belief and say, "Jones has the memory of an elephant" without believing that elephants have prodigious memories (Searle (1979b), pp. 88–90). Also notice that the argument about the rose is valid, and typically such arguments will be valid although again they may not, and need not always be. There is no reason why a good metaphor cannot trade on some subtle fallacious pattern of reasoning. Consider the metaphor, "Mary is a block of ice." As John Searle has argued, there is no similarity between Mary, in the sense in which she is cold, and a block of ice, in the sense in which it is cold. Thus, the comparison theory of metaphor is false because it holds that all metaphors trade on similarity and not just most of them. Nonetheless, the sentence "Mary is a block of ice" can be used successfully as a metaphor. The explanation, I think, is that the metaphor trades on an equivocation on "cold":

> Mary is a block of ice.
> Blocks of ice are cold.
> Therefore, Mary is cold.

"Cold" is equivocal; it means "low in temperature" in the major premise and "unresponsive" in the conclusion.

The second thing to notice about the argument we are considering is that the first premise has its literal meaning. If "My love is a red rose" did not have its literal meaning, then it would not play its proper role in the argument. If, in the first premise, "red rose" did not mean what it normally does, then the first premise jointly with the second premise would not entail the conclusion and the point of the metaphor would not be conveyed. Moreover, if "red rose" did not have its normal meaning, then there would be no way for the audience to determine what form the second premise of the argument should take. Donald Davidson has argued at length that sentences used metaphorically retain their literal meaning (Davidson (1978), pp. 31–47; Searle (1979b), p. 77; Cohen (1975), 670). He also holds that sentences used metaphorically say what they literally mean. He does not, however, commit himself on the more difficult issue of whether a speaker who utters a metaphor says anything. I have argued that such a speaker does not say-that s completely, but does perform some acts that count as parts of saying-that.

Third, notice that the second or major premise expressing the salient features of the rose ends with an ellipsis. Peter Geach distinguishes between two kinds of pronouns: pronouns of laziness and others. We can make an analogous distinction for types of ellipsis: dots of laziness and others. Dots of laziness are a kind of abbreviation. They mark a context that could be filled out if it were desired or necessary, as in the sentence, "The fifty states of the USA are Alabama, Alaska, Arkansas, . . ." The other kind of dots indicate a context that cannot be completed, as in "The natural numbers are 1, 2, 3, . . ." All sentences of natural languages are finite in length and there are an infinite number of natural numbers, so no sentence can specify them all. The dots at the end of the major premise are not dots of laziness. There is no way to fill out the sentence completely and determinately. What a person means by an utterance is not always, if ever, wholly determinate. Usually, the border of what a speaker means is penumbral. Also, since a speaker and his audience are likely to differ about how many features of a rose should be included in the major premise and people will differ about which proposed features are actual features of roses, it is to the communicative advantage of both speaker and audience to leave the major premise disjunctively indeterminate. This kind of indeterminacy does not constitute a defect in our analysis of metaphor. Just the opposite. Most metaphors, and, more generally, most cases of conversational implication, exhibit just this kind of indeterminateness and for the reasons given above. Grice thinks that conversational implications generally should be formulated as open disjunctions of propositions and this seems to me to be largely correct. The disjunctive sentences are clearly inclusive disjunctions; so it is possible, indeed, it is intended, that more than one of the disjuncts are true; yet, should one turn out to be false or should the audience either dispute the truth of one of the disjuncts or not take one as partially constituting the premise, the truth of the premise is still safeguarded by the other disjuncts. The view that the supplied premise (or premises) is an open disjunction also helps us pinpoint one objectionable feature of the comparison view of metaphor. According to the comparison view, the meaning of every metaphor can be rendered by some literal paraphrase. Further, it implies, if it does not say, that the literal paraphrase is a determinate and precise sentence. It is this part of the theory that is objectionable. Metaphors are typically vague and indeterminate. This is not a defect. This indeterminateness is one of the more intriguing features of metaphors; it is what encourages the audience to play with and explore the concepts involved; to look for relationships between things not previously countenanced (Black (1979), 28).

Fourth, the argument about the metaphor involving the red rose can be used to answer a criticism against the interaction view of metaphor. That criticism briefly is that the key term employed in that view is metaphorical, and hence defective as an analysis. What literal sense, to put the objection interrogatively, can be given to the notion that the terms of a metaphor interact (Searle (1979b), p. 92)? Our theory supplies an answer: Notice first that understanding a metaphor requires that the audience must supply one or more premises that will work in conjunction with the metaphor that will (seem to) entail the conclusion, that is, the proposition that expresses the point of the metaphor. Further, and more importantly, such an argument will often be a syllogism, and what will allow the two premises to work jointly is the metaphorical term, which occurs as the middle term of the syllogism. Middle terms are those that mediate the two other terms of the syllogism or, we might say, interact with both premises. There is, perhaps, a stronger sense of interaction to be noted; it concerns the principle of selecting the missing premise. In formulating the missing premise, the audience must take into account the following constraints: whatever term is selected, it must be relevant to the topic, be salient and contribute to yielding a true conclusion.

III. Metaphor and Other Figures of Speech

Metaphor is a figure of speech, and it may be instructive to compare it to three other figures of speech. One crucial mark of a metaphor, I have claimed, is that it would be false, if it were asserted. However, a speaker who uses a metaphor does not assert it, but, by flouting the first maxim of quality, only makes-as-if-to-say what the metaphor expresses. The correct treatment of hyperbole is strictly analogous to metaphor. Hyperboles, like metaphors, are cases of flouting the first maxim of quality. A person who speaks hyperbolically, that is, who consciously and intentionally exaggerates what he knows to be the truth and intends his audience to recognize this, does not say-that but only makes-as-if-to-say.

Hyperbole should be contrasted with simple overstatement, by which a person unconsciously or unintentionally expresses a proposition that is stronger than the evidence warrants. The same proposition can be overstatement in one person's mouth and hyperbole in another's. A person who states "Every American who wants to be successful can be" without realizing that circumstances of nature and society prevent some people from achieving their full potential has simply overstated the truth. However, a person who both realizes the truth and intends his audience will understand it may express the same proposition and thereby speak hyperbolically for effect. Hyperbole is a rhetorical device; overstatement is a mistake. Hyperbole differs from metaphor in that the expressed hyperbolic proposition always entails the proposition that should have been expressed and does not require any additional premises as metaphors do. If someone says, "Jones has never been late to anything in his life," he probably means, "Jones is almost never late for anything" and the former entails the latter.

There is a curious asymmetry between metaphor and hyperbole on the one hand, and meiosis on the other, in two ways. First, meiosis, unlike hyperbole and metaphor, does not contravene a maxim of quality but a maxim of quantity: Contribute as much to the conversation as is required. Meiosis contributes too little. While an hyperbolic proposition entails what ought to be said, meiosis is entailed by what ought to be said. Second, because the proposition the speaker expresses is not false, there is no need to interpret it as not being said-that.

Finally, consider irony. Ironical utterances, like metaphors and hyperboles, appear to contravene a maxim of quality. The contravention is, however, only apparent and not genuine. A person who speaks ironically is not saying what is obviously false; for, if he were, he would be conveying something that is explicitly contradictory. For example, if the disgruntled worker who uttered the sentence, "This is a *fine* country," and meant that his country is not a fine country, were saying that his is a fine country, then he would be contradicting himself. Ironical utterances, like metaphors and hyperboles, constitute cases of making-as-if-to-say; the speaker means just the opposite of what he makes-as-if-to-say.

IV. Nonstandard Metaphors

I have now concluded my treatment of standard metaphors, that is, those metaphorical propositions which would be false if asserted and which, by flouting the first maxim of quality, are cases of making-as-if-to-say. (Thus, "metaphor" no longer means "standard metaphor.") I need now to discuss the nature of nonstandard metaphors, that is, metaphorical propositions, which, if asserted, would be literally true. The first thing to say about such metaphors is that they are rare. The second thing is that they must be treated, because they are genuine cases of metaphor. The third thing is that their treatment is more complicated than that of standard metaphors. It is difficult to think of good examples of nonstandard metaphors. Here is the best that I have been able to come up with. Suppose Princess Grace of Monaco is speaking with an American friend about her daughter Caroline. She might say, "Caroline is our princess." Here we have a case of a nonstandard metaphor. Since Caroline is a princess by virtue of her birth to a princely family, Grace's utterance, if asserted, would be literally true. Grace means it, however, metaphorically. The metaphor operates in the following way. When Grace utters "Caroline is our princess," the American must interpret what Grace means. The American reasons that, if Grace means (or means only) that Caroline is the daughter of a prince, then her utterance is defective because it flouts the first maxim of quantity since it is mutually obvious to Grace and the American that Caroline is the daughter of a prince. Consequently, the American reasons that, since Grace is not (simply) stating the obvious, she must be implying something. Since the assumption that the proposition expressed is (simply) true would make it defective, the audience supposes that the proposition is false in order to test the consequences. If

V   Metaphor   87

Grace intends the American to suppose the proposition is false, then the first maxim of quality is being flouted in that way. Hence, Grace must mean her utterance to be construed metaphorically. Using a folkloric belief as the major premise, the American constructs the following syllogism:

Caroline is a princess.
Princesses are beautiful or admired or well-loved or slightly spoiled or . . .
Therefore, Caroline is beautiful or admired or well-loved or slightly spoiled or . . .

What unites the standard and nonstandard cases of metaphor is the role that falsity plays in generating the metaphor and the characteristic form of conversational implication, leaning on either true or folkloric or mythic or communal beliefs.

A less clearcut case of a nonstandard metaphor is provided by Julia Driver's poem, "The Prostitute," which begins "I am stripped, / an old screw." Taking "stripped" literally to mean "deprived of clothes" and "screw" as "woman who engages in sexual intercourse", we can suppose the sentence is literally true but in this sense plays little or no part in its metaphorical interpretation. The metaphorical interpretation depends upon another interpretation of the meaning of the sentence. In addition to the meaning already cited, the sentence can mean, "I am an old metal fastener with a defective spiral ridge running around it." In this latter sense, it is patently false of the speaker, flouts the first maxim of quality and invites a standard metaphorical interpretation. This example is interesting, however, because the first and second sense of the sentence are not independent. The two senses of "screw" in the poem are etymologically related. The reading of the sentence, "I am stripped, an old screw," that is literally true invites, at least by association, the reading of the sentence that is patently false and metaphorical. (Much more could be said about the metaphor; for example, a stripped metal fastener is virtually useless as is an old prostitute.)

I have claimed that nonstandard metaphors are genuine metaphors but rare and derivative upon standard ones. My view is importantly different from the view that the comparatively rare metaphors that are or would be literally true if asserted are not importantly different from the statistically more numerous cases of metaphors that are or would be literally false if asserted. This latter view is defective for two reasons. First, this view cannot adequately explain how speakers can expect their audience to understand that a metaphor is being broached. On my view, an audience knows that a standard metaphor is being broached largely by the patent falsity of the metaphorical proposition. And if a metaphorical proposition does not appear to be patently false, then there must be some other mechanism that eventually leads the audience to suppose that the literally true proposition must be supposed to be false in order to understand what the speaker means. On my view this other mechanism is the flouting of some conversational maxim — it might be any of the maxims other than the first maxim of quality — that forces the audience to suppose that the utterance is patently false and hence to be interpreted as a standard metaphor would be.

Second, the view that some literally true metaphors are merely statistically rare and not conceptually derivative has led some theorists mistakenly to classifiy as metaphors utterances that are not metaphors. I shall use some of Ted Cohen's work as an example. Cohen gives three examples of allegedly true metaphors: "No man is an island"; "Jesus was a carpenter"; and "Moscow is a cold city." (Cohen (1975), 671). Each of these sentences must be given a different treatment.

As for "No man is an island," my view is that it is not a metaphor at all. It is true and not false that no man is an island. This is not to imply that Donne's line is not a figure of speech. It is. "No man is an island" is trivially true, and for that reason it is a case of meiosis. One might wonder how such a trivial truth could be so poetically powerful? The answer is that it is powerful in the richness of its associations, conveyed by conversational implication. In saying, "No man is an island," Donne is saying something trivial. The reader must, consequently, muse about the relevance of a triviality; he reasons, presumably, in a way analogous to a case of metaphor:

> No man is an island.
> Every island is separated from every other thing of its own kind, does not depend upon any other thing of its own kind for its existence or well-being, and is not diminished by the destruction of any other of its own kind; . . .
> Therefore, no man is separated from every other thing of its own kind, does not depend upon any other thing of its own kind for its existence or well-being, and is not diminished by the destruction of any other of its own kind; . . .

This argument is invalid; yet not the less effective as poetry for all that. In short, while what Donne has said is trivial; what he has linguistically communicated *via* conversational implication is not at all trivial; but, on the contrary, profound.

Concerning "Jesus was a carpenter," a speaker who says this speaks truly. Perhaps, however — and this seems to be Cohen's point — the speaker might well mean more than he says. He might mean that Jesus fashions valuable things out of unfashioned worthless things. If this statement of what the speaker additionally means seems itself metaphorical, it can be paraphrased in ways to eliminate those elements: Jesus causes things that have no value in themselves to become things that do have value in themselves. What is important to notice is that we have specified what the speaker means by specifying that the speaker *means what he says* and *means more than what he says*. And this specification does not commit us to holding that "Jesus is a carpenter" is a metaphor. For, to appeal to the classic formula, "to utter a metaphor is to say one thing and to mean something else" (i.e., something inconsistent with what you say.) In the case under consideration, the speaker does not mean something inconsistent with what he said, merely something additional, just as anyone conversationally implying something means something additional to what he says.

Finally, "Moscow is a cold city" is not a metaphor; it is ambiguous, perhaps, a pun. It has two literal readings: "Moscow is a city that often has low temperatures" and "Moscow is not a cordial city." "Cold," in the latter sentence is a dead metaphor; but dead metaphors are not metaphors.

V. Generalizing the Theory

In section II, I said that *if* we accept Grice's formulation of the maxim of quality, then every metaphor is (or is thought to be) literally false or is supposed to be false. However, as we saw in Chapter Two, his formulation of the maxim of quality is not correct. Recall that the problem is that it is too narrow. As Grice formulates them, "Do not say that which is false," and "Do not say that for which you lack evidence," the maxims apply only to speech acts that have truth values, for example, statements and assertions. Many speech acts do not have truth values, for example, questions, promises and requests. All of this is important for our theory because many metaphors are embedded in utterances that would not have truth values if uttered literally, e.g., the Dutch uncle's utterance, "I promise I will clip that butterfly's wings." So, such simple cases cannot be explained in our original formulation about standard and nonstandard metaphors. However, the proplem is easily corrected by replacing Grice's too narrow maxims of quality with a sufficiently broad one and generalizing our initial formulation to accord with the broader maxim of quality.

Earlier, I suggested that Grice's maxims of quality should be replaced by this one: Do not participate in a speech act unless you satisfy all the conditions required for its successful and nondefective performance. This maxim is obviously broad enough to cover the entire spectrum of speech acts. The question now is, what was the intuition behind the distinction between standard and nonstandard metaphors? We can get at it if we consider the following sentences that might be uttered in the Dutch uncle situation.

> I state that Mary will have her wings clipped.
> I promise that Mary will have her wings clipped.
> I ask whether Mary will have her wings clipped.
> I insist that Mary will have her wings clipped.

In each case, the same proposition is involved: that Mary will have her wings clipped. Yet, in each case the force of the utterance would be different if the sentence were uttered literally. Searle would say that each utterance involves the same propositional content and each attempted speech act would be defective for the same reason if the relevant sentence were uttered literally. In each case, what Searle calls "the propositional content condition" would be flouted. These are cases of standard metaphors. That is, a standard metaphor is one in which the propositional content condition is flouted. Nonstandard metaphors are those in which the propositional content is supposed to be flouted. This formulation of the distinction between standard and nonstandard metaphors is unavoidably stated in technical terms in order to describe the phenomenon of metaphor correctly and with the required generality.

VI. Reply to Objections to a Pragmatic Theory of Metaphor

The theory of metaphor I have been advancing is blatantly pragmatic. Since some distinguished theorists have claimed that metaphor is a semantic phenomenon, their claims should be discussed, if only briefly. Max Black is perhaps the most distinguished philosophical proponent of this view. He says that in a metaphor, the focal or metaphorical term "obtains a new meaning, which is not quite its meaning in literal uses, not quite the meaning which any literal substitute would have (Black (1954), p. 39). This is in line with his general view that metaphor is a semantic phenomenon: "'metaphor' must be classified as a term belonging to 'semantics' and not to 'syntax' . . ." (Black (1954), p. 39). When Black expressed this view, there was no well-developed pragmatic theory such as Searle's revision of Austin's theory of speech acts and Grice's theory of linguistic communication; so it is not surprising that Black opts for a semantic theory against a syntactic theory and does not consider the possibility of a pragmatic theory. And it is not surprising that his arguments in behalf of a semantic treatment are not very telling against a pragmatic theory. He holds that "The chairman plowed through the discussion" and "The poor are the negroes of Europe" (attributed to Chamfort) are "unmistakeably *instances* of metaphor (Black (1954), p. 26). They are such only in context. We can imagine a crazed chairman driving a plow through a meeting of his committee; in which case the first sentence, if asserted, would be literally true. And we can imagine a slightly different history of Europe, in which the statement made by "The poor are the negroes of Europe" would be literally true and not a metaphor. The upshot is that whether a sentence is used literally or metaphorically depends upon the context of its use, and is, I maintain, a fit subject for a pragmatic theory.

Recently, L. Jonathan Cohen has also urged that metaphor be given a semantic treatment. According to Cohen, a pragmatic treatment, more specifically, a treatment of metaphor within a theory of speech acts, falls to the following objection:

A supposed speech act of metaphorizing would differ from standard types of speech act in an important respect. If Tom utters the sentence
(6) I am sorry,
he may well be apologizing. But, if I utter the sentence
(7) Tom said that he was sorry,
I am not apologizing myself; I am just reporting Tom's apology. The original speech act is overridden by the passage from oratio recta to oratio obliqua. Now metaphor behaves quite differently. When Tom describes his friend by saying
(8) The boy next door is a ball of fire,
Tom's description can be fully understood only by someone who understands the metaphor. But equally, if I myself report later
(9) Tom said that the boy next door is a ball of fire,
my report of Tom's utterance can also be fully understood only by someone who understands the metaphor. The metaphor is not overridden by the passage from oratio obliqua: the oratio obliqua sentence contains the same element of metaphorical meaning that the oratio recta contained. Arguably, therefore, metaphorical meaning inheres in sentences, not just in speech acts (Cohen (1979), p. 65).

Cohen's objection to a pragmatic theory turns on the claim that there are several respects in which metaphors do not parallel expressions of sorrow. A short reply to his objection is that since a speech act theory does not consider a metaphor on a par with expressions of sorrow — the latter but not the former are illocutionary acts — it would not be surprising if there were a lack of parallel. Interestingly enough, Cohen is wrong about the lack of parallels. As Cohen says, when Tom uses (8) to describe his friend, his description can be fully understood only by someone who understands the metaphor. Similarly, what Tom means by (6) can be fully understood only by someone who understands that Tom is not simply expressing his sorrow but also apologizing. the reason that the parallel holds up, even though metaphors are not illocutionary acts, is that both (6) and (8) involve the same mechanisms of conversational implication. Both metaphors and expressions of sorrow involve indirect speech acts: the performance of one linguistic act indirectly by performing another. An expression of sorrow is often an indirect way of apologizing, just as asking a question ("Can you pass the salt?") is often an indirect way of making a request ("Please, pass the salt."). A metaphor is always an indirect way of communicating some proposition. In further reply to Cohen, there is also a parallel between reports of metaphors and reports of expressions of sorrow. Cohen is correct to observe that a report of an expression of sorrow is not itself an expression of sorrow. However, he is wrong to hold that a person who reports a metaphor is himself metaphorizing, to use Cohen's word. A person who utters (9) does not speak metaphorically in reporting a metaphor. In short, *pace* Cohen, a metaphor in oratio recta is overridden by the metaphor in oratio obliqua. So the objections of Black and Cohen do not seem to stand in the way of the kind of pragmatic theory I have presented.

VII. A Comparison with Searle's Theory of Metaphor

There are same important similarities between my theory of metaphor and that of John Searle. The spirit is the same. Both are pragmatic theories that exploit features of Grice's theory of linguistic communication. We also differ in several significant respects. My theory is logically stronger than Searle's in three important ways. First, Searle claims that the stimulus to treat a sentence as being uttered metaphorically is the result of "falsehood, semantic nonsense, violations of the rules of speech acts, or violations of conversational principles of communication" (Searle (1979b), p. 105). My view is stronger in that I claim that all standard metaphors flout one maxim, the maxim of quality and all nonstandard metaphors must be supposed to contravene it. Second, Searle does not make clear whether, when a speaker utters a sentence s metaphorically, he is saying-that s or only making-as-if-to-say it. I have argued for the latter view, while also explaining how a speaker communicates some parts of what he says. Third, I have specified that the premises that are added to the metaphor, in order to infer what the point of the metaphor is, are constrained by three principles: they must involve features or properties that are salient to the metaphorical term; they must fulfill the maxim of relation by being relevant to the topic of the conversation; and they must help form a premise that tends to yield a true conclusion.

There is one respect in which Searle's theory has a superficial appearance of being stronger than mine. In contrast with my principles of salience and relevance and truth-producing premises, Searle specifies nine supposed principles for computing the features relevant to the metaphor. Yet, upon reflection, these nine principles turn out to be vacuous. Searle intends his nine principles to constitute at least a partial answer to the question, How is it possible for the hearer who hears the utterance "S is P" to know that the speaker means "S is R"? (Searle (1979b), p. 134). I want to show that Searle's nine principles fail to answer this question in any part, because the principles are so weak as to permit any possible feature or property of a thing to be a value of R.

Any feature or property will either be true of an object or false of it; and Searle allows any feature or property whether true or false of an object to play a role in the interpretation of a metaphor. This is objectionable because it fails to limit the possible features or properties of an object to those that are relevant to a metaphorical interpretation of a sentence. A theory of metaphor must provide principles that specify which features or properties might be relevant to a metaphor in order to allow the audience to know which features or properties the speaker means to imply by the metaphor. We can see this argument against Searle's principles more clearly by considering what he says about the metaphorical applicability of all those features or properties that are true of an object and then all those features or properties that are false of an object. According to Principle 1, a feature or property could be true of the object by definition; according to Principle 2, a feature or property could be contingently true of an object. Since every feature that is true of an object is either necessarily true, that is, true by definition, or contingently true, Searle has in no way restricted the actual features of an object to those that might play a role in a metaphor.

What about features that are not true of an object? Again, Searle allows such latitude that no feature is excluded from possibly playing a role in a metaphor. Citing Principles 3 and 4 is sufficient to show this. Principle 3 allows features that are often said of or believed to be true of an object; Principle 4 allows features that a thing does not have as well as those that are not even like any feature it has. In short, Searle's theory suffers from being too weak for failing to explain when a feature or property might play a role in a metaphor and when it would not.*

---

* Most of this chapter was first published in *Journal of Literary Semantics*, Vol. XIII/1 (1984) and reprinted by permission of the publisher, Julius Groos Verlag, Heidelberg/Germany.

Chapter Six: Applications to Problems in Logic

I. The Problem of a Taxonomy for Informal Fallacies

Perhaps the most unsatisfactory part of the traditional curriculum of informal logic is its treatment of the so-called informal fallacies. (Since I shall not be discussing formal fallacies in this chapter I will hereafter use "fallacies" to refer to informal fallacies.) Fallacies seem to resist an illuminating and perspicuous categorization and characterization. There is a quite banal consideration that makes the search for an adequate taxonomy seem doomed to failure. While there are a few principles of correct reasoning, the number of incorrect patterns of reasoning are unlimited. In other words, there is no underestimating the ability of human beings to invent new ways of making mistakes. This seems to be the view of H. W. B. Joseph, who is quoted as saying, "Truth may have its norms, but error is infinite in its aberrations, and they cannot be digested in any classification" (quoted by Hamblin (1970), p. 13). The belief that there cannot be a theoretically sound taxonomy of fallacies is caused, I think, by the false idea that the principles for a taxonomy of fallacies would have to be based upon what is common to the fallacies, and that the only thing that could be common to fallacies would be the kinds of mistakes that make them fallacies. Since there is little that is common to the fallacies, there cannot be a sound taxonomy of fallacies. Other philosophers are more sanguine about the possibility of categorizing fallacies on the basis of the kind of error involved (Kahane (1982), p. 208). Howard Kahane thinks fallacies can be divided either according to the logical error committed or to the psychological cause for the error. But I do not find the resulting taxonomy very illuminating.

I agree that kinds of mistakes cannot supply sound principles for a taxonomy of informal fallacies. Nonetheless, it does not follow that there can be no adequate theory of informal fallacies. A different principle of categorization, one based upon something other than the kind of mistake made, must be found. All fallacious reasoning involves a departure from or a violation of some rule of correct reasoning. Thus, it is a mistake to try to devise a taxonomy based upon principles involving positive features inhering in fallacies. Rather, the correct way to find a taxonomy for informal fallacies, I suggest, is to find one or more theories that describe the rules that informal fallacies violate.

One hindrance to finding a suitable taxonomy for informal fallacies is that philosophers have not known where to locate informal fallacies and an important reason for this is that until recently there has been no general theory within which fallacies could be located. In other words, until recently no one had spelled out the rules that many or most of the fallacies violated. There is now such a theory.

I want to suggest that a taxonomy of informal fallacies should be part of some theory related to a theory of speech or speech acts. The reason for this is that the informal fallacies typically involve unacceptable features of arguments in ordinary language and such arguments are used for persuasion. "Arguing", as it is used here in its ordinary sense, should not be confused with presenting a formal proof. Arguing stands to presenting a formal proof as genus to species. "Arguing" is the name of the illocutionary act or sequence of illocutionary acts that gives linguistic expression to reasoning. There are many different kinds of reasoning, of which devising a formal proof is just one sort. As "arguing" is the name of an illocutionary act, so "persuading" is the name of its correlative perlocutionary act. So it is not odd to think that a taxonomy of fallacies will be subsumed under some theory related to speech acts. It will not, however, be the theory of speech acts itself. Rather, a taxonomoy of fallacies should be part of a broader theory of conversation. More particularly, I want to suggest that Grice's theory of conversation, and, specifically his conversational maxims, provide the structure for an illuminating taxonomy for informal fallacies.

II. The Taxonomy

Listed below are Grice's conversational maxims, divided into his four categories, and the fallacies, if any, that contravene each.

Quality
1. Do not say that which is false.
2. Do not say that for which you lack adequate and appropriate evidence.
   a. hasty generalization
   b. false cause
   c. composition
   d. division
   e. ad ignorantiam
   f. ad populum
   g. ad verecundiam

Quantity
1. Contribute as much as is necessary for the conversation at the stage it is required.
   a. suppressed evidence
2. Do not contribute more than is necessary at the stage it is required.
   a. Complex question

VI Applications to Problems in Logic

Relation
1. Be relevant
   a. ad hominem abusive
   b. ad hominem circumstantial
   c. tu quoque
   d. ad baculum
   e. ignoratio elenchi
   f. ad misericordiam
   g. begging the question

Manner
1. Be clear.
2. Be brief.
3. Be orderly.
4. Avoid ambiguity.
   a. amphiboly
   b. equivocation
   c. accent

This taxonomy of fallacies requires some explanation. Two general features of this classification stand out. First, some maxims have no fallacies listed under them. We need to ask why this is so. Second, two maxims, the second maxim of quality, and the maxim of relation, contain the bulk of the fallacies. Again, we need to ask why this is so.

III. Maxims without Fallacies

Concerning the first point, the maxims that do not have any fallacies listed under them are those that are not deceptive in the characteristically fallacious way: that is, they do not tend to lead one away from the truth. The first maxim of quality, "Do not say that which is false," is the limiting case. What is false does not in itself tend to *lead one away from* the truth. It is already "away" from the truth. Someone might object that an untruth has a great propensity to lead one to more untruths; indeed, even a person who reasons validly from an untruth will derive many more untruths. My reply is that, although an untruth may lead to other untruths, the initial untruth is not itself a fallacy, and, given that the inference drawn from an untruth is valid, there is still no fallacy involved. The content of the first maxim of quality plays its role in the concept of soundness: a valid argument with *true premises*.

The first three maxims of manner do not have fallacies listed under them because they largely do not bear upon the thing that bears a truth value, namely, the content of what is said, but upon how what is said is said. The fourth maxim, as we shall see, does.

IV. Maxims with Fallacies

Each of the four categories of maxims have some fallacies listed under them although the bulk of them cluster under two maxims: the second maxim of quality and the maxim of relation. This clustering can in large part be explained. Given that I am right in claiming that fallacies concern considerations that mislead one about the truth-value of some proposition, it should not be surprising that those maxims that have the most to do with the assignment of truth values should suffer most of the fallacies.

I will now discuss my taxonomy in more detail. The sole fallacy listed under the first maxim of quantity is that of suppressed evidence. The truth-value of a proposition cannot be rationally assessed if only part of the evidence relevant to it is adduced, hence the courtroom requirement to tell the whole truth. For, in saying less than what is required in the context, the audience rightly assumes that a stronger proposition is either not true or not known by the speaker to be true, and, in that way, is deceived. The maxim, "Contribute as much as is necessary for the conversation at the stage it is required," demands that all the relevant evidence be produced. Violating that maxim, when determining the truth of a proposition, involves one in the fallacy of suppressed evidence. In addition to the fallacy of suppressed evidence or possibly as a species of it, I think there should be a fallacy of understatement, of which the following would be an instance. Suppose a close acquaintance — I cannot say "friend" — of Mr. and Mrs. Jones, sees them check into a motel. If this person says to someone, "I saw Jones and a woman check into a motel last night," in most circumstances the speaker will be (conversationally) implying that Jones checked into the motel with someone other than his wife. Such an implication may well lead the audience to adopt a false belief.

The second maxim of quantity also categorizes a fallacy, the fallacy of complex question. Someone who perpetrates this fallacy surreptitiously introduces into the conversation propositions that exceed what is required and acceptable. The question, "Do you still beat your wife?", when it is an instance of the fallacy of complex question, conversationally implies the proposition that the addressee does beat his wife, and this proposition counts as being more than is necessary at that stage of the conversation, because at that stage that proposition has not been mutually accepted. It is important to recognize that the same sort of error involved in the fallacy of complex question can infect virtually any kind of speech act. A person who says, "You will stop beating your wife" or "I order you to stop beating your wife" or "I promise to help you stop beating your wife," when the assumption that the addressee has beaten his wife is not mutually accepted, is equally fallacious. All of these fallacies involve an illicit presuppositon. Thus, as a generic term for fallacies falling under the second maxim of quantity, I would suggest "Fallacies of Illicit Presupposition," of which the fallacy of complex question is one kind.

The eight fallacies listed under the second maxim of quality –

a. hasty generalization;
b. false cause;
c. composition;
d. division;
e. special pleading;
f. ad ignorantiam;
g. ad populum;
h. ad verecundiam;

– have this in common, that they violate standards of evidence and, in that way, tend to lead to false belief. One important aspect of this fact is that informal fallacies, contrary to the received view about them, do not concern bad inferences, that is, in general they do not name mistaken ways of moving from the truth of one proposition to the truth of another. Rather, they name mistaken ways in which people move from evidence to belief in the truth of a proposition. And evidence typically does not consist of propositions but of nonlinguistic entities. Granted that the evidence for a belief is typically *expressed* by sentences, the evidence itself generally is not a sentence. Thus, to exploit a hackneyed example, a person who comes to believe that all the marbles in a large, opaque jar are black on the basis of randomly drawing out two black marbles is guilty of hasty generalization. But notice that the fallacy consists of forming a belief that outruns the evidence and the evidence is not a proposition but draws from a jar. Of course, one could redescribe the instance of the fallacy by saying that the proposition that the only two draws from the jar produced two black marbles led someone to believe the proposition that all the marbles in the jar were black. But this description is tendentious and reducible to the original one.

Earlier I recommended that fallacies should be categorized on the basis of the rules they violate. A corollary of this is that fallacies that violate the second maxim of quality should be understood as violating rules of evidence. Hasty generalization, special pleading, and false cause and possibly composition and division are violations of rules of evidence best formulated by the philosophy of science. The fallacies of ad ignorantiam, ad populum and ad verecundiam seem less specific to characteristically scientific thought and more akin to our everyday, nontechnical standards of evidence.

The idea that fallacies violate a *rule* of evidence presupposes that for each fallacy there is a legitimate way of using such evidence. Thus, there must be nonfallacious ways of thinking that might be called nonhasty generalization, the nonfallacy of true cause, general pleading, etc. And others have pointed out that sometimes a whole will have a certain property just because each of its parts has that same property; and sometimes the converse holds. It just depends upon what kind of thing and what kind of property is involved. The fallacies of composition and division result from mistaking when properties of parts and wholes apply to wholes and parts, respectively. Similarly, sometimes the opinion of an authority is a reliable guide to the truth value of a proposition: when the authority is speaking about a topic within the area of his expertise, in a discipline within which authorities largely agree. Authorities are not infallible, but they need not be. The opinion of an authority is a kind of evidence and evidence is inherently fallible. (Evidence should not be confused with evidentness.) A person who thinks that the opinion of an authority gives him good reason to think such and such thinks correctly; a person who thinks that the opinion of an authority guarantees the truth of such and such reasons badly and commits the fallacy of authority. The opinion of an authority can be misused, but the possibility of misuse presupposes a correct use. The shared opinion of a large number of people is analogous to the opinion of an authority, when the opinion reports their common experience. Value judgments are not such reports and hence appeals to the people on such matters are typically not reliable. On many other matters, however, people are reliable and an individual who refuses to take their opinion as strong evidence for a truth is a fool or an intellectual snob.

The fallacy of ad ignorantiam violates a principle relating to the burden of proof. If a person asserts a proposition, then the burden of proof falls on him and not on his audience. He does not prove his own proposition if his audience is unable to prove the contrary; to think that he does is to commit the fallacy of ad ignorantiam.

The maxim of relation has been criticized for being too vague. This objection has some force. However, the correct reaction to it is not to abandon Grice's maxims but to give them more content. For our purposes, the vague maxim, "Be relevant" is sufficient since we are principally concerned with finding a general rubric for fallacies. A more serious objection in this context is the following: Fallacious reasoning concerns the relation of evidence to truth; and this fact is reflected in the fallacies falling under the second maxim of quality. However, the maxim of relation concerns the relation of one speech act to another as regards not the truth of the speech act but as regards the coherence and continuity of the conversation. The belief that the maxim "Be relevant" subsumes the fallacies of relevance is an instance of the fallacy of equivocation. What is relevant to the truth of a proposition is one thing; what is relevant to the coherence of a conversation is another. My reply to this objection is that while the distinction between relevance to truth and relevance to the coherence of a conversation is a genuine one, the terms are not mutually exclusive. Sometimes what is relevant to the truth of a proposition is also required for the coherence of the conversation. Consider a clear case of ad hominem circumstantial: "It is not surprising that Chief Jones recommends higher salaries for police officers. He would directly benefit from such a move. Thus, we must reject his recommendation." The fact that Jones stands to benefit from the salary in-

VI Applications to Problems in Logic

crease is logically irrelevant to the issue of whether the increase is justified or not. However, it also constitutes a kind of conversational irrelevance. For Jones's possible benefit in fact is irrelevant to the topic of the conversation, because the topic of conversation is just the issue of whether the salary increase is justified or not. Contrast the fallacies that violate the maxim of relation (such as ad hominem) with the fallacies that violate the second maxim of quality. The difference is that evidence misused against the maxim of relation is not relevant to the truth of the proposition involved, while the evidence misused against the second maxim of quality is relevant but not sufficient for establishing the truth of the proposition at issue. Finally, in this regard, we should also mention that Grice views the conversational maxims as one realization of very general maxims of rationality (Grice (1975), p. 47). There is no reason to assume that what is conversational cannot also be rational.

The fourth maxim of manner, "Avoid ambiguity," contains fallacies, because ambiguity, unlike the first three maxims of manner, concerns not just how what is communicated is communicated, but the very content of what the audience takes to be communicated. Ambiguity can lead a person to be deceived about the truth value of a proposition, because an ambiguous sentence is one that proffers two propositions as if they were one. The fallacy of ambiguity results when an ambiguous sentence expresses both a true proposition and a false proposition and the latter is mistaken for the former.

Ambiguity can result in three different ways, because three different components determine the sense of a sentence: syntax, semantics and phonology. Corresponding to these three components are three fallacies. The fallacy of amphiboly is a fallacy that results from a syntactic or structural ambiguity. Amphibolies are standardly represented as simple minded fallacies. In fact, when they occur, they are very deep and difficult to extricate (see for an example Martinich (1976), 183−201). Equivocation is a fallacy that results from a subtle semantic ambiguity. The fallacy of accent is a fallacy that results from a phonologically based ambiguity. For example, it is true and not fallacious to assert, "We should not speak ill of our friends." But, it is (or can be) fallacious to assert, "We should not speak ill of our *friends*" since such an utterance, with "friends" contrastively stressed, conversationally implies something that is false, namely, that it is permissible to speak ill of one's enemies. Yet, to forestall the opinion that the fallacy of accent is merely a textbook fallacy, let me mention a recent incident in which an instance of it plays a central role. John Searle and Daniel Dennett are arguing, as I write this, about the supposed cognitive capabilities of computers (Dennett and Searle (1982), 56−57). Searle claims that they cannot duplicate human abilities. In the course of championing the cause of computers, Dennett misquoted an argument of Searle and has admitted the error but dismissess it as trivial and of no consequence. Dennett reports his error in this way: "Here are the facts. We *do* misquote him [Searle] in Reflection, alas; we have him saying 'a few slips of paper' where he in fact says 'bits of paper'," (Dennett and Searle (1982), 56) and Dennett denies that the misquotation of "bits" for "slips" is important. Searle does not accept Dennett's account, which, as we shall see, involves the fallacy of accent. Searle conceded that substituting "bits" for "slips" was an unimportant error; but pointed out that it was not the error that exercised him. The important error, the one that Dennett does not call attention to, is the omission of "a few" from the phrase "a few slips of paper." Searle indicates this fact by the use of contrastive stress. He concedes that the misquotation would be unimportant if only "a *few* slips of paper" were involved. However, the issue, in fact, involves, "*a very large number* of bits of paper" (Dennett and Searle (1982), 56). Notice how Searle again relies upon contrastive stress to highlight Dennett's commission of the fallacy of accent. We can see that Dennett does commit this fallacy by considering that his claim that his misquotation of Searle is unimportant makes sense only if we read the misquotation with stress on "slips": "we have him saying 'a few *slips* of paper where he in fact says '*bits* of paper'." If the stress fell on "a few" — "we have him saying "*a few* slips of paper' where he in fact says 'bits of paper'" — Dennett's claim that the misquotation is unimportant would become implausible. It is only Dennett's commission of the fallacy of accent that makes his defense seem cogent.

V. *The Relation of a Standard Taxonomy to the New One*

My taxonomy for fallacies will have to stand or fall on its own. However, it is worth noting an external fact that makes my taxonomy plausible. One standard treatment of fallacies divides them into fallacies of relevance and fallacies of ambiguity (Copi (1972), pp. 72–73). This division accords with my taxonomy. What I have done essentially is to locate these two types of fallacies within a more general theory, a theory of conversation, and to make the division more precise by placing some of the fallacies of relevance under the maxims of quality and some under the maxims of quantity. I think such relocation and precision is a theoretical advance.

VI. *Violating a Maxim*

Each fallacy involves a failure to fulfill some maxim. We have been more precise than this about the kind of failure. We have distinguished four different ways in which a maxim can go unfulfilled: violating, flouting, opting out and suspending.

Of these four ways of not fulfilling a maxim, a speaker who argues fallaciously violates a maxim. He does not flout a maxim since a fallacy cannot be intended to be recognized and a person who flouts a maxim does intend the contravention of the maxim to be recognized. Similarly, a person who argues fallaciously is neither opting out of nor suspending a maxim. For, if a person opts out of a maxim, he again intends the contravention to be recognized; and, if he suspends one, then the maxim cannot be breeched since it is not operative.

Although specifying that a person who argues fallaciously violates a maxim makes the notion of committing a fallacy more precise than it otherwise might be, it does not characterize a fallacy. Lying, for example, involves violating the first maxim of quality, and lying, despicable as it is, is not a fallacy.

VII. Formalism and Informalism

Although the theory of conversational maxims is of tremendous importance for the analysis both of everyday conversation and of literary works (Grice has used it to explain the intelligibility of various figures of speech, such as irony, metaphor, meiosis and hyperbole), the original motive for its construction involved a dispute in the philosophy of logic. This dispute concerns the relative merits of artificially constructed formal systems and natural languages. The "formalists," such as Bertrand Russell, W. V. Quine, and the early Wittgenstein, prefer formal systems because of their precision and explicitness, which serve the needs of sciences very well. Natural languages, in their view, are at best rough approximations to the ideal, badly in need of regimentation, but more or less adequate for the rough-and-tumble of non-technical discourse; at worst, they are strictly unintelligible. (Quine, for instance, holds that most modal sentences — ones involving logical necessity or possibility — are incoherent). On the other hand, the "informalists," such as Austin, Strawson, and the later Wittgenstein, prefer natural languages because of their richness and versatility, arguing that people need language for many purposes that formal systems cannot possibly serve, and pointing out that there are many valid inferences that formal systems cannot accommodate.

To the formalists' charge that natural languages are inexact, the classic reply, due to Wittgenstein, is that what counts as exactness in one kind of endeavor may be not only different but inappropriate and inhibiting in another kind. There is no absolute notion of exactness that can be set up as an ideal:

> What does the word 'exactness' mean? It is real exactness if you are supposed to come to tea at 4.30 and come when a good clock strikes 4.30? Or would it only be exactness if you began to open the door at the moment the clock began to strike? But how is this moment to be defined and how is 'beginning to open the door' to be defined? Would it be correct to say, "It is difficult to say what real exactness is, for all we know is only rough approximations"?

To the formalists' charge that natural languages are inexplicit, the proper reply is that any natural language has in it the resources for being as explicit as any formal system, since technical vocabularies and styles are part of natural languages. The idea that natural languages are by definition less explicit is caused by a confusion between natural languages and so-called "ordinary language," that is, roughly, the non-technical part of a natural language. It is true that speakers of a natural language typically choose to use sentences that are much less explicit than the formulas of a formal system; this is not, however, a defect of natural languages, but rather a virtue. Most thoughts that speakers wish to express can be expressed much more economically if they are not made fully explicit; human beings have a very limited amount of time on this earth and would not be spending their time well if all of their sentences had the explicitness characteristic of formal systems. For most purposes, it is a good thing that we are able to say

> Jack should go to the store this morning.

rather than

> Jack Jackson, eldest son of John Herbert Jackson and Ovis-Ann Dunlap Jackson, should go to the Rylanders grocery store in the Springdale Shopping Center in Austin, Texas, USA, between 0700 and 1200 hours, Central Standard Time, on March 2, 1984.

Not only is life too short for such needlessly explicit utterances, but the stores are not open long enough.

It must be admitted that these replies are not likely to satisfy a thoroughgoing formalist, who will find in them much that is tendentious and controversial. We have not raised this issue in order to resolve it completely, but rather in order to relate it to the conversational maxims. Formalists and informalists alike usually take the position that there are important semantic differences between the symbols used in typical formal systems and their counterparts in natural languages. As Grice says,

> It is a commonplace of philosophical logic that there are, or appear to be, divergences in meaning, between, on the one hand, at least some of what I shall call the FORMAL devices — $\sim$, $\vee$, $\supset$, (x), $(\exists x)$, ιx (when these are given a standard two-valued interpretation) — and, on the other, what are taken to be their analogs or counterparts in natural language — such expressions as *not, and, or, if, all, some* (or *at least one*), *the* (Grice (1975), p. 41, with some obvious misprints corrected).

Grice's purpose in constructing his theory of conversational maxims was to show that the stronger form of this commonplace is false: He wanted to argue that the formal symbols and their natural-language counterparts do *not* diverge in meaning. Further, he wanted to explain the apparent divergences in terms of the conversational maxims; he wanted to say that what is taken to be part of the meaning of a word in a natural language should in many cases be explained as a conversational implicature. In the next three sections, we shall consider three apparent semantic divergences between formal systems and natural languages; our objective will be to judge how plausibly the conversational maxims proposed above account for these apparent divergences.

VIII. Conjunction and a Maxim of Manner

A typical formal system (let's call it "Languish") will contain a symbol for conjunction — say, the ampersand (&). Syntactically, the ampersand joins together two sentences — say, A and B — to form a new sentence, which may be written thus:

$$A \& B$$

Semantically, the sentence $A \& B$ is true just in case A is true and B is true. This information is typically presented in tabular form:

A	B	$A \& B$
T	T	T
T	F	F
F	T	F
F	F	F

It is easy to prove that conjunction in Languish is commutative: a sentence of the form $A \& B$ is true just in case the corresponding sentence of the form $B \& A$ is true.

The ampersand corresponds to the sentential conjunction 'and' in English. That is, when going from English to Languish, one typically translates 'and' with &. In many cases the resulting translation is completely unobjectionable. The sentence 'Lulu is sad and Jerome is happy' is quite properly translated into Languish as, say, $p \& q$, where p corresponds to 'Lulu is sad' and q to 'Jerome is happy'. And there is no problem here with commutation: Just as $p \& q$ is equivalent to $q \& p$, in the sense that these two formulas always have the same truth-value, so 'Lulu is sad and Jerome is happy' seems to be equivalent to 'Jerome is happy and Lulu is sad'.

However, this is not always the case. There is a difference between saying

(1) Mary became pregnant and Joseph married her.

and saying

(2) Joseph married Mary and she became pregnant.

Similarly, there is a difference between saying

(3) Murray took off his socks and got into bed.

and saying

(4) Murray got into bed and took off his socks.

Formalists and informalists alike want to say that commutation does not hold in English, since (1) is not equivalent to (2) and (3) is not equivalent to (4), even though commutation does continue to hold for the translations of these sentences into Languish (Strawson (1952), p. 81). Formalists and informalists alike attribute the differences between (1) and (2) and between (3) and (4) to a characteristic of 'and' that is not shared by the ampersand: 'And', it is held, sometimes specifies a temporal ordering of the events expressed by the conjuncts.

Grice's view is that (1) and (2) mean the same thing, as do (3) and (4). He would admit that they diverge, and even that they diverge in meaning; however, the difference is not in word- or sentence-meaning, but in speaker-meaning. A speaker $S1$ who uttered (1) would typically mean something different from a speaker $S2$ who uttered (2). However, both speakers would be *saying* the very same thing, because their utterances are equivalent; the order of the clauses in a conjunctive sentence is irrelevant to its (sentence-) meaning. Hence the difference must lie in what $S1$ and $S2$ conversationally implicate. In other words, the difference has nothing to do with the semantic conventions governing 'and', but lies rather in the conversational conventions that $S1$ and $S2$ follow. The relevant conversational maxim is a Maxim of Manner: Be orderly. This maxim could be said to have several sub-maxims, one of which has to do with temporal order: "Express events in the order in which they occurred." That is, if event $E1$ happened before event $E2$, express $E1$ before expressing $E2$. Of course, this sub-maxim, like all maxims, can go unfulfilled for various reasons; in epics, indeed, it is a convention to begin not at the beginning, but *in medias res*. (Even there it is usual for the middle events to be taken up in sequence until a convenient flashback point is reached, after which the events are again recounted chronologically.) For the most part, however, the maxim of orderliness is observed; hence, if we assume that $S1$ and $S2$ are observing the Cooperative Principle and have no reason not to fulfill the Maxims of Manner in particular, $S1$ conversationally implicates that Mary became pregnant before Joseph married her, while $S2$ implicates the opposite. Notice that since these are only conversational implicatures, they can be cancelled; there is no contradiction in saying, "Mary became pregnant and Joseph married her, but not necessarily in that order."

This treatment of 'and' also recommends itself because it does not share certain drawbacks of the alternative explanation on which the formalists and informalists are agreed. The latter view posits two meanings for one word, which is uneconomical, to say the least; it would be better if we could account for the differences between (1) and (2) and between (3) and (4) without having to recognize both an "atemporal" 'and' and a "temporal" one, and Grice's account does this. Secondly, if there is a meaning of 'and' that temporally orders the events expressed by its conjuncts, it is odd that we have such sentences as 'Mary became pregnant and *then* got married'. If 'and' already meant 'and then', the word 'then' would be doing no work in that sentence; it would be redundant.

IX. Conditionals and a Maxim of Relation

A conditional sentence is one in which one clause expresses a condition under which another clause is, would be, or might be true. There are many types of conditional sentences in English, and most are very complicated; for instance, counterfactual conditionals, in which the verb in the subordinate clause is in the subjunctive mood ("If Humphrey had been elected president in 1972, the Watergate scandal would never have occurred," "If I were President, the tax credit for energy-saving devices would be greater"), are especially interesting and important because of the role they play in the formulation of scientific laws, yet they are notoriously difficult to analyze. Even conditionals in which all the verbs are in the indicative mood are not unproblematical. We shall be concerned only with conditionals of this latter kind.

Let us use the horseshoe, $\supset$, as the analogue in Languish of the 'if . . . then . . .' construction. Like the ampersand, the horseshoe will link together two sentences, A and B, to form a compound sentence $A \supset B$. The sentence that goes on the left side of the horseshoe is the one that corresponds to the subordinate clause of the English sentence (the part that immediately follows 'if'); the main clause goes on the right of the horseshoe. Semantically, a sentence of the form $A \supset B$ is true just in case A is false or B is true; that is to say, its truth-table is:

A	B	$A \supset B$
T	T	T
T	F	F
F	T	T
F	F	T

The difficulty is that the truth-values of English conditionals, unlike those of sentences of the form $A \supset B$ in Languish, are not determined solely by the truth-value of the clauses. The cases in which the truth-value of the English sentence does not seem to match the truth-value of the corresponding formula of Languish fall into three classes:

(a) *Both clauses are false.* According to the last line of the truth-table, $A \supset B$ is true whenever A and B are both false. So a sentence like

(7) If Nixon is president in 1980, then everyone is prospering.

gets translated into a *true* formula of Languish. Yet (7) seems false, inasmuch as Nixon's being president in 1980 is not sufficient to guarantee prosperity for all. Hence (it is argued) the horseshoe, though it is in some ways analogous to 'if . . . then . . .', is in this case an inaccurate semantic model. (Formalists will charge that the English construction embodies a confused notion of causal connection; informalists will disparage the Languish connective as a simplistic distortion.)

(b) *The subordinate clause is false, the main clause true.* The third line of the truth-table specifies that the Languish formula is true in this case. On the other hand, the English sentence

(8) If Nixon is president in 1980, then not everyone is prospering.

is at best controversial; it doesn't seem entirely impossible that everyone should prosper even if Nixon is president in 1980. But perhaps one's assessment of (8) depends on one's evaluation of Nixon's character and abilities; as president in 1980, considerations of national security might force him to sabotage the prosperity of the people on his "enemies list." So let's take a less controversial conditional:

(9) If pigs have wings, then so do pelicans.

(9) seems false because pelicans' having wings and pigs' having wings are utterly unrelated. Yet the corresponding formula in Languish is true.

(c) *Both clauses are true.* Even when both clauses of the English conditional are true, the conditional as a whole sometimes strikes people as false if there is no connection between the clauses. For example,

(10) If Nixon is not president, then Monday follows Sunday.

According to the first line of the truth-table, the corresponding formula of Languish is true.

As in the case of 'and' and &, the exponent of a Gricean theory of conversational maxims will account for these phenomena not by drawing semantic distinctions between 'if . . . then . . .' and the horseshoe, but by bringing in the notion of speaker-meaning. A speaker who uttered any one of the sentences (7) through (10) would be *saying* something true, just as the truth-table for conditionals says. But what a speaker *means* includes more than just what he *says*; a speaker who uttered any one of these sentences would typically be conversationally implicating a falsehood. The implicature arises from the Maxims of Relation, and specifically maxim C2, "Express yourself in terms that will enable your hearer to tie your contribution into the conversational context." One of the consequences of this maxim is that consecutively uttered clauses should have some topical relationship. Since the hearer is entitled to assume, in the absence of any indication to the contrary, that the speaker is observing this maxim, the speaker who utters, say, sentence (9) conversationally implicates that there is some connection between pigs' having wings and pelicans' having wings — which is false. Similarly, the utterer of sentence (8) implicates that there is some connection between Nixon's being president in 1980 and someone's adversity; if (8) seems false, it is because we are not entirely willing to go along with the speaker on this point.

This consequence of maxim C2 does not apply only to conditionals. Someone who uttered the conjunctive sentence

Mary is happy and three is a prime number.

or the disjunctive sentence

Mary is happy or stars shine brightly.

would, except in special cases, conversationally imply something false, since the hearer would suppose that the speaker was observing maxim C2.

Of course, not every failure to fulfill maxim C2 results in a false statement. One can *flout* the maxim and thereby emphasize the truth of a conditional. When someone says, "If Nixon was an honest president, then I'm a monkey's uncle," the flagrant irrelevance of the two clauses underscores the truth of what was *said*. The speaker is exploiting the fact that conditional sentences in English conform to the truth-table presented above, counting on the hearer to reason that because the speaker has patently contravened C2, no real or imaginary relation between the clauses should be sought; and, given that the speaker is fulfilling the Maxim of Quality "Say what is true," and that the consequent is obviously false, the speaker must believe that the subordinate clause is false as well. That is, the speaker is conversationally implicating that Nixon was not an honest president.

X. *Disjunction and a Maxim of Quantity*

Languish also contains a symbol for disjunction — say, the wedge (v). Once again, the wedge combines with two sentences, A and B, to form a new sentence $A \vee B$. Semantically, a sentence of the form $A \vee B$ is true just in case either A is true or B is true or both. Here is its truth-table:

A	B	$A \vee B$
T	T	T
T	F	T
F	T	T
F	F	F

The wedge corresponds to 'or' in English; that is, in going from English to Languish, one typically translates 'or' with v. So for example the sentence 'Either the Steelers will win the AFC championship or the Cowboys will win the NFC championship' is translated into Languish as, say, $p \vee q$, where *p* corresponds to 'The Steelers will win the AFC championship' and *q* to 'The Cowboys will win the NFC championship'.

This much is unproblematical. The difficulty arises with sentences such as

(11) Either the Steelers will win the AFC championship or the Oilers will win the AFC championship.

(12) Either Reagan will be re-elected to the presidency in 1984 or Walter Mondale will be elected to the presidency in 1984.

On the face of it, these sentences are disjunctions, and should be translated into formulas of Languish of the form $A \vee B$. The objection to such a translation has to do with the fact that in each case it is impossible for both disjuncts to be true; the Steelers and the Oilers cannot both win the AFC championship, nor can Reagan and Mondale both be elected president in 1984.

There are two ways of putting this objection; let us take up the weaker version first. It might be claimed that the Languish disjunctions imply that it is possible for both disjuncts to be true at the same time, while the English sentences clearly do not imply this. In this form the objection is based on a misunderstanding of the way in which a truth-table describes the semantics of a connective. The fact that the truth-table for disjunction contains a line on which both A and B are assigned the value T does not imply that no matter what A and B are, it is possible for them to be true simultaneously, or even that it is possible for them to be true at all. The truth-table simply tells you what value to assign to the disjunction when you are dealing with two sentences that *are* both true. In other words, since the truth-table has to be applicable no matter what A and B are, it covers all the possible combinations of truth and falsity; but that doesn't mean that all those possibilities can arise in any one case.

Here's still another way of putting the same point. A formula of Languish of the form $A \vee B$ *does not say that it is possible for both disjuncts to be true; it says that either* both disjuncts are true *or* the first is true and the second false *or* the first is false and the second true. When one of these is ruled out (say, by the meaning of 'win' and the rules of the National Football League), all that happens is that one of the other alternatives must be true in order for the disjunction to be true; the disjunction does not become false or nonsensical, as it would if it implied something false.

The other version of the objection is harder to deal with: It is that the English sentences imply that it is not the case that both disjuncts are true, while the corresponding formulas of Languish do not. That is, sentence (11) is supposed to imply

(13) It is not the case that both the Steelers and the Oilers will win the AFC championship.

and (12) to imply

VI Applications to Problems in Logic 111

> (14) It is not the case both that Reagan will be reelected to the presidency in 1984 and that Walter Mondale will be elected to the presidency in 1984.

This seeming disparity has led some logicians to propose that the English word 'or' has two meanings, one of which is accurately rendered by the Languish v and the other by a connective w with the following truth-table:

A	B	A w B
T	T	F
T	F	T
F	T	T
F	F	F

Such sentences as (11) and (12) can then be translated using this second kind of disjunction. Standard logical rules will ensure that the Languish translations of (11) and (12) do indeed entail the Languish translations of (13) and (14) respectively.

The fact that there are two Latin words for disjunction, *vel* (which corresponds to v) and *aut* (which corresponds to w) has sometimes been adduced in support of this hypothetical ambiguity of English 'or'. This, however, is a weak and inconclusive argument. Linguists have established (what is, perhaps, obvious to anyone who has become intimately acquainted with more than one language) that the semantic correlations between natural languages are imperfect. There is no reason why a distinction that is marked in the vocabulary of one language should have to be present in the semantics of a single word in another language, even when the languages are cousins, as English and Latin are.

Accordingly, the question boils down to whether it is possible to explain the relationship between (11) and (13) and between (12) and (14) without supposing that 'or' is ambiguous. Now, on Grice's view, 'or' has only one meaning, the one represented by the wedge. This means that the Languish translation of (11) does not imply the Languish translation of (13); but this is all right, since sentence (11) does not, in fact, logically imply sentence (13). The inference that (13) is true has nothing to do with (11); it is based directly on the rules of the NFL. Those rules entail that in a given season the AFC has only one winner. Similarly, the Constitution of the United States makes it impossible for two candidates to be elected to the presidency at the same time, so that (14) is known to be true independently of (12). If these facts are evident both to the speaker and to the hearer, it is unnecessary for either party to call any special attention to them, and indeed there is a Maxim of Quantity, "Do not make your contribution more informative than is required," that would militate against any such remark. Far from being necessary in order to represent 'or' in (11) and (12), the connective **w** is actually *incorrect* as a translation of that 'or', both on logical grounds (since (11) does not by itself imply (13)) and because it incorrectly suggests that the utterer of (11) is contributing the information expressed by (13), which would be a violation of the Maxim of Quantity.

Another Maxim of Quantity, "Make your contribution as informative as is required," is also relevant to our understanding of the divergence between what a speaker *says* with the word 'or' and what he implicates. In standard situations, if a speaker says

(15) John is either at home or at work.

he conversationally implicates that he does not know which. But if he utters (15), he does not *say* that he does not know which, and he may in fact know which. He might go on, without contradicting himself, to cancel the implicature by saying, "But I'm not at liberty to tell you which," or, playfully, "Guess which."

Chapter Seven: Utterer's Meaning and Communication

I. Communicative and Non-Communicative Meaning

In Chapter Three, we approached the notion of speaker-meaning through speech-act theory, breaking it down into its elements (as represented in the table in section VI). We now turn to the question of distinguishing the sort of meaning that is involved in acts of communication from what has sometimes been called "natural meaning."

Grice begins his 1957 paper "Meaning" by contrasting sentences like

(1) Those three rings on the bell (of the bus) mean that the bus is full.

and

(2) That remark, "Smith couldn't get on without his trouble and strife," meant that Smith found his wife indispensable.

with sentences like

(3) Those spots mean measles.

and

(4) The recent budget means that we shall have a hard year.

We intuitively sense that there is an important difference between what the word 'mean' means in sentences (1) and (2) and what it means in sentences (3) and (4). Grice distinguishes these two senses of the word 'mean' as the natural sense and the non-natural sense, and marks the non-natural sense with the subscript 'NN'. Because we shall be quoting from Grice's paper, we shall acquiesce in the use of the subscript, although the choice of terminology seems unfortunate. Human beings are, of course, part of nature, and communication is part of the nature of human beings, so there are at least two senses in which meaning in the "non-natural" sense is natural; moreover, the use of the negative term suggests that there is something deviant or decadent — "unnatural" — about non-natural meaning. For these reasons we have elected to use the term 'communicative' instead of 'non-natural'.

Grice mentions five differences between sentences in which 'mean' is used in the natural sense and sentences in which it is used in the communicative sense ('mean$_{NN}$'):

(i) A sentence of the form 'x means that p', where x is to be replaced by a noun-phrase and p by a sentence, entails the corresponding sentence of the form 'p' just in case 'mean' is used in the natural sense. For instance, the sentence 'Those spots mean that you have the measles' entails the sentence

'You have the measles'. If a doctor says "Those spots mean that you have the measles," and you don't have the measles, then what the doctor said was false and you need a second opinion. In cases of non-natural meaning, the entailment does not hold: Sentence (1) does not entail 'The bus is full', for it is possible for the bell to ring three times even when the bus is not full, if for example the conductor makes a mistake or rings the bell unintentionally.

(ii) A sentence of the form 'x means that p' can be paraphrased by a sentence of the form 'what is meant by x is that p' just in case 'mean' is used in the *communicative* sense. We cannot go from 'Those spots mean that you have the measles' to 'What is meant by those spots is that you have measles', because the latter is incoherent, but we can go from sentence (1) to 'What is meant by those three rings of the bell is that the bus is full'.

(iii) When a sentence of the form 'x means that p' is uttered, 'mean' is used in the communicative sense, and the speaker (normally) implies that *someone* meant that p by x; when 'mean' is used in the natural sense, there is no such implication. Someone who says "Those spots mean that you have the measles" does not imply that anyone means that you have the measles; but someone who utters sentence (1) does imply that someone means that the bus is full. (Notice, however, that this implication is not a semantic fixture, and can be cancelled; if the wind causes the bell to ring three times, the speaker does not imply that the wind is an intelligent being who means that the bus is full.)

(iv) A sentence of the form 'x means that p' can be paraphrased as 'x means "p"' just in case 'mean' is used in the communicative sense. We cannot go from 'Those spots mean that you have the measles' to 'Those spots mean "You have the measles"', but we can go from sentence (1) to 'Those three bells mean "The bus is full"'.

(v) A sentence of the form 'x means that p' can be correctly paraphrased into a sentence of the form 'The fact that . . . means that p' just in case 'mean' is used in the natural sense. We can go from 'Those spots mean that you have the measles' to 'The fact that you are covered with red spots means that you have the measles'; but we cannot go from sentence (1) to 'The fact that the bell has rung three times means that the bus is full'. This latter attempt at paraphrase is not incoherent, but it does not mean the same thing as sentence (1); it implies a natural connection between two facts. We might say "The fact that the bell has rung three times means that the bus is full" if it happened that, quite by accident, a bell had gotten hooked up to the suspension system of the bus, and because of certain physical facts about the bulk of human beings, the volume of the bus, and the resilience of its springs, the bell rings when the bus is full and not otherwise. In this case, there is a natural connection between the ringing of the bell and the bus's being full; and we are using 'mean' in the natural, non-communicative sense.

VII Utterer's Meaning and Communication

These five differences direct one's attention to the fact that we ascribe communicative meaning only to things that result from the deliberate actions of people. Measles are not communicatively meaningful because no human being creates or causes measles; bell-ringing is communicatively meaningful because there is (usually) someone who deliberately rings the bell for some intelligible reason. We conclude that communicative meaning is to be explained in terms of intentions and intentional actions.

II. Grice's Analysis of Communicative Meaning

We saw in section I that the difference between natural and communicative meaning is to be explained in terms of intention. Another indication of the link between meaning and intention is that in some sentences the word 'mean' is synonymous with 'intend':

(8) I did not mean (intend) to hurt you.
(9) He means (intends) well, but he's clumsy.

Accordingly, one might propose the following analysis of communicative meaning:

(10) An utterer U means $_{NN}$ something by uttering x if, and only if, U intends the utterance of x to have some effect (on the interpreter of the utterance).

However, analysis (10) is too weak; there are cases in which a person acts so as to produce some effect on another person, but does not *communicate* with that other person and hence does not mean$_{NN}$ anything by his action. Consider, for example, an episode from *Othello*: The villain, Iago, plants Desdemona's handkerchief in the chambers of another man, intending to get Othello to believe that Desdemona has been unfaithful to him; tragically, this ruse succeeds. Obviously, although Iago intends his action to have some effect on Othello, he is not communicating with him; he does not mean$_{NN}$ anything by the handkerchief or by leaving the handkerchief in Cassio's chambers.

One reason why Iago's action is not an example of communicative meaning is that he acted surreptitiously; communication, on the contrary, must be in some sense open. This does not mean that the participants must be honest and above board, since even a lie or a misleading remark is a communication; but at least the utterer must be willing to acknowledge the action in question as his own. Indeed, for an utterer to have meant$_{NN}$ something, he "must have intended an 'audience' to recognize the intention behind the utterance" (Grice (1957), p. 440). Since Iago certainly would not have wanted Othello to recognize the intention behind his leaving the handkerchief in Cassio's chambers, or even to realize that Iago had put it there,

Iago's action was not a case of communication. We can add this as a second condition in the analysis of communicative meaning:

(11) An utterer U means$_{NN}$ something by uttering x if and only if:
(a) U intends the utterance of x to have some effect on the interpreter; and
(b) U intends the interpreter to recognize intention (a).

It turns out that analysis (11) is still too weak, as Grice points out:

> Consider the following cases:
> (1) Herod presents Salome with the head of St. John the Baptist on a charger.
> (2) Feeling faint, a child lets its mother see how pale it is (hoping that she may draw her own conclusions and help).
> (3) I leave the china my daughter has broken lying around for my wife to see. Here we seem to have cases which satisfy the conditions so far given for meaning$_{NN}$. For example, Herod intended to make Salome believe that St. John the Baptist was dead and no doubt also intended Salome to recognize that he intended her to believe that St. John the Baptist was dead. Similarly for the other cases. Yet I certainly do not think that we should want to say that we have here cases of meaning$_{NN}$ (Grice (1957), p. 440).

Now, in each of these examples we can say that something was *meant*: The head of St. John the Baptist on the charger meant that he was dead; the child's paleness meant that she was faint; the broken china meant that the daughter had broken it (and that she was in trouble). However, the meaning in each case is not communicative meaning, but natural meaning, since what is meant is a matter of the laws of physics or physiology, not a matter of intentions. This is not to deny that Herod and the other agents involved had certain intentions; the point is rather that it is not these intentions that lead us to say that meaning was involved. Herod, the child, and the father each deliberately and openly let someone know something, and got someone to think something; but communication requires something more. What is it?

In this connection Grice invites us to compare the following two cases:

> (1) I show Mr. X a photograph of Mr. Y displaying undue familiarity to Mrs. X.
> (2) I draw a picture of Mr. Y behaving in this manner and show it to Mr. X. I find that I want to deny that in (1) the photograph (or my showing it to Mr. X) meant$_{NN}$ anything at all; while I want to assert that in (2) the picture (or my drawing and showing it) meant$_{NN}$ something (that Mr. Y had been unduly familiar), or at least that I had meant$_{NN}$ by it that Mr. Y had been unduly familar. What is the difference between the two cases? Surely that in case (1) Mr. X's recognition of my intention to make him believe that there is something between Mr. Y and Mrs. X is (more or less) irrelevant to the production of this effect by the photograph. Mr. X would be led by the photograph at least to suspect Mrs. X even if instead of showing it to him I had left it in his room by

accident; and I (the photograph shower) would not be unaware of this. But it will make a difference to the effect of my picture on Mr. X whether or not he takes me to be intending to inform him (make him believe something) about Mrs. X, and not to be just doodling or trying to produce a work of art (Grice (1957), p. 440, with the correction of an obvious misprint in the original).

In order for communication to occur, then, the utterer must intend that his interpreter be affected because he recognizes that the utterer intends him to be so affected. This third intention can be added to our analysis of communicative meaning:

(12) An utterer U means$_{NN}$ something by uttering x if and only if:
(a) U intends the utterance of x to have some effect on the interpreter;
(b) U intends the interpreter to recognize intention (a); and
(c) U intends the interpreter to be thus affected at least partly because the interpreter recognizes intention (a).

Thus, when Herod presents Salome with the head of St. John the Baptist on a charger, he does not mean$_{NN}$ that St. John the Baptist is dead, because condition (c) is not satisfied: Herod knows that Salome will recognize that Herod is letting her know that St. John the Baptist is dead, but this recognition will not play any part in her coming to know that St. John the Baptist is dead; she will know that he is dead simply from seeing his severed head on the charger, regardless of Herod's intentions. Similarly, the child who lets her mother see how pale she is intends her mother to comfort her, but she does not care whether her mother comforts her because she is pale or because her mother figures out that that is what she wants; and the father who leaves the broken cup on the floor, although he does intend to let his wife know that their daughter has broken a cup, does not intend that his wife's recognition of this intention play any part in her coming to know that their daughter has broken a cup. Thus condition (c) is not satisfied in any of Grice's three cases.

Analysis (12) is a formulation of the account of meaning$_{NN}$ that emerges from Grice's 1957 paper. It serves as a sort of reference point, a basic account that others can take up, refine, and elaborate. Let us consider a few of the refinements that have been proposed.

In a subsequent paper (Grice (1969), pp. 152–153), Grice discusses a kind of example that was proposed to him in conversation by J. O. Urmson, showing that analysis (12) is still too weak. He does not present Urmson's example, but from what he does say, one can guess that it goes something like this: A group of industrialists calls on the newly elected governor, a man by the name of Jones. They discuss with him certain legislative items in which they have an interest, and in the course of the conversation they pile fifty thousand dollars in unmarked hundred-dollar bills on his desk. It is clear that they intend the money to have some effect on Jones (namely, that he will look more favorably on the legislation they are interested in). It is also clear that they intend Jones to recognize their intention, and to look more favorably on their legislation precisely because he recognizes their intention. Thus all three conditions of analysis (12) are satisfied; and yet it does not seem that by piling fifty thousand dollars on Jones' desk, the industrialists meant$_{NN}$ that Jones should look more favorably on their legislation.

This example reveals that the original analysis is incorrect insofar as it fails to make clear the connection between the utterance itself and the utterer's intention (b). The utterance is supposed to be the instrument of communication, the means by which the utterer gets the interpreter to recognize what he has in mind. This difficulty is easily rectified; we need only rewrite condition (b) of analysis (12) as follows:

(b*) U intends the interpreter to recognize intention (a), at least partly because of the utterance of x.

Another way of improving on analysis (12) would be to write into it a specification of *what* the utterer U means$_{NN}$ by uttering x. There does not seem to be any easy way to do this, given the variety of perlocutionary effects that U may intend to produce in the interpreter. Initially (as we saw in a different connection in section XIII of Chapter Two), Grice held that the indicative mood is linked to belief; therefore, the utterer of a sentence in the indicative mood usually intends to get the interpreter to share his belief that the sentence is true. There are, however, many counterexamples that disprove this contention. For instance, a student who is asked by his teacher when the Battle of Waterloo was fought and replies, "1815," is not trying to get the teacher to believe the answer; he knows perfectly well that the teacher already knows the answer. Similarly, if A reminds B of some fact that B knows but has put out of his mind for the moment, A is not trying to get B to share A's belief; and so on. These examples, and several others directed to the same points, are discussed in Grice (1969), pp. 166–173.

We shall return to the problem of stating what the utterer means$_{NN}$ by uttering x in section VI. Meanwhile, we shall consider two other challenges to analysis (12); each is formidable enough to require a section of its own.

III. Strawson's Critique of Grice's Analysis

In "Intention and Convention in Speech Acts" (1964c), Strawson argues that analysis (12) of section III is still too weak, and that at least one more condition must be added. The argument takes the form of a schematic description of a counterexample. Calling the utterer "S," the interpreter "A," and conditions (a), (b), and (c) of analysis (12) "(i_1)," "(i_2)," and "(i_3)" respectively, Strawson reasons as follows:

VII Utterer's Meaning and Communication

S intends by a certain action to induce in A the belief that p; so he satisfies condition (i_1). He arranges convincing-looking 'evidence' that p, in a place where A is bound to see it. He does this, knowing that A is watching him at work, but *knowing also that A does not know that S knows that A is watching him at work.* He realizes that A will not take the *arranged* 'evidence' as genuine or natural evidence that p, but realizes, and indeed intends, that A will take his arranging of it as grounds for thinking that he, S, intends to induce in A the belief that p. That is, he intends A to recognize his (i_1) intention. So S satisfies condition (i_2). He knows that A has general grounds for thinking that S would not wish to make him, A, think that p unless it were known to S to be the case that p; and hence that A's recognition of his (S's) intention to induce in A the belief that p will in fact seem to A a sufficient reason for believing that p. And he intends that A's recognition of his intention (i_1) should function in just this way. So he satisfies condition (i_3).

S, then, satisfies all Grice's conditions. But this is clearly not a case of attempted *communication* in the sense which (I think it is fair to assume) Grice is seeking to elucidate (Strawson (1964c), p. 156).

Strawson himself does not attempt to construct an example that conforms to this description, and in fact it is not at all easy to do so. There is an inherent implausibility in one element of Strawson's account: Why should S think — and how could he *know* — that A would recognize the evidence as bogus and yet use it to form a belief? We are asked to suppose that A's general grounds for thinking that S would not mislead him are so strong that even a transparent deception cannot overcome them. This willingness to trust S is worthy of a Tertullian. (Tertullian declared that he believed in Jesus's resurrection because it was absurd.) It is hard to imagine that S could count on it, to the extent of incorporating it into his plans.

Perhaps it is not quite impossible to draw up an example that fits Strawson's description, however. The following *nearly* plausible example is due to Maureen Paskin:

Suppose that Jerome and Murray are very good friends. They know each other very well, they trust each other completely, and neither would ever do anything to hurt the other, or even to mislead him, without having a very good reason. Murray strongly believes in fidelity, and Jerome knows this. Jerome also knows that Murray's wife, Lulu, has been unfaithful to him, and he thinks that Murray should know about it, too. (Jerome doesn't like Lulu — he thinks that Murray deserves better — and he knows that Murray will divorce Lulu if he finds out that she has been unfaithful.) Finally, Jerome knows that Murray is particularly touchy on the subject of fidelity, and in particular that Murray would not let himself believe that his wife had been unfaithful if someone (even Jerome) just told him so. (Even though he trusts Jerome completely, he would repress this information and argue that Jerome was mistaken.) But Jerome does not want Murray to find out about Lulu's infidelity by discovering her in her lover's arms; he is afraid that Murray's temper will get out of control if he finds this stranger embracing his wife, with tragic consequences.

Thus, in order to get Murray to believe that his wife has been unfaithful to him, Jerome adopts the following plan: he somehow inveigles Lulu into having a fling with him, one time only, and arranges for Murray to discover them *in medias res* (without letting Murray know that he has arranged this discovery). He intends by this action to induce in Murray the belief that Lulu has been unfaithful to him, that is, that she has had real affairs in the past. Murray knows that Jerome would never betray him by having a real affair with Lulu, that is, an affair that went on for some time, and Jerome is well aware of this; accordingly, he does not assume that Murray will accept what he sees as genuine evidence that Lulu has had real affairs in the past. But Jerome realizes, and indeed intends, that Murray will recognize that the whole episode is a set-up (but not that Jerome *intended* him to recognize it as a set-up); and Jerome realizes and intends that Murray will infer that Jerome is trying to let him know that Lulu has been unfaithful to him in the past. That is, Murray is supposed to reason: "Jerome would never betray me by having a long-term affair with Lulu; but he is trying to make it look as though there has been just such an affair. Why? He can't expect me to believe that *he* has been having an affair with Lulu; he must be trying to tell me that she has been having an affair with someone else. But he wouldn't be trying to tell me such a thing, especially in such a drastic way, unless it were true; if he merely thought that Lulu *might* be unfaithful, he would surely have approached the subject in a less indelicate and less hurtful way."

Thus Murray's recognition of Jerome's intention to make him believe that Lulu has been unfaithful to him will in fact seem to Murray to be a sufficient reason for believing that Lulu has been unfaithful to him; and Jerome counts on this when he carries out his plan. If we return to analysis (12) of section III, we see that all three conditions are met: Jerome intends his action to have some effect on Murray, he intends Murray to recognize this intention, and he intends Murray to be affected at least partly because of his recognition of Jerome's intention.

If this is indeed a case that fits Strawson's description, Strawson's claim is that Jerome is clearly not trying to communicate with Murray, in the sense that Grice is trying to explain. But is it so clear that no communication takes place? One might very well argue that Jerome *is* communicating with Murray, albeit in an unorthodox way; and the unorthodoxy is necessary because of Murray's unusual psychology and system of beliefs. It does not seem wrong or incoherent to say that by seducing Lulu and arranging for Murray to discover them, Jerome meant$_{NN}$ that Lulu had been unfaithful to Murray in the past. But if he did, then Strawson has not succeeded in producing a counterexample; his claim that the conditions that make up the analysans could be satisfied by a situation to which the analysandum does not apply is incorrect, since the analysandum *does* apply.

Even if Strawson's claim that Jerome is not communicating with Murray is true, there is another problem with his counterexample: It is not instructive. If Jerome is not communicating with Murray, why not? What feature of communicative meaning is absent from the situation? What fourth condition must be added in order to strengthen the analysis? According to Strawson, the example shows that "we must add to Grice's conditions the further condition that S should have the further intention (i_4) that A should recognize his intention (i_2)" (Strawson (1964c), p. 157). In other words, we should add the following to analysis (12):

(d) U intends the interpreter to recognize intention (b*).

In order to mean$_{NN}$ something by x, U must intend the interpreter to recognize that U intends him to recognize that U intends x to have some effect on him.

Now, it is true that this condition is not fulfilled either in Strawson's abstract description (remember, Strawson stipulates that S knows that A does not know that S knows that A is watching him forge the evidence) or in the Jerome-Murray example (for Murray is not supposed to realize that Jerome intended him to recognize that the whole episode was stage-managed). But does this really constitute the difference between meaning$_{NN}$ something and not meaning$_{NN}$ it? Suppose we change the example so that Murray is supposed to realize exactly what Jerome has done and why. Would this make Jerome's course of action any more communicative? Strawson's supposed counterexample does not justify the conclusion that he draws from it.

There is another case (fortunately, a much simpler one) that seems to lend more direct support to Strawson's fourth condition. Suppose that the secretary of state of the United States (let's call him Mr. K) has arranged to have the telephone of his friend H tapped. (Even though H has always been a veracious and loyal friend of K's, he is suspected of sabotage and treason because of his access to top secrets.) Suppose further that H knows that K is tapping his phone, but that K does not know that H knows this. H might exploit this situation in order to pass information along to K that K would not believe if H gave it to him face-to-face. For instance, H might mention in the course of a telephone conversation with a third party that he (H) had used his contact in Congress, unbeknownst to K, to avert an embarrassing investigation of the State Department by the House Judiciary Committee. In this case, H's utterance meets Grice's original three conditions: H intended to induce the belief that he had done K a big favor; H intended K to recognize this intention; H intended K to believe that H had done him a favor because of K's recognition of H's intention to induce this belief. Yet it is clear that H has not communicated with K; he has communicated with the third party to whom he is speaking, and gotten K to understand what he has said to this third party. This seems to support Strawson's fourth conditoin, because in this example the fourth condition is not satisfied, and it would make a big difference if it were; if Mr. K caught on that H intended him to recognize that H was trying to induce the belief that he (H) had done him (K) a favor, H's whole project would fail. K is likely to believe what H says only as long as he believes that H does not know that his remarks are being overheard.

In spite of all this, the example does not really tell against Grice's original analysis. It is true that all three conditions of analysis (12) are satisfied, but in this case too the analysandum applies to the situation: H does in fact mean$_{NN}$ something by his utterance. Something *is* communicated – to the third party, if not to Mr. K. What the example really shows is that it is necessary to be more specific about who the interpreter that is referred to in the analysis is supposed to be.

In order for communication to occur, it is not enough that there be someone to interpret the utterance; the interpreter must also be privy to the attempted communication, and realize that he is privy to it, and be intended to realize that he is privy to it. Eavesdroppers are never fit receivers of communication. When an eavesdropper is affected by a conversation, it is not because he is a participant in it, but because he has tapped into it (or, sometimes, has been caught in it against his will).

If we narrow the discussion to linguistic communication, then we might call the generic class of perceivers of utterer's meaning "listeners," and distinguish two species of listeners: "hearers" and "overhearers." The hearers are those listeners who are privy to the attempted communication; the overhearers are intruders, people who are not intended to be in on the conversation. Within the species of hearers there are two subspecies: the addressees and the audience. A wedding ceremony makes the force of this latter distinction clear. When the minister asks, "Do you, N. N., take this man to be your lawful wedded husband," and so on, the bride is the addressee; the witnesses, who are required for the speech act, are nevertheless only audience. (If they were addressees, the consequences would be fearsome to imagine.) Thus the overall breakdown of those who perceive a speaker expressing a meaning is:

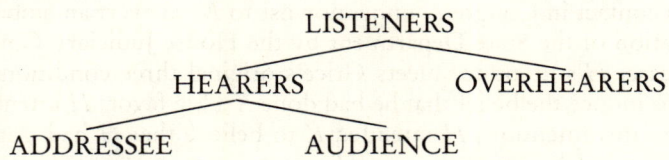

IV. *Searle's Purported Counterexample*

John Searle has criticized Grice's account of communicative meaning on the ground that "it fails to account for the extent to which meaning can be a

VII Utterer's Meaning and Communication

matter of rules or conventions. This account of meaning does not show the connection between one's meaning something by what one says, and what that which one says actually means in the language" (Searle (1969), p. 42). In other words, by discussing only the utterer's intentions and not the semantic conventions of the language he uses, Grice appears to leave open the possibility that anyone could in suitable circumstances mean anything by any utterance whatever. Searle finds this fantastic and thus implies that the analysis (12) is too weak. To illustrate this point, he supplies the following "counterexample":

> Suppose that I am an American soldier in the Second World War and that I am captured by Italian troops. And suppose also that I wish to get these troops to believe that I am a German soldier in order to get them to release me. What I would like to do is to tell them in German or Italian that I am a German soldier. But let us suppose I don't know enough German or Italian to do that. So I, as it were, attempt to put on a show of telling them that I am a German soldier by reciting those few bits of German I know, trusting that they don't know enough German to see through my plan. Let us suppose I know only one line of German which I remember from a poem I had to memorize in a high school German course. Therefore I, a captured American, address my Italian captors with the following sentence: *Kennst du das Land wo die Zitronen blühen*? Now, let us describe the situation in Gricean terms. I intend to produce a certain effect on them, namely, the effect of believing that I am a German soldier, and I intend to produce this effect by means of their recognition of my intention. I intend that they should think that what I am trying to tell them is that I am a German soldier. But does it follow from this account that when I say, *Kennst du das Land . . . etc.*, what I mean is, "I am a German soldier"? Not only does it not follow, but in this case I find myself disinclined to say that when I utter the German sentence what I mean is "I am a German soldier", or even "Ich bin ein deutscher Soldat", because what the words mean and what I remember that they mean is "Knowest thou the land where the lemon trees bloom?" Of course, I want my captors to be deceived into thinking that what I mean is: "I am a German soldier", but part of what is involved in that is getting them to think that that is what the words I utter mean in German (Searle (1969), pp. 44–45).

According to Searle, this scenario is a counterexample, because the American soldier's saying "*Kennst du das Land*," and so on, satisfies Grice's conditions for communicative meaning, and yet the soldier does not mean

(13) I am a German soldier.

as Grice would claim, but rather

(14) Knowest thou the land where the lemon trees bloom?

Searle's contention is that the semantic conventions of German prevent the soldier from uttering "*Kennst du das Land*," and so on, and yet meaning (13).

Here Searle is making one minor mistake and two major ones. The minor mistake is that the analysandum in (12), "*U* means something by uttering *x*," does hold true even in the scenario he presents. Grice and Searle agree that the American means *something* by this utterance; the disagreement is over *what* he means. However, it is important to understand the sources of this disagreement even if analysis (12) is not directly affected; so we shall proceed to the more substantive difficulties in Searle's view.

The first of the two major mistakes is that Searle supposes that Grice's analysis applies only to cases of *linguistic* communication, cases in which an elaborate system of semantic convention is available to determine the meaning. But Grice's account is supposed to be an analysis of communicative meaning in general, in or out of language. It cannot, therefore, be right to object that Grice does not take into account the semantic conventions of the language the utterer uses, for in many cases the utterer does not use a language at all.

This confusion shows up particularly clearly a few pages after the quoted passage, where Searle prefaces a table comparing his proposal and Grice's with the words, "We can summarize the difference between the original Gricean analysis of meaning nn and my revised analysis of the different concept of saying something and meaning it as follows . . . ." (Searle (1969), p. 49). If Searle is analyzing a concept *different* from Grice's, he is not offering a *revised* analysis of the original concept; if he is *revising* Grice's analysis of a given concept, he cannot also be analyzing a *different* concept. It is only by running together general communicative meaning and linguistic meaning that Searle could arrive at the idea that he is "revising an analysis of a different concept."

The second mistake lies in Searle's assumption that the semantic conventions of a language are constraints that restrict what a speaker can mean by his utterance. If this were so, everyone would have to speak literally all the time; there would be no figures of speech, no irony or sarcasm, no "in" jokes, and no modernist poetry, because all of these phenomena depend on the possibility of using expressions of a language in ways that go against the semantic conventions of that language. Obviously there are cases in which what a speaker means by something diverges from what the sentence he utters conventionally means; one cannot determine what a given speaker means solely from what his utterance means, as Searle supposes.

Indeed, a speaker can use any utterance whatever to mean$_{NN}$ anything whatever — if he has previously agreed with the hearer on a code. Semantic conventions are useful generalizations; they tell what speakers *normally* mean by a given expression, in the absence of any contrary indication. But they are not binding, and it is easy to free oneself from them.

Searle's basic charge, that analysis (12) fails to show the connection between what the utterer means and what the utterance itself means, is correct, but it is not an effective criticism of (12), which is only supposed to

VII Utterer's Meaning and Communication

give the conditions under which an utterer means$_{NN}$ something. Relating this analysis of utterer's meaning to other senses of 'meaning' is a separate project, to which we now turn.

V. Four Notions of Meaning

Different contexts containing the word 'mean', in its communicative sense, must be differently analyzed. We have seen in the preceding sections how to analyze 'U means$_{NN}$ something by uttering x' in terms of U's communicative intentions; we can now use this notion to help us analyze related notions of communicative meaning that show up in other linguistic contexts.

First, let's take utterer's meaning. Assuming that U means$_{NN}$ something by uttering x, what is it that he means? The basic form for the analysandum here is 'By uttering x, U means$_{NN}$ that p', where the position marked with the letter p is to be filled with a sentence of English.

As we saw in section V, there is a disagreement here between theorists who hold that what a speaker means on a particular occasion is determined by the semantic conventions of the language in which he speaks and those who hold that what he means is determined by his communicative intentions. The difference shows up in cases where the speaker's communicative intentions are at odds with the semantic conventions of his language. Consider once again the Charlie Chaplin example from section III of Chapter One, in which Charlie says, "This is a *fine* country," in a way that unmistakably manifests disgust. The issue is whether it is possible for Charlie to mean by this sentence that the country he is in is awful. It is evident that this is precisely what has taken place. Hence we take the position that the semantic conventions of a language, although they set certain norms for communication in that language, do not determine what speakers mean on particular occasions.

When the problem of determining what the utterer means$_{NN}$ came up at the end of section III, we noted that adapting analysis (12) was a little bit tricky, because of the variety of possible perlocutionary effects that the utterer might be intending to produce. It would not do, for example, to give the following analysis:

(15) By uttering x, an utterer U means$_{NN}$ that p if and only if:
 (a) U means$_{NN}$ something by uttering x;
 and
 (b) the effect that U intends his utterance of x to have on the interpreter is that the interpreter believe that p.

Admittedly, this could be the correct account for many utterances of declarative sentences. A case in which it gives the right result is the Tank McNamara example at the end of section I of Chapter IV. You will recall that Tank set out to say that the vice-president of the United States was ambitious, but actually produced the utterance "The president of the

United States is vicious." Since the effect that Tank intends his utterance to have on his hearers is that they believe that the vice-president of the United States is ambitious, analysis (15) correctly entails that by his utterance Tank means that the vice-president of the United States is ambitious. A second example is the case Searle describes in the long quotation in section V. Analysis (15) yields the conclusion that the American soldier meant$_{NN}$ that he was a German soldier; and we have held that this is so, in spite of Searle's reservations.

Unfortunately, many examples exist to show that analysis (15) is too strong. Two were mentioned briefly back in section III: The schoolboy who answers his teacher's question about the date of the battle of Waterloo is not trying to get her to believe that the battle was fought in 1815, since he knows that she already knows when the battle was fought; he is trying to demonstrate to her that he also knows when the battle was fought. Nevertheless, what he means by his utterance ("1815") is that the battle was fought in 1815, not that he knows that the battle was fought in 1815. Likewise, in the other example, when A reminds B that p, he is not trying to get B to believe that p, since B already believes that p.

A short way to deal with these and similar examples is to replace condition (b) of analysis (15) with a requirement that the utterer intend to induce, not belief, but understanding of his own belief that p. In other words, the analysis would come to look like this:

(16) By uttering x, an utterer U means$_{NN}$ that p if and only if:
    (a) U means$_{NN}$ something by uttering x;
    and
    (b) the effect that U intends his utterance of x to have on the interpreter is that the interpreter believe that U believes that p.

(Cf. Searle (1971a), pp. 8–9; Dalrymple (1978), p. 159; and Grice (1969), pp. 171–2). This account still works for the more usual cases in which the interpreter does not already believe that p, because normally if the interpreter comes to believe that U believes that p, he will thereby have some reason to believe that p. Therefore, if the utterer U intends the interpreter to believe that U believes that p, then normally he also intends the interpreter to believe that p; he intends that the first belief will provide the grounds for the second.

Analysis (16) is still inexact in one important way. The utterer wants to get the interpreter to believe that he (the utterer) has a certain sort of relationship to the proposition that p, but the relationship is not necessarily belief. The schoolboy wants his teacher to think that he *knows* when the battle of Waterloo was, not just that he *believes* that it was in 1815. Or take another of Grice's examples:

Mother: "It's no good denying it: you broke the window, didn't you?"
Child: "Yes, I did." (Grice (1969), p. 167)

It is not quite right to say that the child intends the mother to believe that he *believes* that he broke the window. The child is *confessing* or *conceding* that he broke the window; what he wants his mother to believe is that he is not going to pretend that he didn't do it.

There is in fact a whole range of what might be called "affirmative relations," in which a person holds or subscribes to a proposition: believing, knowing, assuming, and the like are all affirmative relations, and stating, conceding, announcing, informing, and the like are speech acts that one performs in order to mark such relations. To weaken (15) enough so that it covers all the cases, we must allow the utterer to intend the interpreter to believe merely that the utterer stands in *some* affirmative relation or other to the proposition that p. Accordingly:

> (17) By uttering x, an utterer U means$_{NN}$ that p if and only if:
> (a) U means$_{NN}$ something by uttering x;
> and
> (b) the effect that U intends his utterance of x to have on the interpreter is that the interpreter believe that U stands in some affirmative relation to the proposition that p.

When someone means$_{NN}$ that p by uttering something, p is the utterer's meaning that we spoke of in the opening sections of Chapter Two.

VI. Utterance Meaning and Timeless Meaning

Our focus has been on what it is for an utterer to mean something; we have been assuming that the primary sense of meaning applies to utterers. That is, our analysandum has been, "An utterer U means something by an utterance x iff. . . ." But by metonymy, we also speak of utterances meaning something and thus we are required to give an analysis for the analysandum, "An utterance x means something iff. . . ." When this analysandum is supposed to apply to one particular *occasion* of its use, then we shall say, following Grice, that we are talking about the utterance's occasion meaning. Because we have taken utterer's meaning to be primary, and utterance meaning secondary, the analysis of utterance occasion meaning is simple and straightforward:

> An utterance x means something (on a particular occasion) iff somebody communicatively meant something by it.

For example (recalling that an utterance, in our extended use of the term, might be a gesture), we can say, "That pointing gesture meant 'M. K. Mooney, please leave now'" iff somebody meant by pointing that M. K. Mooney was to leave at that time.

The meaning that an utterance has on a particular occasion is not however the only sense of meaning that an utterance might have. When utterers over a period of time repeatedly use an utterance in the same way, the utterance acquires a meaning independent of the meaning it has on a particular occasion; it acquires a kind of timeless quality, which Grice calls "timeless utterance meaning" and explicates as

> "x means$_{NN}$ (timeless) that so-and-so" might as a first shot be equated with some statement or disjunction of statements about what 'people' (vague) intend (with qualifications about 'recognition') to effect by x (Grice (1957), p. 442; I have corrected an obvious misprint).

The vague and tentative character of Grice's analysis is obvious and invites precision. What Grice seems to have missed in his original analysis, although he later used it (Grice (1968)), is that an utterance which acquires timeless meaning in the way he describes (in virtue of speaker meaning) has a meaning in virtue of a convention, and hence might well be termed "conventional meaning," which could be analyzed as follows:

> An utterance x conventionally means something iff utterers have a convention to mean something by x.

This analysis is not circular, it merely requires an analysis of a convention. Further, there is a promising theory of what a convention is. Although it is outside the scope of this work to explain what a convention is, we can give the briefest summary of a promising theory devised by David Lewis:

> Roughly, a convention is a behavioral regularity which a community maintains in order to coordinate the actions of its members for their own good; for such coordination each member must know that all, or, at least, very many, in the past have acted in a certain way which has succeeded in coordination and each expects the others to continue the regularity. (See Bennett (1976), pp. 176–177; and Grice (1968) p. 62.)

One might be afflicted with one of two temptations: one might want either to conflate occasion-meaning and timeless-meaning or to reduce one to the other. Yielding to either one would be a philosophical sin. We need the distinction to explain one of the linguistic misfortunes that befell Alice while talking to Humpty Dumpty:

> "There's glory for you!"
> "I don't know what you mean by 'glory,'" Alice said.
> Humpty Dumpty smiled contemptuously. "Of course you don't – till I tell you. I meant 'there's a nice knock-down argument for you!'"
> But "glory' doesn't mean 'a nice knock-down argument,'" Alice objected.
> "When *I* use a word," Humpty Dumpty said, in rather a scornful tone, "it means just what I choose it to mean – neither more nor less."
> "The question is," said Alice, "whether you *can* make words means so many different things."
> "The question is," said Humpty Dumpty, "which is to be master – that's all."
> Alice was much too puzzled to say anything (*Through the Looking-Glass*, chapter 6).

VII Utterer's Meaning and Communication

Alice's puzzlement is due to her failure to distinguish two kinds of meaning. Both Alice and Humpty Dumpty are saying true things about meaning, but while Alice is talking about the timeless meaning of words, Humpty Dumpty is talking about their occasion-meanings (or, equivalently, about what the people who utter the words mean). On a given occasion, a word means just what the speaker intends it to mean — neither more nor less, as Humpty Dumpty says; for better or worse, the utterer's meaning is the occasion-meaning of the utterance. Of course, if you capriciously use utterances unconventionally, to mean things that they do not ordinarily mean, you will find it difficult to make yourself understood, because interpreters generally make use of the very conventions you are contravening as they try to make sense of what you say; but if, like Humpty Dumpty, you are indifferent to others, you *can* make words mean as many different things as you please. The assumption behind Alice's remarks is that meaning is a social construction over which no single person has absolute authority; this is true for timeless meaning, but not for occasion-meaning.

In this case Humpty Dumpty goes against the conventions that govern the use of the word 'glory' willfully, simply in order to assert his mastery. This is not a good reason for contravening social conventions, but then Humpty Dumpty is little concerned with the amenities of discourse. Human speakers frequently contravene semantic conventions, too, but they generally have better reasons. When a convention has been established, one can exploit it in the very act of flouting it, as we have seen in Chapter Two; just as someone who goes against the Conversational Maxims can communicate something by doing so, someone who flouts a semantic convention can express something more than what his words literally mean. ("There's glory for you," a speaker at an antinuclear rally exclaims, pointing to a poster that shows Hiroshima destroyed.)

So far we have accounted for utterer's meaning, occasion-meaning, and timeless meaning. But communication is by definition a two-sided affair; it requires an utterer and an interpreter. If there is no one to receive the message, or if no one who receives it understands it, there is no communication. These truisms need to be repeated because they are often forgotten; philosophers have tended to concentrate on the work of the utterer and to neglect the work of the interpreter.

Fortunately, it is possible to define interpreter's meaning quite briefly; it is simply what the interpreter who recognizes that the utterer means$_{NN}$ something by his utterance takes to be the utterer's meaning. (No one who does not recognize that U means$_{NN}$ something by x qualifies as an interpreter.) In most cases the interpreter does not have to go through any conscious process of inference; interpretation is easy enough for us that it becomes a matter of habit as we learn the language and learn about one another. Since the utterer's meaning is often the same as the timeless meaning of his utterance, this timeless meaning is the usual starting-point for interpretation; but of course the interpreter modifies it, using his knowledge of the context of utterance, the idiosyncracies of the utterer, and so on, in order to reconstruct the utterer's meaning more accurately.

An act of communication in which the interpreter succeeds in reconstructing a meaning which exactly matches the utterer's meaning may (if everything goes right) be called nondefective; to the extent that utterer's meaning and interpreter's meaning diverge, the act of communication is *defective*.

Of the four notions of meaning$_{NN}$ developed in this section, only timeless meaning belongs to semantics, to the philosophy of language in the narrower sense; utterer's meaning, interpreter's meaning, and occasion-meaning are all pragmatic notions, belonging to the philosophy of communication. (This is another reason why it is important not to confuse occasion-meaning and timeless meaning.)

Part II: Reference

Chapter Eight: Reference, Existence and Descriptions

I. The Paradox of Reference and Existence

There are a number of philosophical problems that give rise to interest in the notion of reference. One of the starkest problems is the paradox of reference and existence.

The Paradox of Reference and Existence
(1) Everything referred to exists.
(2) "The golden mountain" refers to the golden mountain.
(3) The golden mountain does not exist.

(1)–(3) form a paradox for two reasons. First, (1)–(3) are inconsistent; for, from (1) and (2), what follows is

(3') The golden mountain exists

and that contradicts (3). The second reason (1)–(3) constitute a paradox is that philosophers have not been able to agree about how to resolve the inconsistency. Meinong and Russell, early in his career, resolved the inconsistency by holding that (3) is false (Russell (1903), p. 449). It was only after Russell discovered his theory of definite descriptions that he offered a different solution to the paradox and held that (2) is false.

The paradox might seem to be childishly easy to solve and yet it, more than any other problem, has motivated philosophical reflection on reference. The reason for the difficulty is that no matter how much philosophers might otherwise disagree, most are committed to the first premise, "Everything referred to exists," which John Searle calls "The axiom of existence." (I think this premise is false, as I shall argue in Chapter 9, section III.) Philosophers are moved to hold the first premise because of a line of reasoning that goes something like this. If a person could refer to what does not exist, then the person would be referring to nothing; and if the person were referring to nothing, then the person would not be referring at all. The supposition that a person can refer to what does not exist, then, must be false; hence, everything referred to exists.

Underlying the paradox of reference and existence is the issue of how language is related to the world. And this concerns the issue of existence and nonexistence, and there is no more philosophical subject than that.

II. Is Word-Meaning or Sentence-Meaning Primary?

Referring, within a theory of communication, is just one part of what a speaker might do when he says something. However, it is not obvious that reference belongs to the philosophy of communication. Before 1950, it was the received opinion, and it is still widely held, that the study of reference belongs to the philosophy of language (in the narrow sense), because, it was held, the meaning of a name is the object it refers to. And the clearest, most forceful statements of this view were those of Wittgenstein in his *Tractatus Logico-Philosophicus* and Russell in various books and articles. 1950 is a watershed year because it dates the publication of P. F. Strawson's "On Referring," which was the first persuasive assault on the referential theory of meaning. The main point of Strawson's article is that referring is something that people, not expressions, do. And he indicates, though obliquely, that referring is part of communication, when, after denying that reference is assertion, he says, "communication is much less a matter of explicit or disguised assertion than logicians used to suppose" (Strawson (1950a), p. 15). Russell was always opposed to the view that referring, in any philosophically interesting sense, is something that people do. Reacting to his immediate predecessors, Mill and Meinong, who thought that the laws of logic are psychological laws, Russell said, "The notion of denoting, like most of the notions of logic, has been obscured hitherto by an undue admixture of psychology. There is a sense in which we denote, when we point or describe, or employ words as symbols for concepts; this, however, is not the sense I wish to discuss" (Russell (1903), p. 53).

But before we can appreciate Strawson's criticisms of Russell's referential theory of meaning, we need to understand what questions a theory of meaning must answer. Conceived as the study of word- and sentence-meaning, a semantic theory should answer at least these two questions:

(I) What is the meaning of a word?
(II) What is the meaning of a sentence?

The answers to these questions are never independent of each other. There is some relation between the meaning of a word and the meaning of a sentence. And what that relation is is partially determined by the answers to two other questions:

(III) Is word-meaning or sentence-meaning primary?
(IV) How do words contribute to the meaning of a sentence?

Although Russell's answers to (I) and (II) will dominate the remainder of this chapter, let's begin with some general remarks about (III) and (IV). There are obviously two possible and incompatible answers to (III): word-meaning is primary, and sentence-meaning is primary. Among American philosophers, W. V. Quine has emphasized the importance and primacy of sentence-meaning (Quine (1960)) and has the promise of a theory that will give detailed answers to (IV). It was left to Donald Davidson, a student of Quine's, to show how this might be done for a large part of language. Davidson proposes that the task of semantics is "to give the meaning of all expressions [i.e. sentences] in a certain infinite set on the basis of the meanings of parts. . . . It behooves us then to rephrase our demand on a satisfactory theory of meaning so as not to suggest that individual words must have meanings at all, in any sense that transcends the fact that they have a systematic effect on the meanings of the sentences in which they occur" (Davidson (1967), p. 451). He goes on to say, "sentences depend for their meaning on their structure only as an abstraction from the totality of sentences in which it features (Davidson (1967), p. 454). Davidson gets this view from Tarski's theory of semantics for artificial languages.

Among the British philosophers, J. L. Austin is the most important proponent of the view that sentence-meaning is primary.

> It may justly be urged that, properly speaking, what alone has meaning is a sentence. Of course, we can speak quite properly of, for example, 'looking up the meaning of a word' in a dictionary. Nevertheless, it appears that the sense in which a word or phrase 'has a meaning' is derivative from the sense in which a sentence 'has a meaning'; to say a word or phrase 'has a meaning' is to say that there are sentences in which it occurs which 'have meanings': and to know the meaning which the word or phrase has, is to know the meanings of sentences in which it occurs. All the dictionary can do when we 'look up the meaning of a word' is to suggest aids to the understanding of sentences in which it occurs. Hence it appears correct to say that what 'has a meaning' in the primary sense is the sentence. And older philosophers who discussed the problem of 'the meaning of words' tend to fall into special errors, avoided by more recent philosophers, who discuss rather the parallel problem of 'the meaning of sentences' (Austin (1940), p. 56).

Grice, like Davidson, has sketched a way of answering question (IV), though his way differs from Davidson's. Grice's work has also inspired Jonathan Bennett to construct an even more detailed analysis (Bennett (1976)).

Russell's theory of meaning, a version of the referential theory, is defined by its view about the meaning of words. The meaning of a word is the object it directly denotes. What Russell says about sentence-meaning is circumscribed by his views about word-meaning. Before explaining his theory, it is worth speculating about what lay behind his preoccupation with the meaning of names. Russell was obsessed with how words attach to the world. His obsession has two roots. The first is that, as a philosophical apologist for science, he was concerned with the truth about reality and a necessary condition for there being such truth, he thought, is that words attach to reality. For, if words do not attach to reality, then no proposition can be true. The second root is that, once, when he was naive about the workings of language, Russell had been duped about how much reality included, and duped, he thought, by language. In his halcyon days of *The Principles of Mathematics,* Russell thought that every singular term, and this includes descriptions — what he called "denoting phrases" — attached to some being. This intoxicated view put him in the company of all manner of things, not just the round square, but also such things of philosophical ill-repute as the existent non-existent and his cousin the non-existent existent.

Where had the callow Russell gone wrong? In *Introduction to Mathematical Philosophy,* Russell attributed the problem to a poor sense of reality, as exhibited by the philosopher Alexius Meinong: "It is argued, *e.g.* by Meinong, that we can speak about 'the golden mountain', 'the round square', and so on; we can make true propositions of which these are the subject; hence they must have some kind of logical being, since otherwise the propositions in which they occur would be meaningless. In such theories, it seems to me, there is a failure of that feeling for reality which ought to be preserved even in the most abstract studies. Logic, I should maintain, must no more admit a unicorn than zoology can; for logic is concerned with the real world just as truly as zoology, though with its more abstract features. . . . A robust sense of reality is very necessary in framing a correct analysis of propositions about unicorns, golden mountains, round squares, and other such pseudo-objects (Russell (1919), pp. 169–170). My own diagnosis of Russell's problem is different. He thought that what guarantees the existence of an object is a certain kind of talk, namely, mentioning or denoting: "to mention anything is to show that it is" (Russell (1919), p. 449). Shortly after saying that "The study of grammar, in my opinion, is capable of throwing far more light on philosophical questions than is commonly supposed by philosophers" (Russell (1903), p. 42), Russell explained that for every denoting phrase there is a denoting concept and the object denoted by the concept. So, for example, for the denoting phrase, "The round square" there is the denoting concept of the round square, which denotes the round square. Thus was Russell duped.

The reason that denoting phrases, such as definite descriptions, are unreliable is that, if they have a denotation at all, they have it indirectly. In the doctrine of *The Principles of Mathematics,* the phrase "the round square" supposedly denotes the round square by way of a denoting concept, namely, the denoting concept of the round square. Even if one abolishes denoting concepts, as Russell later did, one still has to account for how descriptions denote in virtue of their parts, and that means to account for how descriptions denote indirectly. Descriptions like "the round square" can give the illusion of denotation. The mere possibility of illusion raises in philosophers the desire for a guarantee, a guarantee against illusion. The only guarantee against the illusion of words attaching to the world is to have a word that attaches directly to the world. Russell thought that names, and, in particular, proper names, come with this guarantee. His obsession with proper names is a corollary of Descartes' worries about the external world; and it is not accidental that Russell should require that the meaning of a proper name be an object known by acquaintance, and should hold that no knowledge of acquaintance is deceptive (Russell (1959), p. 119). For Russell, then, descriptions, and definite descriptions especially, are the bad guys. They are the ones that subvert our confidence that language attaches to the world. They masquerade as names of things, when, in fact, they name nothing. Thus Russell sets himself two tasks. The first task was to unmask the masquerader, to prove that descriptions are not names; that is the force of his remark, "The first things to realize about a definite descriptions is that it is not a name" (Russell (1918), p. 224). The second task was to describe the nature of definite descriptions.

One of Russell's proofs that definite descriptions are not names involves the view that the contribution a definite description makes to a proposition is different from the contribution a name makes, even when both denote the same object. Russell casts this proof in the picturesque terms of different entities entering into propositions. And he means this picturesque language literally. But this is not his most famous proof that descriptions are not names. His most famous proof, one in which he takes his revenge against definite descriptions, goes by way of a lemma: *Definite descriptions mean nothing*. But this lemma raises a question. Given that descriptions mean nothing, what contribution do they make to the meaning of sentences? This question forces Russell to change his focus from word-meaning to sentence-meaning. Definite descriptions, Russell holds, are, unlike names and sentences, "incomplete symbols;" they do not have a meaning of their own, but they contribute to the meaning of the sentence in which they occur. Further, since they do not have a meaning of their own, they cannot be defined absolutely but only as they occur within the context in which they have a meaning, i.e. sentences. Russell calls such definitions, contextual definitions. He explicates sentence-meaning in terms of truth-conditions, not in terms of what entities enter into a proposition. And it is the interrelation of the notions of sentence-meaning and truth-conditions that has attracted the theoretical interests of many philosophers. This, as much as Tarski's work, lies behind Donald Davidson's project of giving the meaning of all the sentences in a language, and not the meaning of each word.

Having completed our Olympian view of Russell's struggles, let's get a better look at some of the individual contests.

III. A Russellian Referential Semantics

Russell's referential theory of word meaning is the most influential theory of meaning in the twentieth century. The greatest merit of this theory is its simplicity; it has but one major tenet: the meaning of a word is the object it directly denotes (refers to). Although simple, three words of this tenet require explanation: "object," "directly" and "denotes." Let's take these words in the order in which they occur.

According to the proper understanding of "object," whatever is an object exists; since whatever does not exist is not an object, it is pleonastic to write "existent object" and self-contradictory to write "nonexistent object." This point, however, raises as many questions as it answers. For we can ask, "What is to count as an existent?" Must something be spatio-temporally locatable in order to count as an existent? Or must it be spatially locatable in the present? If either of these definitions is accepted, what is to be said about numbers and concepts, neither of which are spatial objects? A general referential semantics does not supply answers to these questions. What counts as an existent object is a question for metaphysics, not semantics. The theory of referential semantics says that only objects can be meanings; it does not also determine which candidates for the office of objects get elected.

The word "directly" must also be correctly understood. Its meaning contrasts with "indirectly" or "mediately." For example, consider the phrase, "the big blue ball." This phrase might denote an object, but would do so indirectly, through the mediation of the concepts expressed by "big," "blue" and "ball." Thus, although the phase might denote an object, that object is not its meaning because it would denote that object indirectly.

Finally, "denotes" means literally "to note or mark out from." It signifies the relation that holds between a word and the object it names. The denotation of a word is the object named by the word. "Denotes," as Russell uses it, means the same as "refers" in one of its ordinary senses. Thus, a word or phrase might denote directly or indirectly for Russell. "Denotes" became archaic sometime before 1950. I use it for two reasons: first because it is Russell's word and second, because it has returned to currency since 1966. Russell uses it because his godfather, John Stuart Mill, used it. But Mill used it to signify the thing a word named, not meant. It was Russell who changed Mill's doctrine and asserted that the meaning of a word is the object the word names.

For many, "name" is synonymous with "name of an individual," and Russell often used it in this way. However, he also uses it in the broader sense in which names include many common nouns, adjectives, prepositions, and even verbs. Because the meaning of a word will in every case be the object it names, if any — hence all and only names are meaningful — we can distinguish different kinds of meanings by distinguishing different kinds of objects. The first kind of object to distinguish consists of particulars or "individuals" to use Russell's preferred term. The second kind of object to distinguish consists of concepts or universals. One might divide concepts into properties, i. e., those concepts that collect objects one at a time (the correlates of "bald" or "green" or "human") and relations, i. e., those concepts that collect two or more objects at a time (the correlates of "hits" and "loves"); but, as Russell points out, this is not a theoretically interesting distinction. We might further distinguish a kind of object for the English equivalent of the sentential connectives of logic ("and," "or," "not," "if") and say that such words name operations, a kind of mathematical object. (Russell would not have approved of this move (1903), p. xi.)

Let's now consider the beginnings of an answer that a referential theory of meaning might give to the question:

What is the meaning of a sentence?

Russell's answer is that the meaning of a sentence is the proposition it expresses. This answer can be misleading because of Russell's inconsistent use of the word "proposition." He sometimes explicitly explains "proposition" to mean "sentence." He says, "We mean by a 'proposition' primarily a form of words which expresses what is either true or false. . . . I think the word 'proposition' should be limited to what may, in some sense, be called 'symbols', and further to such symbols as give expression to truth and falsehood. Thus 'two and two are four' and 'two and two are five' will be propositions, and so will 'Socrates is a man' and 'Socrates is not a man'" (Russell (1919), p. 155). But in fact he only sometimes uses it to mean "sentence;" he regularly uses "proposition" and for that matter "statement" to mean "the meaning of a sentence." In discussing Russell, I shall use "proposition" as he in fact usually uses it, not as he says he will use it.

It is convenient to consider the meaning of a sentence, that is, a proposition, to be an ordered collection of entities, which always includes at least one concept (i.e. some kind of universal, either a property or relation) and often one or more particulars. For example, let's begin with the simplest case, that of a subject-predicate sentence, say, "Socrates is human." This sentence consists of three words, "Socrates," "is" and "human." Two of these words have a meaning in Russell's technical sense of meaning. The meaning of "Socrates" is Socrates; the meaning of "human" is humanity. The verb "is" in subject-predicate sentences does not have a meaning and hence does not introduce an entity into a proposition; that is, its propositional counterpart will not be an entity.

Let's now consider the next simplest case, a binary relational sentence such as, "Socrates taught Plato." This sentence also consists of three words, "Socrates," "Plato" and "taught." Each of these words has a meaning in Russell's technical sense of meaning. The meaning of "Socrates" is Socrates, the meaning of "Plato" is Plato, and the meaning of "taught" is — we will ignore tense — the concept or binary relation of teaching, which also expresses the propositional tie just as "is" expressed the tie in "Socrates is human."

So far, with the exception of the verb "is" when it occurs in monadic subject-predicate sentences, we have dealt exclusively with sentences consisting solely of names, that is, with words that have a meaning and contribute to the meaning of a sentence by introducing an entity into the proposition, that is, the meaning of the sentence. We come now to the first of the two kinds of complex sentences. The first kind is a sentence containing the word "a," such as "Socrates is a man." One might think that this sentence is formally the same and even synonymous with one considered earlier, "Socrates is human," and hence express the same proposition. But this is not so. Russell says, "'Socrates is a man' is no doubt *equivalent* to 'Socrates is human' but it is not the very same proposition" (Russell (1919), p. 172). To say that the sentences are equivalent is to say they are true or false in the same circumstances; it is not to say (and does not follow) that they have the same meaning or express the same proposition. "Socrates is a man" differs from "Socrates is human" in two respects. First, as Russell says, "The *is* of 'Socrates is human' expresses the relation of subject and predicate; the *is* of 'Socrates is a man' expresses identity" (Russell (1919), p. 172). That is, the latter sentence is synonymous with "Socrates is identical with a man." Second, "Socrates is human" contains an adjective, "human," which is the *name* of humanity. But "Socrates is a man" does not contain a word or phrase that is the name of humanity. Neither "man" nor "a man" is. The consequence of thinking so is absurd. For it would mean that "Socrates is a man" means "Socrates is identical with humanity"! As great as Socrates was, he was never humanity itself.

From what we have said so far, the contributions "Socrates" and "is identical with" make to the proposition should be clear. It is not so clear what contribution "a man" makes. One might think that the nonlinguistic counterpart of "a man" is some individual man. But which man? It cannot be Socrates. For, suppose the sentence were "Fido is a man." Would "a man" still denote Socrates? Of course not. "Fido is a man" does not mean that Fido is Socrates. Thus, by parity of form "Socrates is a man" does not mean that Socrates is Socrates; in other words, the meaning of the phrase "a man" does not change just because some other word in the sentence changes. The phrase "a man" does not denote Socrates in "Socrates is a man." Russell is contrasting the contribution "a man" makes to a proposition with the contribution made by a proper name. In the sentence "I met Jones," Jones himself enters into the proposition. In contrast, Jones does not enter the proposition expressed by "I met a man" even if Jones is the man I met. "But we may go further: not only Jones, but no actual man, enters into my statement. This becomes obvious when the statement is false, since then there is no more reason why Jones should be supposed to enter into the proposition than why anyone else should" (Russell (1919), p. 168). Nor is it acceptable to say that "a man" introduces a man who is no particular man. For Russell has specified the following adequacy condition on any analysis of propositions: "In obedience to the feeling of reality we shall insist that, in the analysis of propositions, nothing 'unreal' is to be admitted" (Russell (1919), p. 170).

What then is the answer to the question, "What contribution does 'a man' make to the meaning of the sentence?" After making some preliminary remarks here, I shall begin his answer in the next section. Russell's general answer to this kind of question consituates the first half of his Theory of Descriptions. The second half of his theory concerns his analysis of the word "the." If devoting two sections to Russell's treatment of the seemingly insignificant words, "a" and "the," seems excessive, I at least have two excuses. First, Russell's treatment of these two words constitutes the most important theory in twentieth century philosophy of language; it has been described, and often endorsed, as "a paradigm of philosophy." Second, Russell thought his theory was so important that he claimed that he would give the doctrine even if, like Socrates after drinking hemlock, he were dead from the waist down and not merely, as was the case, in prison for his pacifism during World War I (Russell (1919), p. 167).

IV. *Russell's Theory of Indefinite Descriptions*

Descriptions present a problem for Russell because he held that the meaning of a name is an object, that a phrase like "a man" seems to be a name, and that there seems to be no object for "a man" to name. We already saw the problem that "a man" presents in "Socrates is a man," but consider the further aggravation with noun phrases of mythic objects ("a unicorn") or contradictory objects ("a square circle"). What object might they name without causing greater grief? One might argue from the principle that there are more objects in heaven and on earth than are dreamt of in philosophy to the conclusion that mythic and contradictory objects *do exist*. Some philosophers have.

Russell might have solved his problem — as others later did — by giving up the idea that the meaning of a word or phrase is an object. But his solution was different. He gave up the idea that phrases like "a man" and, more generally, noun phrases beginning with an article, are names at all. In other words, the thread guiding Russell through this philosophical labyrinth was the idea that noun phrases are not names. I call this a "guiding thread" and not a solution, because while this idea gives Russell some sense of direction, it does not itself constitute a solution. A solution requires that he give an account of the contribution that indefinite descriptions make to a proposition, the meaning of a sentence. To give it a name, Russell's solution is his theory of indefinite descriptions. "An indefinite description is a phrase of the form 'a so-and-so'" (Russell (1919), p. 167), says Russell, by which he means phrases consisting of the indefinite article followed by a noun or noun phrase.

Russell's solution might be divided into two steps: first a paraphrase of the sentence containing the problematic phrase into another sentence that does not contain the problematic phrase; and second, an unproblematic account of how the words of the latter sentence contribute to the meaning of the sentence.

Let's consider Russell's solution to "Socrates is a man" in light of this two step process. First then, "Socrates is a man" needs to be rewritten in a way that preserves meaning while eliminating the noun phrase, "a man." To this end, Russell suggests as the paraphrase, the sentence, "Socrates is identical with something and it is human." Second, each word of this sentence either contributes a philosophically acceptable entity or serves a philosophically acceptable purpose in the proposition. Roughly, "something and it is human" replaces "a man." The essence of the change is the substitution of the adjectival "human" for the noun phrase "a man." For, according to Russell, adjectives are names that introduce philosophically innocuous entities, namely, concepts. Moreover, this point is generalizable; for any noun phrase there is always a corresponding adjectival form either existing or inventable.

The verb "is" in "Socrates is a man" expresses a propositional tie; "and," "something," and "it" are acceptable because they are acceptable to mathematical logic, the paradigm of rigor and respectability for Russell. This is not to say that the notions are easy to understand. At the beginning of a chapter devoted to the topic, Russell once wrote, "The variable is perhaps the most distinctively mathematical of all notions; it is certainly also one of the most difficult to understand" (Russell (1903), p. 89). He ends by saying about his explanation, "may some reader succeed in rendering it more complete, and in answering the many questions which I have had to leave unanswered" (Russell (1903), p. 94). With that I beg off explaining Russell's doctrine.

As for "and," we shall construe it as introducing the mathematical operation of conjunction as an entity for exegetical purposes. "Something" and "it" indicate that some object belongs in the proposition without specifying any particular object — Russell's unfortunate phrase is "denote an ambiguous object" — and that is just what we want them to do. We are, in effect, saying that Socrates is Mr. X or, more perspicuously, x. But our x is not wholly unspecified. For we know that x stands in the subject-predicate relation to the property of being human. We can also handle denoting phrases that denote nothing, such as, "a unicorn," on this theory. The sentence, "I met a unicorn," is equivalent to the sentence, "I met something unicornal." About these sentences, Russell had written, "'I met a unicorn' or 'I met a sea-serpent' is a perfectly significant assertion, if we know what it would be to be a unicorn or a sea-serpent, *i. e.* what is the definition of these fabulous monsters. Thus it is only what we call the *concept* that enters into the proposition. In the case of 'unicorn', for example, there is only the concept: there is not also, somewhere among the shades, something unreal which may be called 'a unicorn'. Therefore since it is significant (though false) to say 'I met a unicorn', it is clear that this proposition, rightly analyzed, does not contain the concept 'unicorn'" (Russell (1919), p. 168).

V. Russell's Theory of Definite Descriptions

Let's now turn to Russell's theory of definite descriptions. A general statement of Russell's theory can be presented in two sentences:

(a) A definite description is not a name.
(b) Sentences containing definite descriptions as the grammatical subject, that is, sentences of the form, "The φ is ψ," where φ is a noun phrase in the singular and ψ is a noun phrase or adjective, are *not* of the subject-predicate form but are complex existential assertions.

Let's consider (a) and (b) in somewhat more detail.

(a) First recall what a name is for Russell. He says, "A name is a simple symbol whose meaning is something that can occur as subject" (Russell (1919), p. 170). Shortly later Russell offers a variation on this. He says a name "is a simple symbol, directly designating an individual which is its meaning . . . (Russell (1919), p. 171). As both statements suggest, his definition of a name has three parts. (i) A name is a simple symbol; (ii) it denotes an individual or particular; and (iii) the individual or particular is directly denoted.

The first part of this definition, (i), specifies a syntactic requirement; it concerns only the form of a name. A "simple" symbol is "one which has no parts that are symbols" (Russell (1919), pp. 170–171). In other words, a simple symbol is a vocabulary item, and not a complex of vocabulary items constructed by concatenation. Russell gives some examples: "Thus, 'Scott' is a simple symbol because, though it has parts (namely, separate letters), these parts are not symbols. On the other hand, 'the author of *Waverley*' is not a simple symbol, because the separate words that compose the phrase are parts which are symbols" (Russell (1919), p. 171). This first condition is important historically because it puts Russell at odds with Mill and Frege, both of whom allowed that there were complex proper names, that is, names whose parts are symbols. Mill called these "many worded names" (Mill (1881), Book I, chapter 2). The second and third parts of Russell's definition of a name specify semantic requirements; (ii) concerns the kind of object that can be a meaning; (iii) concerns the relationship that holds between the name and the object. Concerning (ii) consider three words, "the," "red" and "Socrates." Each of these words satisfies condition (i), that is, each is a simple symbol. But only "Socrates" is a proper name because only "Socrates" denotes a particular or individual object. "The" denotes no object at all, and "red" denotes the concept red, which is a universal. Concerning (iii), recall that descriptions do not directly denote objects. They denote them indirectly in virtue of the concepts they express. "The author of *Waverley*" denotes Scott in virtue of his falling under the concept of being the sole author of *Waverley*.

(b) In a sentence of the form, "The φ is ψ," where φ is a noun phrase in the singular and ψ is a noun phrase or adjective, "The φ" looks like it is the subject of the sentence, contrary to Russell's claim that it cannot be the subject because it is not a name. And Russell concedes that a phrase of the form, "The φ," is the *grammatical* subject of the sentence. What he denies is that it is the real or logical subject. If Russell is to make good his claim that a phrase of the form, "The φ," is not the subject in a sentence of the form, "The φ is ψ," he will have to explain what it is; that is, he will have to analyze it in such a way that it no longer even appears to be a subject expression. This analysis is the heart of his theory of definite descriptions.

It was Russell's theory of sentences and propositions that a subject-predicate sentence has as its meaning a particular (denoted by the subject) and a concept or property (denoted by the predicate), related in a certain way. It is obvious that, if we replace the name, "Socrates," with another name, say "Plato," which denotes a different individual, then the resulting proposition is not identical with the original one. Russell's own example of this concerns the sentence, "Scott is the author of *Waverley*." He says, "And if we put anyone other than Scott in the place of 'the author of *Waverley*', our proposition would become false, and would therefore certainly no longer be the same proposition" (Russell (1919), p. 171).

Now does the proposition change if we replace one name with another name that denotes the same thing? Russell says "No." Suppose we were to replace the name "Plato" with another name of his: Aristocles. Since the meaning of "Aristocles" is Plato, the proposition expressed remains the same. Similarly, there is no change in the proposition expressed if the second occurrence of "Scott" in "Scott is [identical with] Scott" is replaced with "Sir Walter" since both names name or mean the same object. The sentence changes but not the proposition. This is what Russell means when he says, "Thus so long as names are used as names, 'Scott is Sir Walter' is the same trivial proposition as 'Scott is Scott'" (Russell (1919), p. 172).

But Russell had earlier remarked that ordinary proper names are usually used as disguised descriptions, and, when they are, replacing one so called name with another so called name will change the proposition. This is his point in the passage: "if 'Scott is Sir Walter' really means 'the person named "Scott" is the person named "Sir Walter"'", then the names are being used as descriptions: i.e. the individual, instead of being named, is being described as the person having that name" (Russell (1919), p. 171).

Now the question is, "Does the proposition change if we replace a name with a description that denotes the same object as the name?" Russell's answer to this is "Yes." He says, "A proposition containing a description is not identical with what that proposition becomes when a name is substituted even if the name names the same object as the description described" (Russell (1919), p. 171). The reason is that since the meaning of a proper name is an individual and the meaning of a definite description is not an individual, replacing a proper name with a definite description must change the meaning of the sentence, that is, must change the proposition it expresses.

Now the question might seem to be, "if the meaning of a definite description is not a particular, what is it?" Russell's answer to this question is "Nothing." Thus, Russell said, "The first thing to realize about a definite description is that it is not a name" (Russell (1918), p. 244); earlier, he had written, "Thus all phrases (other than propositions) containing the word *the* in the singular) . . . have a meaning in use, but not in isolation" (Whitehead and Russell (1910), p. 67) and later "The central point of the theory of descriptions was that a phrase may contribute to the meaning of a sentence without having any meaning at all in isolation" (Russell (1959), p. 85). The phrase, "have a meaning in use" suggests that definite descriptions have a meaning; but this suggestion is cancelled in both versions of Russell's argument, which alike conclude "'the author of *Waverley*' means nothing." Russell's argument might be put as follows:

0. If "author of *Waverley*" means anything, then it means either what "Scott" means or something other than what "Scott" means.
1. If "the author of *Waverley*" means something other than what "Scott" means, "Scott is the author of *Waverley*" is false.
2. "Scott is the author of *Waverley*" is not false.
3. If "the author of *Waverley*" means what "Scott" means, then "Scott is the author of *Waverley*" is a tautology.
4. "Scott is the author of *Waverley*" is not a tautology.
   Therefore,
5. "The author of *Waverley*" does not mean what "Scott" means (from 3 and 4).
   Therefore,
6. "The author of *Waverley*" does not mean something other than what "Scott" means (from 1 and 2).
   Therefore,
7. "The author of *Waverley*" means nothing (from 0, 5 and 6).

One plausible attack on Russell's argument is to say that premise 1 is false. "Scott" and "the author of *Waverley*" mean different things, yet it is true that Scott is the author of *Waverley*. In other words, the antecedent "'The author of *Waverley*' means something other than what 'Scott' means" is true, but the consequent "'Scott is the author of *Waverley*' is false" is false. Of course, Russell would disagree. He holds that the antecedent is false. But on what grounds? If it is on the grounds that "the author of *Waverley*" means nothing, then he begs the question. (One might think that the conditional is true for a different reason. One might argue that since the speaker means Scott when he uses the phrase "the author of *Waverley*" just as he means Scott when he uses the name "Scott," "the author of *Waverley*" and "Scott" mean the same thing, namely, Scott. This argument is importantly fallacious. It slides from what a speaker means to what a phrase means; it simply does not follow that if a speaker means something by his words, then the words have that very meaning.)

Some have defended Russell by claiming that by "means" he means "names," and hence by the antecedent Russell means "'the author of *Waverley*' names nothing other than Scott." This defense has the ill consequence of making Russell's conclusion trivial. For then 7 means only "'the author of *Waverley*' names nothing," and, given Russell's definition of "name," no one would dispute this.

There is a more devastating attack on Russell's argument that sidesteps the whole convoluted issue of what Russell means by "means" (Stroll (1975)). Stroll points out that if Russell's argument were good, an argument of the same form could be used to prove that names have no meaning. One simply interchanges "Scott" and "the author of *Waverley*":

0′. If "Scott" means anything, then it means either what "the author of *Waverley*" means or something other than what "the author of *Waverley*" means.
1′. If "Scott" means anything other than what "the author of *Waverley*" means, then "Scott is the author of *Waverley*" is false.
2′. "Scott is the author of *Waverley*" is not false.
3′. If "Scott" means what "the author of *Waverley*" means, then "Scott is the author of *Waverley*" is a tautology.
4′. "Scott is the author of *Waverley*" is not a tautology.
5′. "Scott" does not mean what "the author of *Waverley*" means.
6′. "Scott" does not mean something other than what "the author of *Waverley*" means.
Therefore,
7′. "Scott" means nothing.

Fortunately for Russell, he does not need the blockbuster conclusion that definite descriptions mean nothing. And, as mentioned earlier, it was only vengeance that drove him to that mad conclusion. All he needs is the sensible view that definite descriptions are not names; that is, that they denote in virtue of their structure and the meanings, whatever they are, of their constituent parts.

The question, then, becomes, what is this structure and what are the constituent parts? Given Russell's previous treatment of names and descriptions, one might well expect more talk of entities entering into propositions; the expectation is frustrated. He says, for example,

> Such a proposition as "Scott is the author of *Waverley*" could not be true if *Waverley* had never been written, or if several people had written it; and no more could any other proposition resulting from a propositional function x by the substitution of "the author of *Waverley*" for x. We may say that "the author of *Waverley*" means "the value of x for which 'x wrote *Waverley*' is true." Thus the proposition "the author of *Waverley* is Scotch," for example, involves:

(1) "x wrote *Waverley*" is not always false;
(2) "if x and y wrote *Waverley*, x and y are identical" is always true;
(3) "if x wrote *Waverley*, x was Scotch" is always true (Russell (1919), pp. 176–177).

What do "true" and "false" refer to? Russell would not say, as Frege would, that they refer, respectively, to the True and the False. What does "always" refer to? Again, Russell would not want to say that it refers to the Always.

One can avoid these problems with an alternative and equally accurate presentation of the theory: The sentence, "The author of *Waverley* is Scotch" means "Something x authored *Waverley* and whatever authored *Waverley* is identical with x and x is Scotch." It is important to notice that this analysis contains no descriptions of any sort. This is important for two reasons. First, since descriptions were to be analyzed, they could not very well appear, in any form, in the analysans. More importantly, no descriptions of any sort appear as the grammatical subject of the analysans. Instead, the description, a noun phrase, gets melted down and recast as quantifiers, connectives and verb phrases. This is important because Russell thought he was misled into thinking that there are objects corresponding to definite descriptions because they could occur as subjects. Russell was not bothered by the presence of "something" and "whatever" because he was not tempted to think that they introduced objects into propositions.

VI. Russell's Solution to The Paradox of Reference and Existence

Recall that the topic of reference was motivated in section I by the paradox of reference and existence:

The Paradox of Reference and Existence
(1) Everything referred to exists.
(2) "The golden mountain" refers to the golden mountain.
(3) The golden mountain does not exist.

Further recall that Russell's solution is to deny (2) with the help of his theory of descriptions. How does the theory of descriptions allow one to hold that (2) is false? To see this, one first has to see what lies behind (1). Recall that traditionally philosophers have held that the basic kind of sentences are subject-predicate ones, and that the subject picks out a particular about which the predicate says something. On this view, then, the subject, "The golden mountain," picks out a particular; what particular? Well, the golden mountain, what else? But, if "the golden mountain" picks out the golden mountain, the latter must exist. For to pick out something that does not exist is, it seems, to pick out nothing. Russell's theory of descriptions stops this juggernauting argument by holding that, contrary to appearances, "the golden mountain" is not the real subject of the sentence; or, to put the point another way, although "the golden mountain" is the grammatical subject of the sentence, it is not the real or *logical* subject of the sentence; for the sentence is not really (logically) a subject-predicate sentence at all. What it is is a complex sentence, part of which asserts existence. What the sentence "the golden mountain is worth a lot of money" asserts is, according to the theory, this: at least one thing is mountainously golden, at most one thing is mountainously golden, and it is worth a lot of money." The same remarks, *mutatis mutandis,* apply to the sentence Russell concentrates on in "On Denoting." Contrary to appearances, "The present king of France," is *not* the real subject of the sentence, "The present king of France is wise." Indeed, the sentence is not of the subject-predicate form but rather is a complex existence sentence, asserting the existence of a monarch of France.

Chapter Nine: A Speech Act Theory of Referring

I. Strawson's Critique of Russell

Although Russell initially had some trouble getting his theory of descriptions into print, the first major challenge to it did not come until 1950, when P. F. Strawson's article "On Referring" appeared.

In order to explain Strawson's objections, let us first consider one more Russellian analysis. The example that Strawson constantly uses is

(1) The king of France is wise.

On Russell's theory, this sentence gets rendered as

(2) Something x is male, reigning in France, and whatever is male, reigning in France, is identical with x; and x is wise.

In order for (2) to be true, there has to be something that is simultaneously (a) at least one thing that is male, reigning in France; (b) not more than one thing that is male, reigning in France; and (c) it must be wise.

Since France is no longer a monarchy, no one currently reigns in France; condition (a), therefore, is not satisfied, so that, according to Russell, (1) expresses a false proposition. But there is something odd about this claim. Here is Strawson's comment on it:

> Suppose someone were in fact to say to you with a perfectly serious air: 'The king of France is wise'. Would you say, 'That's untrue'? I think it is quite certain that you would not. But suppose he went on to *ask* you whether you thought that what he had just said was true, or was false; whether you agreed or disagreed with what he had just said. I think you would be inclined, with some hesitation, to say that you did not do either; that the question of whether his statement was true or false simply *did not arise*, because there was no such person as the king of France. You might, if he were obviously serious (had a dazed astray-in-the-centuries look), say something like: 'I'm afraid you must be under a misapprehension. France is not a monarchy. There is no king of France.' . . .

The sentence, 'The king of France is wise', is certainly significant; but this does not mean that any particular use of it is true or false. We use it truly or falsely when we use it to talk about someone; when, in using the expression. 'The king of France', we are in fact mentioning someone. The fact that the sentence and the expression, respectively, are significant just is the fact that the sentence *could* be used, in certain circumstances, to mention a particular person; and to know their meaning is to know what sort of circumstances these are. So when we utter the sentence without in fact mentioning anybody by the use of the phrase, 'The king of France', the sentence does not cease to be significant: we simply *fail* to say anything true or false (Strawson (1950a), pp. 12–13). The difference in approach is striking. Whereas Russell considers a sentence like (1) as an abstract entity, Strawson's method is to imagine the circumstances in which the sentence might be used, and to describe what would happen in such circumstances as sensitively and as thoroughly as he can. In part, this difference in method is due to the fact that Strawson is much more concerned than Russell with natural language, and in particular with English. By 1950, it was becoming clear that the logically perfect language is a myth, and that some of Russell's arguments for its superiority are due to misguided idealism rather than to any objective merits. But a more important reason for Strawson's less abstract way of inquiring into definite descriptions is that unlike Russell he is clear on the distinction between an expression (or a sentence) and a *use* of that expression. As we saw in Chapter Eight, Russell abstracts from the use of language, and tries to give an account of language in itself; the point that Strawson is making is that no such account can include a satisfactory theory of descriptions. Russell gets the wrong answer from this theory, because he is trying to answer a question of pragmatics by semantic means.

There is another way of putting the same point. The question whether a given sentence is significant, and, if so, what it means (in the "timeless" sense) is semantic; it has to do with what the prevailing conventions of the language are. On the other hand, the question whether a given expression refers to anything, and, if so, to what, belongs to the philosophy of communication; one can reasonably ask it about an expression as used on a certain occasion or in a certain way, but not about an expression in the abstract. We saw this in Chapter Seven; the attempt to set up a notion of denotation (or "timeless" reference) that would be related to occasion-reference as "timeless" meaning is related to occasion meaning cannot succeed.

What Strawson is willing to concede is that the utterer of (1) normally cannot make a true assertion unless Russell's three conditions are met, that is, unless there is an x such that x is wise, x is male and reigns in France, and no one other than x is male and reigns in France. However, if, as is now the case, no one reigns in France, the utterer of (1) does not make a *false* assertion, according to Strawson, because he does not make any assertion at all; his attempt to assert something (if that is indeed what he is trying to do) is a failure. The condition that there be one and only one king of France is not part of the meaning of sentence (1), even though the utterer of (1) implies, in some sense, that it is true.

Strawson's view is sometimes construed as a semantic theory of descriptions, as an alternative to Russell, according to which simple sentences containing vacuous descriptions have no truth-value (rather than being simply false). As Strawson explains in (1964b), however, the crucial issue is not whether sentences like (1) have truth-values, but whether someone who asserts that the king of France is wise thereby *asserts* that there is one and only one king of France or whether he refers to him and merely implies his existence.

II. Presupposition, Entailment, and Implicature

One reason why this crucial issue is somewhat intractable is that it is not quite clear what is meant by the word 'imply', as Strawson uses it. His first attempt at explaining the term goes like this:

> To say 'The king of France is wise' is, in some sense of 'imply', to *imply* that there is a king of France. But this is a very special and odd sense of 'imply'. 'Implies' in this sense is certainly not equivalent to 'entails' (or 'logically implies'). And this comes out from the fact that when, in response to his statement, we say (as we should) 'There is no king of France', we should certainly *not* say we were *contradicting* the statement that the king of France is wise. We are certainly not saying that it is false. We are, rather, giving a reason for saying that the question of whether it is true or false simply does not arise (Strawson (1950a), p. 12).

The philosophical use of a word in some special and odd sense is generally perceived (and rightly so) as a stop-gap measure, especially when the word in question normally has a meaning that is relatively clear and well-defined. One suspects that despite his explicit distinction of the two senses, the writer is trying to exploit the clarity of the word in its normal sense to make his own usage seem clearer. Hence Strawson's notion of implication calls out for definition and explanation.

Shortly after "On Referring" appeared, Strawson tried to answer this call. Wanting to sharpen the contrast with "logical implication," he abandoned the word 'imply', replacing it with 'presuppose', and offered the following definition of presupposition:

> A statement $S1$ presupposes a statement $S2$ just in case if $S1$ is true or false, then $S2$ must be true (Strawson (1952), p. 175).

Under this definition, the statement that the king of France is wise presupposes the statement that there is a king of France, because if the former statement is either true or false, then the latter statement must be true. (And since there is no king of France, the statement that the king of France is wise is neither true nor false; hence we arrive at the position taken in the quotation in section I.)

Strawson wanted his notions of presupposition and entailment to be logically independent. But, as many critics have pointed out, they are not.

For the standard logical definition of entailment is that $S1$ entails $S2$ just in case it is necessary that if $S1$ is true, then $S2$ is true. And, whenever $S1$ entails $S2$, $S1$ also presupposes $S2$, according to Strawson's definition.

Not everyone finds this result unintuitive, but much of what Strawson had to say about presupposition has to be modified, or at least rephrased, if presupposition includes entailment as a special case. I shall take a different line. I hold that the distinction between presupposition and entailment is one version of a distinction made rather more broadly in Chapter Two: the distinction between conversational implicature and conventional (or linguistic) implication.

What a speaker conventionally implies is determined by the semantic conventions governing the words he utters. For example, if Ovis-Ann says, "Jerome is a bachelor," she conventionally implies (though she does not say) that Jerome is not married; her statement *entails* that Jerome is not married. On the other hand, if in the course of a discussion about recent weddings Ovis-Ann says to her unmarried daughter, "Jerome is a bachelor," in a certain tone of voice, she may be conversationally implicating that her daughter needs a husband and suggesting Jerome as a suitable candidate. This connection is not semantic; conversational implicatures are determined by the conversational maxims — in this case, the Maxim of Relation. (Ovis-Ann's remark would not tie in with the rest of the discourse without the link that the presupposition provides.)

My claim is that in Strawson's example, the man who says, "The king of France is wise," conversationally implicates that there is a king of France. In Chapter Two, we saw that conversational implicatures are calculated by appealing to the Cooperative Principle, "Make your conversational contribution such as is required, at the stage at which it occurs, by the accepted purpose or direction of the talk exchange in which you are engaged." What is the purpose of a conversation in which the sentence 'The king of France is wise' is uttered? In the scenario that Strawson offers, it is not easy to tell, since he doesn't give any of the conversational context; but at least we can judge that the utterer is trying to make an assertion. Asserting is an illocutionary act that requires the kind of rhetic act discussed in section I of Chapter Eight: propounding a categorization. Thus the speaker can succeed in making his assertion only if he introduces an object to be placed in a category and a category in which to place that object. The subject expression in this case, 'the king of France' — is the part of the sentence by which the speaker introduces the object. Now, if the speaker says, "The king of France is wise," and intends to make an assertion, he is contravening the Cooperative Principle unless he thinks that there is a King of France, an object that can be introduced for categorization by means of the expression 'the king of France'. Otherwise, he is frustrating his own purpose and the purpose of the conversation in which he is participating. Since the only way to interpret the speaker's utterance in accordance with the Cooperative

Principle is to ascribe to him the belief that there is a king of France, the speaker conversationally implicates that there is a king of France.

Does he also implicate that there is no more than one king of France? This is a little bit trickier. The Cooperative Principle requires the maker of an assertion to introduce the object that he proposes to categorize in such a way that the hearer can be expected to know who or what it is. One way of ensuring this is to choose as the subject term a definite description that fits only one entity. More frequently, however, the hearer can be expected to know or to infer which of a number of entities that fit the description is the object for categorization. For example, the subject expression in the sentence 'The garbage bag needs to be taken out' is a definite description that is hardly unique in its application; but when this sentence is uttered the hearer is not likely to have any trouble deciding which of the many garbage bags in existence is being referred to. In general, then, the utterer of a definite description does not presuppose that the description fits only one thing, but rather that the hearer will be able to single out the intended referent from the class of things that the description fits. There need not be only one king of France (fortunately enough, since the description, though it fits no one in the contemporary world, does fit many people in history as a whole).

The conclusion, then, is that on the issue that Strawson identified as crucial, his objection to Russell is sound: Someone who asserts that the king of France is wise does not thereby assert that there is a king of France, but only implies it, or (more precisely) conversationally implicates it. The point Strawson missed, in contrasting his notion of implication or presupposition with (logical) entailment, is that the relation between what is asserted and what is implied is a matter of conversational maxims and not of semantic conventions.

III. The "Axiom of Existence"

To many philosophers of language it has seemed obvious that it is impossible to refer to things that do not exist. This view has been especially common among formalists, but there are also informalists who accept it. A prominent instance is John Searle, who calls the thesis that whatever is referred to must exist the "axiom of existence" and says that it "is an obvious tautology since it says only that one cannot refer to a thing if there is no such thing to be referred to" (Searle (1969), p. 77). By 'tautology', Searle means a logically true statement; without even knowing what kind of a relation reference is, Searle is suggesting, one can deduce that anything that is referred to has to exist in order to stand in the relation.

However, Searle's claim that the axiom is a tautology is erroneous. Compare the axiom with the following statements:

(3) Whatever is sought must exist.
(4) Whatever is imagined must exist.
(5) Whatever is proven not to exist must exist.

If Searle's reasoning were sound, one could establish any of these theses by saying that one cannot seek or imagine a thing or prove that it does not exist if there is no such thing to be sought, imagined, or proven not to exist. But this is absurd. One can seek something that does not, in fact, exist; the fact that there is no such thing as one is seeking does not make it impossible to seek it; and similarly in the other cases. The deduction is unsound, therefore, and this means that the exactly analogous inference about referring is also unsound. The "axiom of existence" may be true or false, but it is not a *logical* truth.

Both Russell and Strawson accept the axiom of existence, too, though in slightly different ways. The easiest way to see this is to consider a couple of unsound arguments for the existence of the king of France. Strawson formulates these arguments when he explains the problem that Russell's theory of descriptions is supposed to solve:

> Let us call the sentence 'The king of France is wise' the sentence S. Then the first argument is as follows:
> (1) The phrase, 'the king of France', is the subject of the sentence S.
> Therefore (2) if S is a significant sentence, S is a sentence *about* the king of France.
> But (3) if there in no sense exists a king of France, the sentence is not about anything, and hence not about the king of France.
> Therefore (4) since S is significant, there must in some sense (in some world) exist (or subsist) the king of France.
> And the second argument is as follows:
> (1) If S is significant, it is either true or false.
> (2) S is true if the king of France is wise and false if the king of France is not wise.
> (3) But the statement that the king of France is wise and the statement that the king of France is not wise are alike true only if there is (in some sense, in some world) something which is the king of France.
> Hence (4) since S is significant, there follows the same conclusion as before. (Strawson (1950a), p. 3)

These are arguments that a follower of Meinong might give in order to establish that the king of France must have some sort of logical being ("subsistence," perhaps, if not real existence).

In opposition to Meinong, Russell would reject these arguments. The first argument is unsound, according to Russell, because premise (1) is false; 'the king of France' is the *grammatical* subject of sentence S, but the grammar of the sentence is misleading and does not accurately represent its logical structure. In the logically perfect language, the equivalent of sentence S would not be a subject-predicate sentence at all. Certainly, therefore, premise (2) is false; sentence S, though significant, does not express a proposition that contains the king of France as a constituent, and is not *about* the king of France in the sense needed for the argument to go through. As for the second argument, Russell would say that the dilemma posed in premise (2) leaves out one alternative; it may be that there is no king of France, in which case it is incorrect to say either that the king of France is wise or that the king of France is not wise. In other words, S can be false even if there is no king of France, contrary to what is inferred from premise (2).

It is noteworthy, however, that Russell accepts the third premise of each of these arguments. The premises he accepts are variants of the axiom of existence. And it is quite natural that Russell should accept the axiom, since by definition an expression that genuinely denotes something denotes an existing thing, something that is "real"; that's the whole point of the passage quoted in section III of Chapter Eight, about the logician's need for a robust sense of reality.

Strawson also wants to reject the Meinongian arguments for the existence of the king of France, but his complaint is more general: He would say that throughout both arguments the sentence S itself is confused with certain uses of that expression. Strictly speaking, it makes no sense to ask what a sentence is about, or whether it is true or false; such questions can be asked about particular *uses* of sentences, but not about sentences in the abstract. The erroneous conclusions arise only because the two kinds of things are run together.

If the arguments are revised to eliminate this confusion, Strawson might very well accept the revised versions:

> (First argument.) The phrase 'the king of France' is the subject of the sentence S. Therefore, whenever someone uses S to make an assertion, the assertion is *about* the king of France. But if there exists no king of France, it is impossible to make an assertion *about* the king of France; therefore, whenever someone uses S to make an assertion, there exists a king of France.
>
> (Second argument.) Whenever someone uses S to make an assertion, the assertion is either true or false. It is true if the king of France is wise and false if the king of France is not wise. But the statement that the king of France is wise and the statement that the king of France is not wise are alike true only if there exists a king of France. Hence, whenever someone uses S to make an assertion, there exists a king of France.

Thus Strawson, too, accepts some form of the axiom of existence; he allows that an assertion can only be *about* existing things, and that in using a definite description, the speaker implies the existence and uniqueness of the thing described.

Neither Russell nor Strawson offers any real justification for their acceptance of the axiom. This is especially surprising, since it flies in the face of common sense; common sense knows that it is possible to refer to all sorts of things that do not exist — fictional and mythological characters, long-gone historical entities and entities yet to come, things that might have existed and things that could never have existed. The axiom is really a metaphysical doctrine to which philosophers are drawn like moths to a flame, and with analogous consequences.

Consider the devastating contradictions that Searle generates as he tries to defend the axiom of existence while still leaving open the possibility of referring to fictional characters:

> References to fictional (and also legendary, mythological, etc.) entities are not counter-examples. One can refer to them as *fictional characters* precisely because they do *exist in fiction*. To make this clear we need to distinguish normal real world talk from parasitic forms of discourse such as fiction, play acting, etc. In normal real world talk I cannot refer to Sherlock Holmes because there never was such a person. If in this 'universe of discourse' I say "Sherlock Holmes wore a deerstalker hat" I fail to refer. . . . But now suppose I shift into the fictional, play acting, let's-pretend mode of discourse. Here if I say "Sherlock Holmes wore a deerstalker hat", I do indeed refer to a fictional character (i.e. a character who does not exist but who exists in fiction). . . .
> The fact that there is such a fictional character as Sherlock Holmes does not commit us to the view that he exists in some suprasensible world or that he has a special mode of existence. Sherlock Holmes does not exist at all, which is not to deny that he exists-in-fiction (Searle (1969), pp. 78–79).

This passage opens with the claim that apparent references to fictional characters are not counter-examples to the axiom of existence. Now, it would seem that there are only two ways of reconciling such apparent references with the axiom: One can either deny that the fictional characters are referred to, or one can affirm that fictional characters exist. Unless one takes one or both of these positions, one is left with references to things that do not exist, and such cases would indeed constitute counter-examples to the axiom. What is surprising about Searle's discussion, then, is the length he goes to in order to *avoid* taking either of these two positions. He concedes that by shifting into a special mode of discourse, one can refer to fictional characters such as Sherlock Holmes; he insists flatly that Sherlock Holmes does not exist. How, then, can he claim to have defended the axiom of existence?

There are three ways in which one might try to defend Searle. First, one might play around with his distinction between two modes of discourse, "real-world" discourse and "let's-pretend" discourse. Searle does claim, after all, that Sherlock Holmes *cannot* be referred to in the first mode of discourse. But it is hard to see how this distinction helps Searle, any more than a distinction between two kinds of rope helps a man who is to be hanged: If he avoids being hanged with a hemp rope, but is hanged with a cotton one, he is hanged nevertheless. Similarly, if Sherlock Holmes is not referred to in "real-world" discourse, but is referred to in "let's-pretend" discourse, then he is referred to, period. It is not as if "let's-pretend" discourse takes place in the fantasy world that it is *about*; "let's-pretend" discourse takes place in the real world, and is just as much in need of theoretical analysis as "real-world" discourse. References in the "let's-pretend" mode are real references.

Nor is it obvious that the distinction that Searle is trying to draw is ultimately a coherent one. Consider Searle's own assertion, "Sherlock Holmes does not exist at all." Is this made in the "real-world" mode or in the "let's-pretend" mode? Presumably it is supposed to belong to the "real-world" mode, since it forms part of a serious philosophical study; and yet it contains an apparent reference to a fictional character. What does Searle think he is doing in that very sentence, if not referring to a non-existent?

Or take the claim that Sherlock Holmes wore a deerstalker hat. Why can't one say this, truthfully, as part of a "real-world" discourse, as an observation about the habitual garb of a fictional character? One can imagine "shifting into a fictional, play acting, let's pretend mode of discourse"; one of the things that one might pretend is that Sherlock Holmes affected blue berets instead of a deerstalker hat. But we do not need to *pretend* that Sherlock Holmes wore a deerstalker hat; that is what he *did* wear, as a matter of fact. Where is the pretense?

A second line of defense is to restate the axiom in two parallel forms:

(6) Whatever is referred to in the "real-world" mode of discourse must (really) exist.
(7) Whatever is referred to in the "let's-pretend" mode of discourse must exist-in-fiction.

Apart from the reservations expressed above about the validity of the distinction between the two modes of discourse, this initially appears to be a more plausible account. It does mean giving up the axiom of existence in its original form, since Searle is quite clear on the point that existence-in-fiction is not a species of existence, so that (7) is really an acknowledgement that it is possible to refer to things that don't exist. And the notion of existence-in-fiction is not intuitively clear; Searle owes us an analysis of it, since he is using 'exist' in a special and odd sense. However, the real problem with (6) and (7) is that they don't cover references to things that neither exist nor exist-in-fiction. For example, Searle holds that "'Mrs. Sherlock Holmes' fails of reference [even in the 'let's-pretend' mode of discourse] for there is no such fictional character." Presumably, then, no such person as Mrs. Sherlock Holmes exists-in-fiction. But surely we can say that if Sherlock Holmes had ever married, Mrs. Sherlock Holmes would not have allowed him to keep his pipe tobacco in an old slipper; and in so saying, we certainly seem to be referring to Mrs. Sherlock Holmes.

The third way of defending Searle is to suggest that perhaps he does not mean quite what he says in this passage. But this is unlikely, inasmuch as Searle has repeated the same views in a later article that explicitly deals with fictional discourse. After asserting that his views "help us to solve some of the traditional puzzles about the ontology of a work of fiction," he comes up with the claim that "Holmes and Watson never existed at all, which is not of course to deny they exist in fiction and can be talked about as such" (Searle (1975b), p. 71). And yet, Searle says, "I did not *pretend* to refer to a real Sherlock Holmes; I *really referred* to the fictional Sherlock Holmes" (Searle (1975b), p. 72). But if Sherlock Holmes was really referred to, then by the axiom of existence, Sherlock Holmes exists.

I suggest, then, that the axiom of existence is indefensible and should be abandoned. Indeed, any theory of reference that entails that whatever can be referred to must exist is thereby discredited, shown to be inadequate; references to non-existent objects are too much a part of our linguistic practice to be disregarded or dismissed as belonging to an unimportant mode of discourse.

IV. Referring: The Speaker and the Hearer

Our goal in the remaining sections of this chapter will be to draw up an analysis of various types of attempted reference with definite descriptions. One way to approach such an analysis would be to try to formulate it at once, saying what constitutes an attempted reference, whether or not it is defective; one can then adjust and refine the first trial formulation in the light of counterexamples, making it weaker or stronger and correcting hasty generalizations. However, a sounder and more common philosophical procedure is to ask what the clearest and most readily identifiable cases of the notion to be analyzed have in common, and to collect these common features in the analysans. We shall begin, therefore, with an analysis of paradigmatic (that is, successful and non-defective) reference; once we have that, we can adapt and extend the analysis to take care of the cases that diverge from the paradigms in various ways.

Here are some cases of paradigmatic reference:

(A) A visitor to Waggener Hall at the University of Texas at Austin enters on the ground floor and pushes a button to call an elevator in order to go up to the third floor. No elevator comes, and eventually he walks up several flights of stairs. Arriving at the third floor, he encounters several people at the elevator landing, with expectant looks on their faces; he tells them, "The elevator isn't working."

(B) A man is assembling a piece of do-it-yourself furniture. He asks his wife, "Would you please bring me the large blue Phillips-head screwdriver from the second drawer of the tool chest?"

(C) A television anchorman begins a report, "The budget that the House Ways and Means Committee approved today provides for a three-year, eighteen-percent tax cut."

In these three examples, there are six definite descriptions in all:

(8) the elevator
(9) the large blue Phillips-head screwdriver
(10) the second drawer of the tool chest
(11) the tool chest
(12) the budget that the House Ways and Means Committee approved today
(13) the House Ways and Means Committee

To what uses are these definite descriptions put? In other words, what are the speakers' intensions in uttering them? What goal are the speakers trying to achieve? How do the definite descriptions function in achieving this goal?

The standard view, which is due largely to Strawson, is that the speaker is picking out or identifying something (see, for example, Strawson (1961), pp. 59–60, and Strawson (1959), pp. 15–19). However, the terms 'picking out' and 'identifying' are ambiguous and vague, while the more precise terms 'selecting', 'distinguishing', 'individuating', and so on do not fit the cases very well. About the best one can do is take the cases one by one and describe what is going on as accurately as possible.

Consider case (A), then. The speaker's overall goal is to pass along the information that the elevator isn't working, so that his hearers won't waste any more time waiting for it. He makes a statement, and this involves propounding a categorization: The elevator is the object categorized, and the category it is put into is the category of nonfunctioning things. His assertion will be of no value, however, unless his hearers understand which object he is categorizing; the point of the definite description is to introduce the object for categorization *and* to do so in such a way that the hearers know which object it is. This is very easy, since the object in question is nearby, and especially since it is probably much in the minds of the hearers already. In fact, the pronoun 'it' would probably do just as well as the phrase 'the elevator' in this context, since the hearers can readily deduce from the context what object the speaker is likely to be talking about.

In (B), the speaker is making a request; he wants his wife to bring him a particular object. Again, it is essential for the success of his communication that the hearer know which object he is talking about; this time, however, the object is not nearby and the hearer is not thinking about it. Hence a more elaborate description is necessary; the speaker tells the hearer where it is, what it looks like, what kind of a thing it is. The three descriptions (9), (10), and (11) work in slightly different ways. (9) is basically informative, giving the hearer data she needs in order to distinguish the desired object from other objects with which it might be confused; she may never have seen the object and need not have known of its existence. (11) is more like 'the elevator' in case (A), in that the speaker expects the hearer to be acquainted with the referent; the problem of distinguishing it from others of its type simply does not arise. (10) is an intermediate case; as in (11), the hearer is probably acquainted with the object referred to, but as in (9), she needs some information about it in order to figure out which of a number of similar items the speaker is talking about.

Finally, in case (C), description (13) is virtually nothing but a label (and it has been argued that such expressions are really names that happen to begin with the definite article); the anchorman assumes that his listeners already know enough about the structure of the House of Representatives to catch the reference. On the other hand, description (12) is used to "advoke" (see Chapter Two, section VI) belief in the committee's budget proposal. Once again the speaker is introducing an object for categorization, and doing so in such a way that his hearers know, in a sense, which object it is. But notice that in this case, as opposed to case (A), the epistemic situation of the hearers with respect to the referent is much weaker; all the average hearer knows about the budget in question is what the anchorman proceeds to tell him.

This phrase 'know which object it is' is very tricky. Initially one is tempted to suppose that there is a single criterion for knowing an object, and that either one knows it or one does not. This, however, is an oversimplification. In some cases, it is enough to be able to name something or someone; if we are looking through an album of photographs of celebrities (without captions), and one of us says, "I know who that is!" he can make good his claim just by naming the person (or, at most, he needs to be able to say in very general terms why the person is celebrated). At a diplomatic soirée at the United Nations, on the other hand, one might find people saying things like, "His name-tag says that he is Taslim Olawala Elias, but I don't know who he is"; "knowing who he is" would require being able to identify him as the Nigerian member of the International Court of Justice.

Such variations can be adduced endlessly, and this has led some philosophers to distinguish two senses of 'identify'. Searle makes the distinction thus:

> At the lowest level, questions like "who?", "what?", or "which one?" are answered [by an identification]. Of course at another level these questions are still open: after something has been identified one may still ask "what?" in the sense of "tell me more about it", but one cannot ask "what?" in the sense of "I don't know what you're talking about". Identifying, as I am using the term, just means answering that question. For example, in an utterance of the sentence "The man who robbed me was over six feet tall" I can be said to refer to the man who robbed me, even though in one sense of "identify" I may not be able to identify the man who robbed me. I may not be able, e.g., to pick him out of a

police line-up or say anything more about him. Still, assuming one and only one man robbed me, I do succeed in making an identifying reference in an utterance of the above sentence (Searle (1969), p. 85).

This distinction is useful as far as it goes; we certainly do not want to say that a speaker can't refer to something unless he can pick it out of a police line-up. However, Searle's analysis really only pushes the problem one step farther back: How can we tell whether questions like "who?", "what?", and "which one?" have been adequately answered? It is not enough for the hearer to be able to make some kind of a reply to such questions, for he can generally do that even if he *doesn't* know what the speaker is referring to. Suppose a speaker of unknown political persuasion begins a speech: "The worst president of the United States not only made money from his high office, but is still profiting from it today." At this point, if one of the hearers is asked who the speaker is talking about, he may without contradiction say, "I don't know who he is referring to; it's 'the worst president of the United States,' but it's not clear yet who he means."

The fact is that identification and the criteria for being able to identify something vary with the purposes of the people involved. It is not that there are two senses of 'identify', or three, or seventeen; it is that identification is relational, and takes different forms as it figures in different sorts of activities. In identifying celebrity photographs, names suffice, because all we are trying to do is to link the picture with our previous knowledge about the celebrity, and the name is sufficient to provide the link; at the diplomatic soirée, however, we want to link the person to his position in the power structure (or so we may assume), and the name is generally not enough to do this (since few people know the names of the justices of the International Court of Justice). In Searle's examples, if the speaker simply wants to tell his friends about his adventure, 'the man who robbed me' is an adequate means of identification; if, however, he wants to press charges, then he is going to have to be able to pick the man out of a line-up.

The only way of generalizing, then, is to say that the goal of an act of reference is to introduce an object for categorization, in such a way that the hearer can make whatever connection with the object is needed. In general, the establishment of this connection does not require the sensible presence, or even the existence, of the referent. In most cases, the speaker wants the hearer simply to *think of* the object in a certain way; this intentional activity requires only an intentional object, not a real one.

So far, this account leaves open the question whether a paradigmatic act of referring takes place if the hearer fails to make the necessary connection. Suppose that the speaker carries out his part perfectly, giving the hearer everything he needs to identify the referent, but the hearer fails to pick up on what the speaker says. Has a paradigmatic act of referring taken place? Many philosophers have held that it does, although this contention is rarely argued for. Keith Donnellan, for example, simply asserts his view:

I do not fail to refer merely because my audience does not correctly pick out what I am referring to. I can be referring to a particular man when I use the description 'the man drinking a martini' even though the person to whom I speak fails to pick out ... any person at all" (Donnellan (1966), p. 205).

Similarly, Jack Meiland says that "Nothing need be done by any hearer in order for a speaker to succeed in referring to an individual. *That is, a statement's being about a particular individual rather than any other individual is independent of anything any hearer does or does not do*" (Meiland (1970), p. 120). Meiland does recognize that there is a "hearer-dependent activity" of "referring a hearer to an individual," but he denies that referring *simpliciter* is the same concept. It is difficult to make out any rationale for this distinction; why should there be *two* notions of referring?

One author who does give an argument on this point is Alfred MacKay, who writes:

> Must we really succeed in making it *known* [to the hearer] what we are talking about? This would mean that we have not succeeded in referring to any object if, say, our audience happens not to have heard us, or perhaps if, unknown to us, our audience does not understand English. The question of whether or not reference is achieved cannot turn on our actually achieving an effect in our audience. Too many extraneous factors can frustrate that (MacKay (1968), p. 197).

Now, if the question is whether referring is a perlocutionary act that cannot take place at all unless the hearer reacts as intended, MacKay is correct in answering "no." However, if the hearer does not identify the object that the speaker is talking about, it is clear that something has gone wrong; we can hardly have a *paradigmatic* (successful and non-defective) act of referring in such a case. In referring, as in many other acts, our aspirations can be frustrated by the failings of another. So in our initial analysis of paradigmatic reference, we must take the role of the hearer into account; to refer is to refer *someone* to an object.

An analogy may help to clarify this point. Everyone agrees that to refer is to refer to some object, for to refer to no object is not to refer at all; similarly, to direct is to direct to something. Moreover, to refer is to refer someone to an object, just as to direct is to direct someone to an object. There is no more difference between referring and referring someone to something than there is between directing and directing someone to something. It does not make sense to talk about giving directions independently of any possible recipient; similarly, it does not make sense to talk about referring independently of any possible hearer.

In summary, then, we have found that the goal of the speaker in an act of reference is to enable the hearer to identify an object for categorization; what is meant by 'identify' here varies with the broader purposes and interests of the speaker. In a paradigmatic act of reference, this goal is achieved; the hearer succeeds in understanding who or what the speaker intends to be categorizing.

V. An Analysis of Paradimgatic Reference

From the discussion in the preceding section, it appears that although it is often convenient and harmless to use 'refer' as a one-, two-, or three-place predicate, the notion to be analyzed is what Russell would call a tetradic relation between a speaker, a hearer, an object, and an expression. The analysans must exhibit the connections among these four elements in terms of the speaker's intentions and the hearer's recognition of them. The analysis I propose, then, is as follows:

(14) A speaker S successfully and non-defectively refers a hearer H to an object O with a definite description D if, and only if,
   (a) S introduces O as an object for categorization;
   (b) S utters D with the intention of getting H to identify O, at least partly by recognizing that S intends him to identify O;
   (c) D fits or applies to O; and
   (d) H identifies O, at least partly by recognizing that S intends him to identify O.

Let us consider some of the implications of this analysis. To begin with, although it requires that S produce D, it does not specify a mode of production; any medium of utterance can be a medium of reference. Second, the production of D must be intentional (no reference takes place if S utters D unintentionally or purposelessly, even if S's utterance enables H to identify an object). Moreover, the speaker's intention must be of the kind specified, which is really threefold: S intends (i) that H identify O, (ii) that H recognize S's intention to get him to identify O, and (iii) that H's identification of O be achieved at least in part through his recognition of S's intention to get him to identify O. In cases of paradigmatic reference, as condition (d) indicates, all of these intentions are fulfilled. Naturally, the route by which H identifies O includes more than just H's recognition of S's intentions; usually he also knows the meaning of the description D, as well as the relevant facts about the conversational context and he counts on S to conform to the Conversational Maxims, and so on. No one of these factors singly would enable H to identify O, but together they are sufficient.

In using the expression 'fits or applies to' in condition (c), we are following Strawson, Donnellan, and others (see, for example, Strawson (1961), Donnellan (1966), or Meiland (1970), pp. 3, 88). It is, perhaps, a more philosophically neutral term than, say, 'true of'. We do not require that a definite description fit or apply to nothing other than O; we leave open the possibility that the fit is not unique, for the reasons discussed in section II. As Searle has pointed out, the definite article is "a conventional device indicating the speaker's intention to refer to a single object, not an indication that the description which follows is true of only one object" (Searle (1969), p. 84). (Actually, it is not the definite article that indicates this intention, but the article plus singular form of the noun that follows it; for the article can also combine with plurals, and the speaker's intention to refer to a single object is equally manifest in indefinite descriptions.)

Returning to the examples of paradigmatic reference in section IV, we see how the analysis applies to them. In case (A) ("The elevator isn't working"), the speaker introduces the Waggener Hall elevator as an object for categorization, utters the phrase 'the elevator' with the intention of getting the people who are gathered on the landing to identify it, and uses a description that fits it (it is an elevator); and the hearers identify the elevator as the object being introduced for categorization, partly from the context, but partly by recognizing the speaker's intentions. This is not, of course, an exhaustive analysis of *all* the speech acts that the speaker is executing as he utters his sentence; what it is supposed to show is that a genuine paradigmatic act of reference does take place in this case.

If all this strikes the reader as exceedingly fine dissection of what is, after all, a very common and obvious phenomenon, that is as it should be. It is a commonplace in philosophy that the most difficult things to examine objectively and analytically are the things of which we have the most experience; their familiarity and nearness make them difficult to focus on. Heidegger once wrote, "What is closest to us is often the farthest away." So it is necessary to check analyses of very ordinary activities, such as referring, with special care, even at the expense of seeming to make a mountain out of a molehill.

Turning to case (B), then, let's take only description (9), 'the large blue Phillips-head screwdriver'. Condition (a) of analysis (14) is met; the speaker introduces the object in question for categorization. (The category is that of "things to be brought to me.") Condition (b) is met; the speaker intends the hearer to identify this object, this time in the sense that she has a sufficiently detailed mental representation of it that she will be able to find it when she looks into the second drawer of the tool chest, and the speaker intends to produce this representation in her by means of his description of the object and her recognition of the intention behind his utterance. Condition (c) is met; the object in question is indeed a large blue Phillips-head screwdriver. And the hearer succeeds in identifying it, so condition (d) is also met.

Similarly, in case (c), the utterer of description (12) is introducing the Ways and Means Committee's budget as an object for placement in the category of things that provide for a three-year, eighteen-percent tax cut. The speaker intends the hearers to identify this object; identification, in this case, consists simply in being aware that there is something that the description fits. Unlike the speaker in case (B), the television anchorman has no relevant motive or purpose beyond simply informing his listeners; it is not necessary, from his point of view, that they be able to distinguish the Ways and Means Committee budget from the superficially similar budget proposal of the O. M. B. So the kind of identification that he intends the hearers to make is much weaker than that kind of identification that the man who needs a particular screwdriver wants to provide. Once again, the description fits the referent, and the hearers identify the referent as the speaker intended.

Perhaps the least satisfactory part of analysis (14) is the use of the word 'identify', which may seem too flexible and indefinite to be correct. In section IV, I tried to explain this notion by means of examples; at this point, it may be helpful to contrast identification in my sense with certain other notions that have been proposed in connection with reference.

In *Individuals*, Strawson develops two notions of "hearer-identification." In the weaker sense, a hearer identifies an object when he is able to distinguish it or single it out from the other objects in the speaker's universe of discourse, the range of objects that figure in what he is saying; in the stronger sense, a hearer identifies an object when he is able to place it in space and time, or to distinguish it from every other particular entity in the entire history of the universe. Neither one of these notions of identification is the one I am using. In the first place, Strawson accepts the axiom of existence, and as a result he considers it plausible to assume that whatever can be referred to is either itself located in space and time or else uniquely related in some way to something that is located in space and time. He builds this condition into both his notions of hearer-identification; I, on the other hand, make no suppositions whatever about the spatial or temporal characteristics of a referent. Second, Strawson's requirement that the hearer be able to distinguish the referent from other things either in the universe of discourse or in the universe as a whole, by means of what he calls an "individuating fact," that is, something that holds true of one and only one object, is too weak, in the same way that Searle's notion of identification, discussed in section IV, is too weak; the hearer may know an individuating fact about something and yet not know, in the relevant way, who or what the individuating fact individuates. (For example, it may be an individuating fact about a person that he is wearing a nametag that says "Taslim Olawala Elias" on it; in the context of the diplomatic soirée, this alone does not enable the hearer to identify him in the relevant way.)

Another notion that bears some relation to identification in my sense but does not match it is Zeno Vendler's 'thinking of' (Vendler (1976), pp. 34–35), which he explains thus:

> In thinking about an individual, person, thing or event, one must recall (or actually experience) an introduction of the individual into one's life history either by itself, or by means of a token (picture, name, descriptions, etc.) which at that time was understood to be linked to that individual via a historical causal chain (Vendler (1976), p. 44).

As we mentioned in section IV, sometimes the hearer's identification of the referent consists in nothing more than his thinking of it in a certain way, and initially this account of Vendler's looks like a plausible description of what this "thinking of" is. Once again, however, it seems to be assumed that whenever one thinks of an individual, person, thing, or event, it must exist or have existed. If Vendler's explanation were correct, there would be no thinking of non-existent objects, or even of things in the future (since we can neither recall nor experience them). Moreover, Vendler's account omits any indication of what the point of "thinking of" is. *Why* do speakers mean for their hearers to think of things? Since this question is answered differently in different cases, the proponent of a pragmatic explanation of "thinking of" must recognize that the character of this activity is relative to the broader context of action within which it takes place. For instance, thinking of water when one is perishing of thirst in the desert is not the same as thinking of water when one is performing an experiment in inorganic chemistry. My notion of identification allows for such variations; although this may make it seem inexact and indefinite, its flexibility is indispensible.

VI. *An Analysis of Successful Reference*

With the analysis of paradigmatic reference behind us, it is necessary to extend and modify it to encompass oblique cases, in order to help fix the limits of the concept of referring as precisely as it allows. For paradigm cases put us in the heart of the concept's country but do not define its boundaries. Defective cases of referring are cases of referring nonetheless, and we must ferret them out. A complete inventory and catergorization of defective but successful reference is beyond the scope of this work. I want to concentrate on one basic way in which reference can defectively succeed.

Thinking of an object *tout court* seems to be incorrigible or infallible. We cannot mistakenly think of something because thinking of what we are thinking of constitutes thinking of that thing. If this is correct, then it is nonsensical to talk about correct or incorrect thought of an object. Correctness or incorrectness arises only when thought is related to something else such as a description. Since in referring the description relates to both a speaker and his hearer, we can speak about both speaker and hearer "thinking of" or identification and about both speaker- and hearer-correct identification. We can speak of a speaker's identification being correct or incorrect relative to the description he uses; his identification is correct just in case the description he uses fits or applies to his intended referent; and otherwise it is incorrect. We need to distinguish then between speaker correct and incorrect reference.

There is an analogous sense in which a hearer's identification can be correct or incorrect. A hearer's identification is correct relative to the object the speaker intends him to identify. It is correct just in case he identifies the object the speaker intends him to identify; and otherwise it is incorrect. Despite the speaker's and hearer's best and most sincere efforts, the hearer might fail to identify the correct object. Incorrect hearer identification has a radically negative effect on an attempted reference; it renders it unsuccessful. Since referring is part of communication and communication involves the transfer of the speaker's thought to his hearer, the attempted reference is unsuccessful if the hearer does not identify the object the speaker intends him to. Doubtless, there are many bizarre cases of unsuccessful reference involving speaker- and hearer-incorrect identification, many of which give rise to a comedy of errors; but there are also many banal instances of such. Suppose (as is the case) Columbus did not discover America but is widely believed to have done so; then, if someone intending to refer to Columbus says, "The man who discovered America was brave," and the hearer identifies Lief Ericsson as the speaker's intended referent, we have a case of unsuccessful reference, which may well go undetected.

Let's now return to the notion of speaker correct and incorrect identification. The analysis of paradigmatic reference is the analysis of speaker-correct identification. The analysis of speaker-incorrect identification is an analysis of the analysandum:

> A speaker S successfully refers his hearer H to an object O with an incorrect description D [just in case]

The analysandum is just like that of paradigmatic reference except for condition c, which gives way to

> c'. D does not fit O.

The Cooperative Principle comes into its own in many cases described by speaker incorrect identification. When the speaker uses a description that does not fit or apply to his intended referent, the hearer has to do more than his normal share of work in order to make the intended communication succeed. He must decide first to overrule the working assumption that the speaker is using a fit description and decide secondly what in fact the speaker's intended referent is. How the speaker decides these matters is complex and far outside the scope of the current discussion.

Chapter Ten:
The Attributive Use and the Speech Act Theory of Referring

I. A Distinction in Search of a Characterization

In his 1966 article "Reference and Definite Descriptions," Keith Donnellan argued that definite descriptions can be used in at least two different ways; they have a "referential use" and an "attributive use." Now, there are in general two ways to establish that a distinction exists; one can either characterize the distinction (that is, give a precise account of the difference between the things distinguished) or illustrate it with examples. Donnellan tries both approaches. In this section, we consider Donnellan's characterizations of the two uses; his examples will be dealt with in sections II and III.

Donnellan initially presents the distinction as follows:

> A speaker who uses a definite description attributively in an assertion states something about whoever or whatever is the so-and-so. A speaker who uses a definite description referentially in an assertion, on the other hand, uses the description to enable his audience to pick out whom or what he is talking about and states something about that person or thing. In the first case the definite description might be said to occur essentially, for the speaker wishes to assert something about whatever or whoever fits that description; but in the referential use the definite description is merely one tool for doing a certain job — calling attention to a person or thing — and in general any other device for doing the same job, another description or a name, would do as well. In the attributive use, the attribute of being the so-and-so is all important, while it is not in the referential use (Donnellan (1966), p. 198).

There are actually three characterizations in this passage, with different defects. The first is the claim that a definite description is used attributively when the speaker states something about whoever or whatever the description fits, referentially when he enables his audience to pick out the person or thing he is talking about and states something about that thing. Now, in the first place, the two kinds of statements that Donnellan speaks of are not mutually exclusive; there is no reason why one cannot both state something about whoever or whatever the description fits and also enable one's audience to pick out that person or thing. Indeed, many paradigmatic acts of referring belong on both sides of Donnellan's distinction as he characterizes it here.

Possibly what is responsible for this overlapping of the two sides of the distinction is the occurrence of the word 'about' in the characterization of each side; if a statement is really *about* some person or thing, then it is hard to resist the thought that the definite description involved is being used to refer to that thing, that is, referentially. Even some of those who accept the referential/attributive distinction concede that attributive uses also involve reference; for example, Dennis Stampe says,

> It is with these *attributives* that I shall be mainly concerned; I shall try to understand how it is that such sentences both refer to and predicate something of a particular subject, *by and while therein* expressing a connection between certain properties of that subject (Stampe (1974), p. 160; see also p. 192, and Margolis and Fales (1976), pp. 289–302).

It is possible to amend Donnellan's first characterization of the attributive use so as to eliminate 'about':

> (1) Whenever anyone uses a description attributively in a sentence of the form 'The φ is ψ', he could equally well have used the corresponding sentence of the form 'The φ, whoever or whatever it is, is ψ'.

(We must imagine that English expressions are inserted in the places marked by Greek letters so as to make 'the φ' a definite description and 'is ψ' a grammatically correct predicate.) This paraphrase has the merit of emphasizing what Donnellan wants to emphasize, namely, the tag phrase 'whoever or whatever'. But does this tag phrase come to anything? Does it distinguish different functions of the description? Unfortunately, no. It is as appropriate to indisputably referential uses of singular terms as to the so-called attributive uses. Suppose, for example, that Tom and Zoe, walking down the street together, pass an unusually distinguished-looking and well-dressed woman, and Zoe exclaims, "The woman who just passed by, whoever she is, is certainly elegant." Or suppose that Professor S and Professor H have been arguing inconclusively over whether a certain man they are observing is a dean or a vice-president of the university, and S says, "Well, whatever he is, the fellow is not to be trusted." In each case, Donnellan would say that the description is being used referentially, and yet the "whoever or whatever" tag fits perfectly into the sentence involved.

The function of the "whoever or whatever" clause in such a phrase is to indicate that the speaker, though he expects the hearer to be able to identify the intended referent well enough for immediate conversational purposes, is unable to supply the hearer with the means of identification needed for some further purpose. In our examples, Zoe implies that the woman who just passed by is a person of some importance, but that she (Zoe) does not know what the woman's claim to distinction might be; similarly, Professor S is in effect conceding that he and H cannot agree on an identification of the man they are observing as the holder of a particular academic post, although it is obviously possible for them to identify him well enough to talk about him (since they are both looking right at him).

Let's turn to Donnellan's second characterization of the distinction he is trying to make. The key notion here is that when a description is used attributively, "the definite description might be said to occur essentially." What does this mean? The idea seems to be that an expression occurs essentially just in case no other expression can "do the same job," or function in the same way in the same context. Definite descriptions used referentially fail this test, because there are other descriptions or names that could be substituted for them without affecting the job done.

By this criterion, however, no description is ever used attributively; for any description, it is always possible to find a synonymous expression that can be substituted in without affecting either the illocutionary force or the propositional content of the utterance (which is what Donnellan probably has in mind when he talks about "doing the same job," although he is not clear on this point). It does no good to reply that in such cases one is simply substituting one attributive use of a description for another, because this is precisely what one is not supposed to be able to do with attributive uses.

Thus Donnellan's criterion must be weakened so as to license the substitution of synonymous expressions even when they occur essentially. There is textual evidence to support this interpretation. For what Donnellan considers important about an essentially occurring expression is not its phonetic or syntactic shape, but its semantic force or meaning; it is the attribute expressed that is important, not the phrase that expresses it. Let us say that all expressions that express the same attribute are "trivial variants" of one another. The revised criterion, then, is that when a description is used attributively, only trivial variants of the description can do the same job, whereas when it is used referentially, non-trivial variants can be substituted for it without affecting either the propositional content or the illocutionary force of the utterance.

Even this revision, however, does not yield any attributive uses of definite descriptions. As I shall argue more fully in section II, there are always non-trivial variants that can do the same job as a given description, even in the cases that Donnellan takes as paradigms of the attributive use. This is sometimes difficult to see, because we tend to think of cases in which the speaker knows next to nothing about the object he refers to, so that the non-trivial variants are in a manner of speaking unavailable to him; there are other ways for him to refer to the same object, but he does not know what they are. It cannot be right, however, to say that there are two uses of definite descriptions that differ only in that in one case the speaker knows less about what the description fits than in the other case. We should say rather that there is a single use of definite descriptions, but in one case the speaker's choice of descriptions is more restricted than in the other.

Incidentally, one consequence of going along with Donnellan's claim that definite descriptions sometimes occur essentially is that the same is true of proper names, for there are uses of proper names that are closely analogous to his examples of attributive uses of definite descriptions. (This is an important point, since Donnellan denies that the referential/attributive distinction applies to proper names.) For example, suppose that a drawing has just taken place for the grand prize in a raffle, and the chairman of the raffle committee announces the winner by saying, "Jane Smith has won the grand prize," If we suppose that the chairman knows nothing more about Jane Smith, then he is unable to replace the name 'Jane Smith' with any other name or description that will do the same job; that is, this occurrence of 'Jane Smith' is essential. Moreover, Donnellan's first criterion of the attributive use is also satisfied in this case, since the chairman is using 'Jane Smith' to state that Jane Smith, whoever she is, has won the grand prize. (We would say, of course, that the 'Whoever' here reflects the chairman's inability to identify the winner except as a name on a ticket stub.)

It might be objected that 'Jane Smith' does not occur essentially because one can replace it with the non-trivial variant 'the winner of the grand prize'. But if one makes the substitution, the chairman winds up saying, "The winner of the grand prize has won the grand prize," and this statement does not have the same illocutionary force as the chairman's actual utterance; it is not an announcement, since it is uninformative. 'Jane Smith' contributes information that 'the winner of the grand prize' does not; thus the latter does not do the same job as the former.

It might also be urged that the description 'the person named 'Jane Smith' could be substituted for 'Jane Smith' without affecting either the propositional content or the illocutionary force of the chairman's utterance. Now, either this new description is a trivial variant of 'Jane Smith', in which case it does not disprove the claim that 'Jane Smith' occurs essentially, or else it is a non-trivial variant, in which case it is hard to see why we cannot supply an equally non-trivial variant for any description whatever, namely, the result of writing the original into the blank of the schema 'the object described by '____''. Thus either we have attributive uses of proper names, or else there are no attributive uses of definite descriptions, under Donnellan's second criterion. I hold that Donnellan is right to reject the first alternative; the conclusion to be drawn from the second, however, is that Donnellan has not succeeded in distinguishing two uses.

Donnellan's third attempt to characterize his distinction concerns the importance of the attribute expressed; he says that when a definite description is used attributively this attribute is "all important," while in referential uses it is presumably only "part important," or perhaps not important at all. A clearer statement of what he has in mind follows a page or so later:

> We can say, I think, that there are two uses of sentences of the form, "The φ is ψ." In the first, if nothing is the φ then nothing has been said to be ψ. In the second, the fact that nothing is the φ does not have this consequence (Donnellan (1966), p. 199).

The question is whether it is possible for a speaker to use a sentence of the form 'The φ is ψ' to make an assertion without saying that something is ψ. If this is not possible, then once again Donnellan's proposed notion of attributive use comes up empty. We have suggested that in any speech act that has propositional content, there is a rhetic act of propounding a categorization, in which one or more objects are introduced. In an assertion of the form Donnellan cites, the speaker categorizes these objects as things that have the attribute expressed by ψ. It is impossible for him to make an assertion without saying that something, to wit, the object categorized, is ψ. Thus Donnellan has not succeeded in distinguishing an attributive use.

This *a priori* objection, however, does not show what is wrong with Donnellan's account or why he should suppose that the distinction he is proposing is needed. For that we must examine some of the examples he brings in to illustrate the supposed distinction.

II. Purported Examples of the Attributive Use

Donnellan's examples are most easily related to the third of the characterizations discussed in section I. According to that characterization, the difference between the two uses of definite descriptions will show up most clearly not in cases of paradigmatic reference, but rather in cases where the definite description does not fit or apply to anything. Thus, in order to show the difference, he constructs two scenarios in which the use of the definite description is defective and in which the consequences of the defect are supposedly different:

> [Scenario I.] Suppose first that we come upon poor Smith foully murdered. From the brutal manner of the killing and the fact that Smith was the most lovable person in the world, we might exclaim, "Smith's murderer is insane." I will assume, to make it a simpler case, that in a quite ordinary sense we do not know who murdered Smith (though this is not in the end essential to the case). This, I shall say, is an attributive use of the definite description. . . .
> [Scenario II.] Suppose that Jones has been charged with Smith's murder and has been placed on trial. Imagine that there is a discussion of Jones's odd behavior at his trial. We might sum up our impression of his behavior by saying, "Smith's murderer is insane." If someone asks to whom we are referring, by using this description, the answer here is "Jones." This, I shall say, is a referential use of the definite description (Donnellan (1966), p. 198).

Donnellan then adds to each scenario the supposition that no one actually murdered Smith, that he committed suicide in such a way that the discoverers of the body, and the police and the public prosecutors, mistook it for a case of murder. It is clear that in each scenario the speaker's use of the definite description is defective, but according to Donnellan the results of the defect are not the same:

In the first case, if there is no murderer, there is no person of whom it could be correctly said that we attributed insanity to him. Such a person could be identified (correctly) only in case someone fitted the description used. But in the second case, where the definite description is simply a means of identifying the person we want to talk about, it is quite possible for the correct identification to be made even though no one fits the description we used (Donnellan (1966), p. 199).

However, Donnellan's claim that it is impossible to identify the intended referent correctly in scenario I and possible to do so in scenario II is vitiated by the fact that his term 'identify' is equivocal. When he talks about the first case, what he means by correct identification is speaker correct identification. In neither scenario is speaker correct identification possible since by hypothesis the description does not fit or apply to anyone and hence condition 3 ("D fits or applies to O") fails to obtain. When he talks about the second case, on the other hand, what he means by correct identification is hearer correct identification. And this is possible in both scenarios. Of course, it is more likely to happen in scenario II, since the hearer (if he has been following the trial, say) knows a lot about Jones, while in scenario I his knowledge is supposed to be extremely incomplete. Still, by appropriately filling in the scenario we can make it quite clear that here too the hearer might be able to identify the intended referent. Suppose that the speaker said that Smith's murderer was insane because of the apparently gratuitous brutalities inflicted on him, as Donnellan suggests; and suppose that the hearer knows that although Smith committed suicide (by an overdose of drugs), it was a third party, Robinson, that multilated the body. In that case, in spite of the misdescription, it is possible for the hearer to infer that the speaker is referring to Robinson.

Since what is impossible in scenario I is also impossible in scenario II, and since what is possible in scenario II is also possible in scenario I, Donnellan has failed to show that the definite description is used in different ways in the two cases. Of course, this is not to say that there are no significant differences between the two; indeed, one of the weaknesses of this pair of examples is that there are so many differences. In scenario I, Smith is one of the *dramatis personae* and Jones is not; in scenario II, the reverse is true. In scenario I, the expression 'Smith's murderer' is, perhaps, a complete novelty; since Smith is only just dead, the problem of identifying Smith's murderer (in the sense of apprehending someone whom that description fits or applies to) has never been raised before. In scenario II, the police, a grand jury, and the public prosecutor have gone on record as believing that Jones is Smith's murderer, which makes it easy for the speaker to refer to Jones by means of this "authoritative" description. The odd thing is that if the difference between the referential use and the attributive use is due to a difference in the intentions of the speaker, as Donnellan claims (Donnellan (1966), p. 207), it ought to be possible to construct a pair of scenarios which

X The Attributive Use and The Speech Act Theory of Referring 175

differ only in that the speaker's intentions are altered. By using two very different scenarios, Donnellan raises the possibility that any significant differences in the communicative force of the description can be explained by citing some factor other than the speaker's intentions.

Donnellan's second pair of contrasting examples is supposed to show that the referential/attributive distinction shows up in questions as well as in assertions:

> Suppose one is at a party and, seeing an interesting-looking person holding a martini glass, one asks, "Who is the man drinking a martini?" If it should turn out that there is only water in the glass, one has nevertheless asked a question about a particular person, a question that it is possible for someone to answer. Contrast this with the use of the same question by the chairman of the local teetotalers Union. He has just been informed that a man is drinking a martini at their annual party. He responds by asking his informant, "Who is the man drinking a martini?" In asking the question the chairman does not have some particular person in mind about whom he asks the question; if no one is drinking a martini, if the information is wrong, no person can be singled out as the person about whom the question was asked. Unlike the first case, the attribute of being the man drinking a martini is all-important, because if it is the attribute of no one, the chairman's question has no straightforward answer (Donnellan (1966), p. 199).

Donnellan has again compromised his claims about illustrating two different uses of definite description by giving us two importantly different scenarios with interlocutors having very different interests and epistemic access to the object of interest. Further, his assessment of the second situation is simply wrong; the chairman's informant will have no difficulty in answering the question in a perfectly straightforward way. If he is a sincerely offended teetotaler who has spotted someone with a martini glass and jumped to conclusions, then he will describe the man (or perhaps name him); if he is a prankster playing some sort of practical joke on the chairman, he will supply the vice-chairman's name without a blush. In either case, although the chairman is misinformed, he does have a particular person in mind when he asks the question; it is just that at that point he cannot supply a description that actually fits or applies to that person, who is known to him only under a misdescription.

A third pair of examples involves commands:

> Consider the order, "Bring me the book on the table." If "the book on the table" is being used referentially, it is possible to fulfill the order even though there is no book on the table. If, for example, there is a book *beside* the table, though there is none on it, one might bring that book back and ask the issuer of the order whether this is "the book you meant." And it may be. But imagine we are told that someone has laid a book on our prize antique table, where nothing should be put. The

order, "Bring me the book on the table" cannot now be obeyed unless there is a book that has been placed on the table. There is no possibility of bringing back a book which was never on the table and having it be what was meant, because there is no book that in that sense was "meant."

One stylistic problem with this pair of examples is that the point of view shifts confusingly; in the first example the reader sees things from the point of view of the person who is trying to obey the order, while in the second he becomes a joint issuer of the command. Let's shift to third person throughout. In case I, Lulu says to her roomate, Elaine, "Bring me the book on the table." Elaine goes to the table — no book. What is it that Lulu wants her to do in this situation? Presumably Lulu is reading, or is going to read, the particular book that is supposed to be on the table, but isn't — could it be that the book she wants is somewhere about? Lying beside the table is a trashy romance of just the sort Lulu reads — that must be what she wants. Elaine returns and asks Lulu, "Is this the book you meant?" And it may be. Case II: Lulu has a prize antique table; nothing is supposed to be put on it. One day Erik, who has come in through the entrance hall where the table is kept, says to Lulu, "Say, I noticed a big, heavy book on that prize antique table of yours in the hall; I thought you never read anything except trashy romances." Lulu's jaw drops; she gets purple in the face, turns to Elaine, and grates, "Bring me the book on the table." Elaine goes to the table — no book. Now, once again, it may be that Erik is playing a joke, in which case it is indeed impossible for Elaine to obey Lulu's order; one cannot bring back a non-existent book. If case II is parallel to case I, however, Elaine looks around and finds a book beside the table. Suppose that she takes this book to Lulu, explaining carefully that it was not *on* the table, but *beside* the table — Erik must have been mistaken. Has she not obeyed Lulu's order? The order is, of course, defective, but it does not seem so radically defective that it cannot be carried out at all.

There is still another possibility. Suppose that when Elaine goes to the table, she finds, not a book, but a large, jagged rock (or a muddy shoe, or a book-end shaped like a book, or some other object that should not be on a prize antique table). In this case it is clear that she can obey Lulu's order by taking whatever is on the table back to Lulu. There is every reason to say that this large, jagged rock is what Lulu "meant," or, rather, referred to.

What makes the second case seem so different from the first in Donnellan's original presentation is, again, the fact that the speaker is supposed to know nothing whatever about the book. If we fill in a little more detail, setting up a situation in which the speaker could plausibly say what he is supposed to say, we find that the two cases are really very much alike, and specifically that in each case there is an "intended referent," although in special cases it may turn out that the object referred to does not exist.

Finally, let us consider a case that causes Donnellan some dismay, because the description seems to be used referentially, but there does not seem to be any referent:

> Suppose that I think I see at some distance a man walking and ask, "Is the man carrying a walking stick the professor of history?" [And suppose] there is nothing at all where I thought there was a man with a walking stick; and perhaps here we have a genuine failure to refer at all, even though the description was used for the purpose of referring. There is no rock, nor anything else, to which I meant to refer; it was, perhaps, a trick of light that made me think there was a man there. I cannot say of anything, "That is what I was referring to, though I now see that it's not a man carrying a walking stick" (Donnellan (1966), p. 206).

What is responsible for Donnellan's puzzlement is his assumption that whenever an act of referring takes place, the intended referent must exist. As we saw in section III of Chapter Nine, this is not the case. The only difference here is that the speaker mistakenly supposes that he is referring to something that does exist; but this error does not prevent him from referring. The reference may even be successful, if, for example, the hearer experiences the same optical illusion. If the speaker then proceeds down the path and investigates the place where he thought there was a man carrying a walking stick, only to find that there is nothing there about which he is willing to say, "That is what I was referring to," he may withdraw or cancel the reference, since his intention to get the hearer to identify an object is likely to dissipate when the object turns out not to exist.

The conclusion to be drawn from this analysis of Donnellan's examples is that although he has demonstrated that definite descriptions can be used in a variety of circumstances, even by speakers who know next to nothing about the intended referents, he has not shown that they can be used in a variety of ways. All the cases he cites in which definite descriptions are used conform to the analysis of referring that we gave in sections V and VI of Chapter Nine.

III. Alternative Analyses of These Examples

Despite the absence of any defensible theoretical base, Donnellan's "attributive use" is firmly entrenched in the philosophy of language; hardly an article is written on the subject of reference that does not include some discussion of it. Because of this entrenchment, it is not enough to refute the referential/attributive distinction; one must also account for its intuitive appeal and provide an alternative explanation for the phenomena that seem to support it.

Much of the plausibility of the referential/attributive distinction lies in the series of contrasting scenarios quoted in section II. But the fact that the scenarios in each pair are different in important ways, ways that affect the nature of the communication that takes place, does not imply either that the same difference is involved in each pair of examples, or that any of the differences involved is relevant to distinguishing between uses of definite descriptions. Neither of these last two propositions is true, as we shall see.

Let's return to Donnellan's first pair of examples, the strange case of "Smith's murderer." We come upon Smith's mutilated body and assume that he has been murdered; further, the speaker surmises (on the basis of his beliefs about the visible mutilation, Smith's likable character, and certain general principles concerning mutilators of likable persons) that Smith's murderer must be insane. The salient fact about this scenario is that the speaker knows almost nothing about the person he is referring to. He didn't see the crime committed; he doesn't know the name of the perpetrator; he could not pick anyone out of a lineup. If we stipulate that the speaker knows the intended referent only under the misdescription 'Smith's murderer', then it is this epistemic impoverishment, rather than any essentiality of the description, that ensures that no other description could 'do the same job." Given any additional knowledge, even of the descriptive sort, other descriptions become available: 'Smith's mutilator', 'the person who attacked Smith', or even (if the speaker is a Sherlock Holmes type) 'the lame Ukrainian scientologist who left a half-smoked Tiparillo among the rhododendra'.

In scenario II, the speaker and the hearer are not similarly deprived. The intended referent, Jones, has been on public display in the courtroom; the label 'Smith's murderer' has virtually been pinned to his lapel by his accusers; the speaker may even have been present at the trial, not just seeing the effects of Jones's putative insanity, but acquainting himself with their cause. Naturally the speaker can use another description to do the same job; he has a large variety to choose from, because he knows much more about the intended referent.

Does the fact that the speaker in scenario II has this epistemic advantage mean that he uses the description in a completely different way? No. In both cases the speaker is introducing an object for categorization, and trying to enable the hearer to identify the object; it is just that in scenario II the speaker has more resources to work with.

A similar epistemic difference between the speakers in the second pair of examples accounts for the intuition that they are not doing quite the same thing with the definite description 'the man drinking a martini'. In the "referential" case, the speaker perceives his intended referent and could, if he chose, use some other description that discernibly fits or applies to the referent in order to get the hearer to identify him. In the "attributive" case, no such option is open to the speaker, because he does not know who he is talking about, except under the description provided by his informant. (Actually, as in all of Donnellan's "attributive" cases, the speaker could in fact resort to alternative descriptions, despite his lack of information: 'the disruptor of the party', 'the unfortunate victim of Demon Rum', 'the insensitive bozo'.) It is therefore unnecessary to posit any difference in use.

In the third pair of examples the seeming difference in the communicative force of the description has an origin of still another sort. The distinction we need in order to explain these cases is Grice's distinction between what a speaker says and what he conversationally implies. In the "referential" example, what the speaker says can be reported thus: The speaker requested the hearer to bring him the book on the table. If there is a book on the table the request can be fulfilled; if there is no book on the table, the request as it is literally expressed cannot be fulfilled, contrary to Donnellan's claim. There is, however, a different request that can be obeyed, a request that is conversationally implied rather than expressly stated: Given that the speaker has an interest in an object that is a book and not merely in any object that happens to be situated on a table, the speaker conversationally implies that a book should be brought to him even if the book is not on the table. Moreover, if the hearer knows that the speaker has an interest in a specific book – say, in our Lulu/Elaine version, *Nurse in Love* – then, if Elaine goes to the table and finds *A Short History of Agricultural Implements* on the table and *Nurse in Love* beside it, she will do better to obey the conversationally implied request, disregarding the literally expressed one.

Analogous remarks apply to the other example in the pair, the "attributive" example. What the speaker says is precisely the same: She requests the hearer to bring her the book on the table. What the speaker conversationally implies is different, because the speaker's interests and intentions are, and are known to be, different. Given that Lulu has an interest in having *no object* on the antique table, and perhaps in examining any clues that would enable her to find out who has been putting things on her table, then what she conversationally implies is that Elaine bring her what is on the antique table (or any clue that is in the vicinity). If Elaine returns and tells Lulu that her request cannot be obeyed, owing to the fact that there are no books on the table, but only a large, jagged rock, Lulu would be justifiably piqued; she would not excuse Elaine's uncooperativeness on the grounds that she had used the description attributively.

In short, the differences that Donnellan points out, when genuine, can be fully accounted for in terms of other distinctions that are needed in a theory of linguistic communication, without positing a distinction between two uses of definite descriptions. Inasmuch as he does not succeed in making this distinction clear either by his characterizations or by his examples, it would be best simply to abandon it.

Chapter Eleven:
The Causal and Description Theories of Reference

I. Donnellan's Causal Theory of Reference

Donnellan presents his article, "Reference and Definite Descriptions," as if it were a piece of arbitration between Russell and Strawson. In fact, he intends it as something different and much more important than that; it was his way of introducing a new and general theory of referring, a theory he likes to call "The Historical Chain Theory of Referring," but which is more commonly called "The Causal Theory of Referring."

One way to put the main thesis of "Reference and Definite Descriptions," is this: there are two different uses of definite descriptions: the attributive and the referential uses. A definite description is supposedly used attributively, as we have seen, if and only if it is used to pick out whoever or whatever fits that description. A description is used referentially if it is used to pick out the object that the speaker has in mind. This way of putting Donnellan's main thesis is perfectly accurate, yet misleading if it is taken to imply that Donnellan has equal interests in both the attributive and referential use. In fact, Donnellan's primary and dominant interest is in the referential use. He discusses the attributive use only in order to put it aside; and it is important for him to point it out in order to put it aside because he thinks that a lot of philosophers, most prominently Russell and Strawson, have confused the attributive with the referential use, and he wants to isolate the referential use.

Donnellan's primary and dominant interest in the referential use comes to the fore in his next major article, "Proper Names and Identifying Descriptions." The ostensible point of this article, like that of "Reference and Definite Descriptions," seems to be purely critical. Viewed as a critical piece, the main point of "Proper Names and Identifying Descriptions" can be put this way: The dominant theory of referring, the Description Theory, is false.

The term "The Causal Theory of Reference" may be misleading. It sounds like a competitor to the "Speech Act Theory of Reference" that I presented in the last chapter. It is not. The two theories are used to answer different questions. The Speech Act Theory attempts to answer the question, "What is reference?". The Speech Act Theory of Reference gives an analysis of the concept of reference and as such it must conform to the adequacy conditions for analysis. For example, the Speech Act Theory cannot use the concept of reference in its analysans without being criticizable for being circular. In contrast, the Causal Theory attempts to answer the question, "Given that a speaker or expression refers to an object, what determines which object is the referent?" (See Kripke (1972), pp. 29, 31−32). As this question indicates, the Causal Theory presupposes, and hence is permitted to use, the concept of reference. A revealing instance of this use of the notion of reference to explicate the causal theory of reference occurs in an essay by Gareth Evans, who discusses the theory as applied to proper names:

> The Causal Theory . . . goes something like this. A speaker, using a name 'NN' on a particular occasion will denote some item x if there is a causal chain of *reference-preserving links* leading back from his use on that occasion ultimately to the item x itself being involved in a name-acquiring transaction such as an explicit dubbing or the more gradual process whereby nicknames stick (Evans (1973), p. 197).

Kripke holds that no theory of reference can use the notion of reference for the reason that such a theory would be circular. It is not clear what he means by this since in his own statement of his theory he uses the notion of reference and acknowledges that its use cannot be eliminated (Kripke (1972), p. 97). He is wrong about the reason as it applies to the question, "Given that a speaker or expression refers to an object, what determines which object is the referent?". An answer to the second question can use the notion of reference, but that notion alone is not sufficient to answer the question. The second question presupposes the notion of reference and asks something more about it; so something more than a mere appeal to the concept is required (cf. Kripke (1972), p. 68−70; 93; 96−97).

The Causal Theory of Reference is the ostensible competitor of the Description Theory of Reference. Indeed, any explanation of the Causal Theory will be incomplete or misleading if it does not contain some discussion of what proponents of the Causal Theory think is wrong with the Description Theory. Consequently, I will proceed to say something about the Description Theory.

II. *The Description Theory*

The Description Theory can be stated briefly as adherence to what Donnellan calls "The Principle of Identifying Description," which he divides into two parts. First, the users of a proper name must be able to supply a set of descriptions in answer to the question, "To whom (or what) does the name refer?". Second, the principle states that the referent of a proper name, if any, is "that object that uniquely fits a 'sufficient' number of the descriptions in the set of identifying descriptions (Donnellan (1972), p. 360). The Description Theory is associated with the jointly unlikely names of Frege,

XI The Causal and Description Theories of Reference

Russell, Strawson and Searle, and it is pretty clear that each of them adhered to the Principle of Identifying Descriptions. Since the Description Theory is most elaborate and explicit in the work of Strawson and Searle, I shall quote from just these two. Strawson says,

> it is no good using a name for a particular unless one knows who or what is referred to by the use of the name. A name is worthless without a backing of descriptions which can be produced on demand to explain the application (Strawson (1959), p. 20).

Searle says

> Suppose we ask the users of the name "Aristotle" to state what they regard as certain essential and established facts about him. Their answers would be a set of uniquely referring descriptive statements. Now what I am arguing is that the descriptive force of "this is Aristotle" is to assert that a sufficient but so far unspecified number of these statements are true of this object (Searle (1969), p. 171).

According to the Description Theory, the object referred to is that object that fits most of the descriptions which the speakers associated with the object. A speaker refers to whatever object those descriptions fit. As regards proper names, associated with each proper name is some cluster of descriptions that "back up" the application of that proper name. A proper name refers to whatever object a weighted most of those descriptions fit. The "weighted most" feature of the Description Theory takes account of the relative importance and diversity of the descriptions that speakers associate with objects. Suppose that Smith and Jones associate the following descriptions with the name "Aristotle":

Smith	Jones
the best student of Plato	the best student of Plato
the teacher of Alexander	the teacher of Alexander
the author of *Metaphysics*	the author of *Metaphysics*
the philosopher from Stagira	the philosopher from Stagira
the husband of Xantippe	the most overrated philosopher

Both Jones and Smith have a mix of true and false beliefs about Aristotle. Yet both refer to Aristotle because most of their associated descriptions and the most important ones fit Aristotle and no one else.

III. Donnellan's Counterexamples to the Description Theory

The main feature of Donnellan's "Proper Names and Identifying Descriptions" is a set of counterexamples to the Description Theory. Viewed solely as counterexamples they are not very interesting. Let's make a more general point. Viewed solely as a counterexample, no counterexample is very interesting. A counterexample shows that a theory is false; but if a counterexample does no more than this, then it is not very interesting because merely to learn that some theory is false is not sufficiently instructive as to what is true to be very interesting. For example, it is very easy — as Donnellan shows — to provide a counterexample to the Description Theory as it applies to what Smith and Jones believe about Aristotle: "*theoretically* Aristotle might turn out to be the person who did *not* write the *Metaphysics*, was *not* the teacher of Alexander, etc.; that is to say, a person who does not fit a sufficient number of the descriptions we, as users of the name would now supply" (Donnellan (1972), p. 367); yet that failure of fit would not prevent us from referring to Aristotle. The reason a mere counterexample is uninteresting is that the number of possible, false theories is infinite, and simply to know that one of an infinite number of theories is false is not very helpful. Also, there is a big difference between a counterexample that can be gotten around by some fine tuning of the theory and a counterexample that goes to the heart of the theory and shows that the theory is fundamentally misconceived. Further, a good counterexample is one that points in the direction of an alternative account of the phenomenon involved. Donnellan's counterexamples are good ones. He presents several. Each is rather artificial and complex, and may easily give rise to the false impression that they are not very interesting. To indicate what his counterexamples are like I will quote one extensively, with the promise that at the end of it I will explain what this counterexample has in common with the others and what about it makes it interesting.

> Imagine the following circumstances: Perhaps in an experiment by psychologists interested in perception a subject is seated before a screen of uniform color and large enough to entirely fill his visual field. On the screen are painted two squares of identical size and color, one directly above the other. The subject knows nothing of the history of the squares — whether one was painted before the other, etc. Nor does he know anything about their future. He is asked to give names to the squares and to say on what basis he assigns the names. With one complication to be noted later, it seems that the only way in which he can distinguish the squares through description is by their relative positions. So he might respond that he will call the top square 'alpha' and the bottom square 'beta'.
> The catch in the example is this: unknown to the subject, he has been fitted with spectacles that invert his visual field. Thus, the square he sees as apparently on top is really on the bottom and vice versa. Having now two names to work with we can imagine the subject using one of them to say something about one of the squares. Suppose he comes to believe (whether erroneously or not doesn't matter) that one of the squares has changed color. He might report, 'Alpha is now a different color'. But which square is he referring to? He would describe alpha as the square on top. And if this is the only uniquely identifying description at his command then according to the principle I am attacking he would have referred to the square that is on top. But given our knowledge of the presence and effect

XI The Causal and Description Theories of Reference 185

of the inverting spectacles and the ignorance of the subject about that, it seems clear that we should take him to be referring to, not the square on top, but the one that seems to him erroneously to be on top — the one on the bottom. We know why he describes 'alpha' the way he does; we expect changes in the square on the bottom to elicit from him reports of changes in alpha, etc. I think it would be altogether right to say that although he does not know it, he is talking about the square on the bottom even though he would describe it as 'the square on top'. If this is right, we seem to have a case in which the speaker's descriptions of what he is referring to when he uses a name do not yield the true referent so long as we stick to what is denoted by the descriptions he gives. The referent is something different and the thing actually denoted is not the referent (Donnellan (1972), p. 368–369).

What this counterexample has in common with the others are two features:

(a) the description the speaker uses does not fit the referent; and
(b) the object referred to is the causal source of the description that the speaker uses.

It is in virtue of feature (a) that the Description Theory is refuted. Feature (a) is the less important one. Feature (b) is the more important. For feature (b) points to the fact that the object referred to is causally related to the speaker. In the cases Donnellan presents in "Proper Names and Identifying Descriptions," the causal connection is close. In many other typical cases of referring the causal connection is often remote. Consider an example. Think back to ancient Egypt. There was a person, whom we know as Moses. He was given some Hebrew name, presumably, shortly after his birth, in some sort of name-creating act, either by dubbing, naming, pointing, or, perhaps, in the course of circumcision. Most, if not all of those who knew him, used that name to refer to him, and used it because others used it. Some of these users handed down that name to other potential users as they were introduced to discourse about that person. Even after that person died, the use of that name to refer continued to be handed down to other users. As the name gets handed down, changes in the name occur. The pronunciation of the language changes; dialects introduce other variations. Some Hebrew users translate the name into another language or transliterate it into another alphabet, and this causes further changes in the phonological and orthographic shape of the name. Other changes occur involving the name. Both by innocent error and the invention of myths, many of the things actually true of Moses get replaced by false beliefs. In the end, that is, today, nothing believed about Moses is true and only remnants, if that much, of the original shape of the name survive in users. And, yet — and this is what gives the Causal Theory of Names its force against the Description Theory, — as different as our descriptions are of Moses from that of his contemporaries, we refer to him (her!?) as successfully as they (Donnellan (1972), p. 362–363). Hopefully, most causal-referential chains are not so misleading as we have supposed the "Moses"-chain to be. I deliberately invented a distorting chain to emphasize that it is the referential links and not the fittingness of the description that is crucial. The vaguely historical account of the use of "Moses" to refer to . . . Moses explains why Donnellan likes the term, "The Historical Chain Theory of Reference." This account of the use of "Moses" is also a vaguely causal account: There was a person whom we know as Moses. He was given some Hebrew name in some sort of name-creating act, and this act of naming *caused* most, if not all, of those who knew him, to use that name to refer to him, and this use *caused* others to use it. ETC. What principally bothers Donnellan about calling the theory "The Causal Theory" is that not "all the links in the referential chain are causal" (Donnellan (1974), p. 216).

It does not bother him that the notion of cause used is vague (Donnellan (1974), p. 18).

Donnellan's Causal Theory of Reference has two parts: one part concerns how the referent of a proper name is determined; the other part concerns how the referent of a definite description is determined. So far we have been talking about the first part. The second part is easy to explain since it is something like a limiting case of the first. Just as no proper name needs to have a backing of definite descriptions that fit the referent, so also no definite description needs to have a definite description — not even itself — that fits the referent. That is the inexplicit, but underlying, point of "Reference and Definite Descriptions." A definite description can be used to refer to something that the description does not fit.

IV. *Kripke's Causal Theory of Names*

Kripke's views about proper names are often associated and even roughly identified with Donnellan's. However similar in some respects they might be, there is a crucial difference between them, a difference of which Kripke is aware (Kripke (1972), pp. 25–27; 87). Putting the difference starkly, we can say that while Donnellan's views belong to pragmatics, Kripke's views belong to semantics. Donnellan discusses the issue of what object a *speaker* refers to when he uses a proper name or definite description in various circumstances. Kripke, on the other hand, discusses the issue of what the meaning of a proper name is; more particularly, he asks, "Do proper names have a sense?" His answer is negative. His positive account of proper names is, roughly, that a proper name denotes the object with which the referential-causal chain begins. Notice again that this link is established by some kind of communicative act. A name n is semantically linked to an object o as part of some action such as dubbing, naming or pointing.

One consequence of Kripke's semantic interests, in contrast with Donnellan's pragmatic interests, is that Kripke's causal theory is a causal theory of proper names only and not a causal theory of definite descriptions. In

XI The Causal and Description Theories of Reference

other words, while Kripke recognizes the pragmatic fact that in some cases a speaker refers to an object that does not fit the description used, he does not count this object as the referent of the description. The referent of the description is whatever object uniquely fits the description. As Kripke puts it: "if you have a description of the form 'the x', and there is exactly one x such that Ox, that is the referent of the description" (Kripke (1972), p. 26; see also p. 87 n. 37). Thus, for Kripke, the referent of a definite description is the object, if any, that the definite description denotes. That is to say, Kripke considers "the Description Theory of Reference" true for descriptions, semantically treated. Definite descriptions are not semantically interesting to Kripke because they have senses; their senses are a function of the senses of their parts and the senses of their parts are not problematic.

Let's return to what Kripke holds about proper names.

> A rough statement of a theory might be the following: An initial 'baptism' takes place. Here the object may be named by ostension, or the reference of the name may be fixed by a description. When the name is 'passed from link to link', the receiver of the name must, I think, intend when he learns it to use it with the same reference as the man from whom he heard it. If I hear the name 'Napoleon' and decide it would be a nice name for my pet aardvark, I do not satisfy this condition (Kripke (1972), p. 96).

Kripke extends his views about proper names to terms for natural kinds, expressed by some count nouns (e.g. "cat" and "tiger"), mass nouns ("gold," "iron" and "water") and adjectives ("red," "hot," and "loud"). Just as proper names denote particulars, independently of the beliefs speakers have of the qualities of those particulars, so also common nouns denote kinds of particulars, independently of the beliefs speakers have of the properties of those kinds. He says,

> we use 'gold' as a term for a certain *kind* of thing. Others have discovered this kind of thing and we have heard of it. We thus as part of a community of speakers have a certain connection between ourselves and a certain kind of thing. The kind of thing is *thought* to have certain identifying marks. Some of these marks may not really be true of gold. We might discover that we are wrong about them. Further, there might be a substance which has all the identifying marks we commonly attributed to gold and used to identify it in the first place, but which is not the same kind of thing, which is not the same substance. We would say of such a thing that though it has all the appearances we initially used to identify gold, it is not gold. Such a thing is, for example, as we well know, iron pyrites or fool's gold. This is not another kind of gold. It's a completely different kind of thing which to the uninitiated person looks just like the substance which we discovered and called gold (Kripke (1972), pp. 118–119; see also pp. 127, 134).

V. Fixing the Referent of a Name

It is important to distinguish between *giving the meaning* of a word and *fixing the referent* of a word. Suppose someone wants to introduce a name into a language. He might do so by pointing to the intended nominatum and uttering the name with the right sort of intention. Alternatively, he might introduce the name via a description or set of descriptions. Thus, someone who introduces the name of Aristotle into discourse by saying, "Aristotle is the greatest man who studied with Plato" fixes the reference of the name "Aristotle." He does not, however, give the meaning of "Aristotle." If "Aristotle" meant "the greatest man who studied with Plato," then the sentence "Aristotle is not the greatest man who studied with Plato" would be a contradiction; it would be synonymous with "the greatest man who studied with Plato is not the greatest man who studied with Plato." Also, if "Aristotle" meant "the greatest man who studied with Plato," then "Aristotle" would denote different people in different possible worlds. But it is false that the denotation of "Aristotle" differs from world to world. It is trivially true to hold that Aristotle is the same person in all the possible worlds in which he exists, although his properties may be quite different (Kripke (1972), p. 57). Similarly, it is possible that the discoverer of Hesperus said, "I shall use 'Hesperus' as a name of the heavenly body appearing in yonder position in the sky," in order to fix the referent of that name (Kripke (1972), p. 57).

Kripke's distinction between fixing a referent and giving the meaning of a term might be used to explain how the Description Theory of Names goes wrong. Proponents of that theory confuse fixing the referent of a name with giving its meaning. They think that the cluster of descriptions associated with a name, say, "Aristotle" or "Moses" gives the meaning of the name when in fact it only fixes the referent by enabling their interlocutors (and themselves) to pick out the referent.

There is an irony, here, however, because, if the error committed by adherents of the Description Theory consists principally in confusing fixing the referent with giving the meaning of a name, then there is more truth to the Description Theory than the adherents of the Causal Theory would allow. For what Kripke seems to allow in virtue of his views about fixing the referent of a name, is that, as Strawson has said, a name is worthless without the backing of a description; what Kripke adds to this view is simply the observation that such descriptions do not give the meaning of the name but only fix its referent. This concession to the Description Theory is actually disastrous for the Causal Theory for this reason. In fixing the referent by using a description to back up his use of a name, a speaker can determine that the object his name refers to is not the object in the causal chain that gives rise to the act of reference. Let me explain this by sketching a counterexample to Kripke's theory of names. Suppose that all that we know about

Aristotle comes from one very large manuscript that contains all his known writings, including a short autobiography, in which Aristotle is referred to only by (the Greek word for) "I". Further suppose that this manuscript was transcribed by Aristotle's slave, who, having completed the manuscript affixed his own name at the end of it. The twist to the story is that Aristotle's slave was named "Aristotle," and it was because his name appeared at the end of the manuscript that later generations down to our own day use the name "Aristotle" to refer to the author of those manuscripts. And, although Aristotle's name is "Aristotle" because of our use of it, that was not the name he went by in ancient Greece. Now, according to the Causal Theory, when we use the name "Aristotle," we refer to Aristotle's slave and not Aristotle, because it is Aristotle's slave who plays the crucial causal role in our use of "Aristotle" to refer. When Aristotle's slave used his own name (also "Aristotle") at the end of the manuscript, he referred to himself and thereby began the causal-referential chain that has come down to us through history. And this is what is wrong with the theory. Although Aristotle's slave used "Aristotle" to refer to himself and began the causal chain, it is not Aristotle's slave that we refer to when we use the name "Aristotle." It is "Aristotle" that we refer to; and it is he whom we refer to because the referent of "Aristotle" is fixed by the description "the author of these manuscripts."

Other counterexamples have been constructed. Gareth Evans points out that originally "Madagascar" named part of the African mainland and not the island. Marco Polo mistook the referent of "Madagascar" and applied it to the island. According to the Causal Theory, "Madagascar" should be the name of part of the mainland still, since Marco Polo's use of it is causally tied to those earlier uses. Since "Magadascar" does not name any part of the mainland, the Causal Theory is false (Evans (1973), p. 202). And Kripke explains how David Lewis has extended Evans's counterexample: "David Lewis has pointed out that the same thing could have happened even if the natives had used 'Madagascar' to designate a mythical locality. So real reference can shift to another real reference, fictional reference can shift to real, and real to fictional. In all these cases, a present intention to refer to a given entity (or to refer fictionally) overrides the original intention to preserve reference in the historical chain of transmission. The matter deserves extended discussion. . . . I leave the problem for further work" (Kripke (1972), p. 163).

VI. *The Olympian Description Theory of Reference*

Discovering that Kripke's notion of fixing the referent of a name resurrects a central aspect of the Description Theory motivates some obvious questions. Although causal relations do not determine what object a speaker refers to, aren't these causal relations in some way relevant to the issue? And, since sometimes a speaker cannot supply a description that denotes the object he intends to refer to, what precise role does a description play in determining the referent? The answer to the first question is affirmative. Of course causal relations are relevant to what object gets referred to. All (or seemingly all) physical reality is inextricably bound up with all sorts of causal relations; so it would be very surprising if humans in communication were not. And we could agree with Kripke that "what is true is that it's in virtue of our connection with other speakers in the community, going back to the referent himself, that we refer to a certain man" (Kripke (1972), p. 94), except that the phrase "in virtue of" is too strong. Further, these causal/referential chains are usually operative in determining what is referred to. However, it is not these causal relations, but the fact that there is a description that could be given — usually if a person knows the historical chain) that determines what object is the referent.

Different intuitions motivate the Causal and the Descriptive Theories of Names (McKinsey (1978), pp. 174–175). The Description Theory is motivated by the belief that the user of a name must *have that object in mind* and having an object in mind requires some description that represents how that object is conceived. The Causal Theory is motivated by the belief that reference to an object is causally linked to previous uses of the name. Although the Causal and Description Theories are inconsistent, it is possible to formulate hybrid theories of reference that accommodate both intuitions (e. g. Devitt (1974), pp. 183–205). However, I think it is a mistake to try to accommodate both intuitions in the standard sort of way, because the two intuitions arise from viewing reference from two radically different perspectives. These two perspectives are a crucial part of the counterexamples constructed by proponents of the causal theory. First, notice that all their counterexamples involve two perspectives. There is the fallible and limited perspective of the users of the names and suppliers of the descriptions. Let's call them "mortals." And there is the infallible, unlimited perspective of the Causal Theorists, who stipulate what mortals say and believe. Let's call them "Olympians." What the Olympians do not seem to recognize is that, while they can make it the case that none of the mortals has a correct description for the referent of the name he uses, the Olympian always does. Recall Donnellan's psychology experiment. The poor subject wearing the inverted glasses is quite benighted. But Donnellan and all his readers are Olympians. We know that the referent of "alpha" is the square on the *bottom*. All the Olympians have an identifying description for "alpha." (In Donnellan's scenario, the scientists are quasi-Olympians since Donnellan has put them in possession of the identifying description. It would be easy, however, to fiddle with the scenario and darken their minds too, if they should suffer from *hubris*.) What is wrong with the Description Theory is that it requires the mortals to have the perspective of Olympians, to have sufficient knowledge that makes them infallible with respect to fixing their referents. But that is an impossible requirement to satisfy. The Causal Theory, in contrast, does not require the mortals to know the causal (or historical) links that are relevant. All the proponents of the Description Theory need to do to save their theory is to take the Olympian point of view. This is the clue we need to solve the problem of how referents are determined.

The answer to the second question is this: For every name there is a description that fixes the referent and thereby determines the referent, and this description is the one that a user of the name could and would give if he knew everything relevant to his use of the name. This is the Olympian Description Theory. It corrects the original Description Theory in two ways. First, it reduces the requirement that the user or users of an name actually be able to give an identifying description of the referent to the requirement that the user or users of a name potentially be able to give one. Second, it eliminates the idea of a cluster of descriptions. This is a good thing too. For the idea of having clusters of descriptions was motivated by the realization that individual speakers would fail to possess the name-fixing descriptions.

It has been suggested that the cluster view was an attempt to circumvent problems with what has been called "the first-in-mind view" of identifying descriptions (Ingber (1979), p. 729), the view that the description that fits the referent is the one that first comes to mind. I think the motivation was deeper. The cluster view attempts to describe the actual practice of mortals in trying to sort out their references, given their limited and fallible perspectives. Mortals, communicating with other mortals, actually do rely upon weighted clusters of descriptions. They do not and cannot have the Olympian view – only God (always) and philosophers (sometimes) – have it; and so the procedure sketched by the original Description Theory is the best available for mortals. Thus, proponents of the Description Theory tried to hedge their descriptions by pooling and weighting the resources of all the speakers. The hedge, however, doesn't work, because in the extreme cases that generate the counterexamples to the original Description Theory pooling descriptions amounts to nothing more than pooling mistakes.

Only one definite description is needed to fix the referent, not a cluster of them; the description chosen will take the causal/historical/referential chain into account; and the description need not be a description actually in the possession of any user of the name, just as the knowledge of the historical chain need not be. Kripke holds that a speaker's intention to refer is tied to chains of references. Thus, typically a speaker's intention to refer is referential, in the sense that the speaker intends his referent to be *the* object referred to by the person from whom the speaker acquired the name. Here we have a kind of Hegelian synthesis of the Causal and Description Theories of Reference.

Bibliography

(The date that follows the author's name is typically the initial date of publication or the date at which the material in that work was first widely disseminated in some form. I have not always given the original place of publication, but only the edition that I have used.)

Alston, William (1964). *The Philosophy of Language* (Englewood Cliffs: Prentice-Hall, Inc., 1964).
— (1974). "Semantic Rules, in Munitz and Unger (1974), pp. 17–48.
Austin, J. L. (1940). "The Meaning of a Word," in Austin (1970), pp. 55–75.
— (1955). How to Do Things with Words, 2nd edition, ed. J. O. Urmson and Marina Sbisa (Cambridge: Harvard University Press, 1975).
— (1956a). "Ifs and Cans," in Austin (1970), pp. 205–232.
— (1956b). "Performative Utterances," in Austin (1970), pp. 233–252.
— (1958). "Performative-Constative," in Caton (1963), pp. 22–54.
— (1970). *Philosophical Papers*, 2nd edition, ed. J. O. Urmson and G. J. Warnock (London: Oxford University Press, 1970).
Ayer, A. J. (1960), "Philosophy and Language," in *The Concept of a Person* (New York: St. Martin's Press, Inc., 1963), pp. 1–35.
— (1977). *Part of My Life* (Oxford: Oxford University Press, 1977).

Bach, Emmon and Robert T. Harms, eds. (1968). *Linguistic Universals* (New York: Holt, Rinehart and Winston, Inc., 1968).
Bach, Kent and Robert Harnish (1979). *Linguistic Communication and Speech Acts* (Cambridge: MIT Press, 1979).
Bennett, Jonathan (1976). *Linguistic Behavior* (Cambridge: Cambridge University Press, 1976).
Bergmann, Merrie (1982). "Metaphorical Assertions," *Philosophical Review* 91 (1982), 225–245.
Black, Max (1954). "Metaphor," in *Models and Metaphor* (Ithaca: Cornell University Press, 1954), pp. 41–60.
— (1979). "More on Metaphor," in Ortony (1979), 1–30.
Boer, Stephen (1972). "Reference and Identifying Descriptions," *Philosophical Review* 81 (1972), 208–228.

Carnap, Rudolf (1935). *Philosophy and Logical Syntax* (London: Kegan Paul, 1935).
— (1937). *The Logical Syntax of Language* (London: Routledge and Kegan Paul Ltd., 1937).

- (1942). *Introduction to Semantics* (Cambridge: Harvard University Press, 1942).
Carr, C. A. (1978). "Expression, Meaning, Conversation and Indirect Speech Acts," *Southwestern Journal of Philosophy*, 89–100.
Carroll, John B. (1953). *The Study of Language: A Survey of Linguistics and Related Disciplines in America* (Cambridge: Harvard University Press, 1953).
Caton, Charles E. (1963). *Philosophy and Ordinary Language* (Urbana: University of Illinois Press, 1963).
Chastain, Charles (1975). "Reference and Context," in Gunderson (1975), pp. 194–269.
Chomsky, Noam (1957). *Syntactic Structures*, (The Hague: Mouton, 1957).
- (1971). "Deep Structure, Surface Structure, and Semantic Interpretation," in *Semantics*, ed. Danny D. Steinberg and Leon A. Jakobovits (Cambridge: Cambridge University Press, 1971), pp. 183–216.
- (1975). *Reflections on Language* (New York: Pantheon Books, 1975).
Cohen, L. Jonathan (1971). "Some Remarks on Grice's Views About the Logical Particles of Natural Language," in *Pragmatics of Natural Languages* ed. Y. Bar-Hillel (New York: Humanities Press), pp. 50–68.
- (1975). "The Semantics of Metaphor," in Ortony (1975), pp. 64–77.
Cohen, Ted (1975). "Figurative Speech and Figurative Acts," *Journal of Philosophy*, 72 (1975).
- (1976). "Notes on Metaphor," *Journal of Aesthetics and Art Criticism* 34 (1976), 249–259.
Cole, Peter (1978). *Syntax and Semantics: Pragmatics*, vol. 7 (New York: Academic Press, 1978).
Cole, Peter and Jerry L. Morgan (1975). *Syntax and Semantics: Speech Acts*, vol. 3 (New York: Academic Press, 1975).

Dalrymple, Haughton (1978). "A Comparison of Mead's Theory of Linguistic Communication with that of Grice and Strawson," in *The Individual and Society*, ed. Michael Jones *et al.* (Norman: The University of Oklahoma Press, 1978), pp. 157–166.
Davidson, Donald (1967). "Truth and Meaning," in Rosenberg and Travis (1971), pp. 450–465.
- (1968). "On Saying That," in Davidson and Harman (1975), pp. 152–161.
- (1970). "Semantics for Natural Languages," in *On Noam Chomsky*, ed. Gilbert Harman (Garden City: Doubleday, 1974), pp. 242–252.
- (1977). "The Method of Truth in Metaphysics," in French, Uehling, and Wettstein (1979), pp. 294–304.
- (1978). "What Metaphors Mean," *Critical Inquiry* 5 (1978), 31–47.
Davidson, Donald and Gilbert Harman, ed. (1972), *Semantics of Natural Languages* (New York: Humanities Press Inc., 1972).

Donnellan, Keith (1966). "Reference and Definite Descriptions," in Rosenberg and Travis (1971), pp. 195–211.
— (1972). "Proper Names and Identifying Descriptions," in Davidson and Harman (1972), pp. 356–379.
— (1974). "Speaking of Nothing," in Schwartz (1977), pp. 216–244.
— (1978). "Speaker Reference, Descriptions and Anaphora," in French, Uehling and Wettstein (1979), pp. 23–44.
Dretske, Fred (1972). "Contrastive Statements," *Philosophical Review* 81 (1972), 411–437.
Dummett, Michael (1956). "Nominalism," in *Essays on Frege*, ed. E. D. Klemke (Chicago: University of Illinois Press, 1968), pp. 321–336.
— (1958). "Truth," in Pitcher (1964), pp. 93–111.
— (1973). *Frege: The Philosophy of Language* (New York: Harper and Row, 1973).
Evans, Gareth (1973). "The Causal Theory of Names," in Schwartz (1977), pp. 192–215.
Findlay, J. N. (1963). *Meinong's Theory of Objects and Complexes*, 2nd ed. (Oxford: Oxford University Press, 1963).
Firth, J. R. (1951). "General Linguistics and Descriptive Grammar," *Transactions of the Philological Society*, 1950 (London: 1951).
Flew, Antony ed. (1951). *Logic and Language,* (Garden City: Doubleday & Company Inc., 1965).
Fodor, Janet Dean (1977). *Semantics: Theories of Meaning* (New York: Thomas Y. Crowell Company, 1977).
Fodor, Jerry A. and Jerrold J. Katz, ed. (1964). *The Structure of Language: Readings in the Philosophy of Language* (Englewood Cliffs: Prentice-Hall Inc., 1964).
Fotion, N. (1971). "Master Speech Acts," *Philosophical Quarterly* 21 (1971), 232–243.
— (1979). "Speech Activity and Language Use," *Philosophia* 8 (1979), 615–638.
Frege, Gottlob (1960). *Philosophical Writings*, ed. Peter Geach and Max Black (Oxford: Basil Blackwell, 1960).
— (1967). "The Thought," in *Philosophy of Logic*, second edition, ed. P. F. Strawson (Oxford: Oxford University Press, 1967).
French, Peter, Theodore E. Uehling, Jr., and Howard K. Wettstein (1979), *Contemporary Perspectives in the Philosophy of Language* (Minneapolis: The University of Minnesota Press, 1979).
Fries, Charles (1954). "Meaning and Linguistic Analysis," in *Theory of Meaning*, ed. Adrienne and Keith Lehrer (Englewood Cliffs: Prentice-Hall Inc., 1970).
Gardiner, Alan H. (1951). *The Theory of Speech and Language*, 2nd ed. (Oxford: Oxford University Press, 1951).

Geach, Peter (1950). "Subject and Predicate," *Mind* 59 (1950), 461–482.
– (1962). *Reference and Generality*, emended edition (Ithaca: Cornell University Press, 1968).
Graham, Keith (1977). *J. L. Austin: A Critique of Ordinary Language* (Sussex: The Harvester Press, 1977).
Green, O. H. (1977). "Semantic Rules and Speech Acts," *Southwestern Journal of Philosophy* 8 (1977), 141–150.
Grice, H. P. (1957). "Meaning," in Rosenberg and Travis (1971), pp. 436–444.
– (1961). "The Causal Theory of Perception," *Proceedings of the Aristotelian Society*, Supplementary Volume 35 (1961), 121–152.
– (1968). "Utterer's Meaning, Sentence-Meaning and Word-Meaning," in Searle (1971), pp. 54–70.
– (1969). "Utterer's Meaning and Intentions," *Philosophical Review* 78 (1969), 147–177.
– (1975). "Logic and Conversation," in Cole and Morgan (1975), pp. 41–58.
– (1978). "Further Notes on Logic and Conversation," in Cole (1978), pp. 113–127.
– (1981). "Presupposition and Conversational Implicature," in *Syntax and Semantics: Radical Pragmatics* (New York: Academic Press, 1981), 183–198.
Gunderson, Keith, ed. (1975). *Language, Mind and Knowledge* (Minneapolis: University of Minnesota Press, 1975).

Hare, R. M. (1952). *The Language of Morals* (Oxford: Oxford University Press, 1952).
Hancher, Michael (1980). "How to Play Games with Words: Speech-act Jokes," *Journal of Literary Semantics* 9 (1980), 20–29.
Harman, Gilbert (1968). "Three Levels of Meaning," in Steinberg and Jakabovits (1971), pp. 66–75.
–, ed. (1974). *On Noam Chomsky* (Garden City: Doubleday, 1974).
Hawkes, Terence (1977). *Structure and Semiotics* (Berkeley: University of California Press, 1977).
Heath, Peter (1974). *The Philosopher's Alice* (New York: St. Martin's Press, 1974).
Hopper, Robert (1978a). "Content, Form, and Implication: The case of the Missing Premises," Speech Communication Association, Minneapolis (November, 1978).
– (1978b). "Logic-In-Use Among Everyday Arguers: The Rules of First-Speak," Speech Communication Association, Minneapolis (November, 1978).
Hymes, Dell (1972). "Review of 'Noam Chomsky', in Harman (1974), pp. 316–333.

Ingber, Warren (1979). "The Descriptional View of Referring: Its Problems and Prospects," *The Journal of Philosophy* 76 (1979), 725–738.

Kempson, Ruth (1975), *Presupposition and the Delimitation of Semantics* (Cambridge: Cambridge University Press, 1975).
– (1977). *Semantic Theory* (Cambridge: Cambridge University Press, 1977).

Kim, Jaegwon (1977). "Perception and Reference without Causality," *The Journal of Philosophy* 74 (1977), 606–620.

Kripke, Saul (1972), *Naming and Necessity* (Cambridge: Harvard University Press, 1980).
– (1971). "Identity and Necessity," in Schwartz (1977), pp. 66–101.
– (1977). "Speaker Reference and Semantic Reference," in French, Uehling and Wettstein (1979), pp. 6–27.

Landesman, Charles (1972). "Remarks on Reference and Action," in MacKay and Merrill (1972), pp. 105–118.

Lewis, David (1974), "Language, Languages and Grammar," in Harman (1974) pp. 253–266.

Lindsay, Peter H. and Donald A. Norman (1977), *Human Information Processing* 2nd edition (New York: Academic Press, 1977).

Linsky, Leonard (1967). *Referring* (London: Routledge and Kegan Paul, 1967).
– (1977). *Names and Descriptions* (Chicago: The University of Chicago Press, 1977).

Lyons, John (1977). *Semantics* vol. 1 (Cambridge: Cambridge University Press, 1977).

MacKay, Alfred (1968). "Mr. Donnellan and Humpty Dumpty on Referring," *Philosophical Review* 77 (1968), 197–202.

MacKay, Alfred F. and Daniel D. Merrill, ed. (1972). *Issues in the Philosophy of Language* (New Haven; Yale University Press, 1976).

McKinsey, Michael (1978). "Names and Intentionality," *Philosophical Review* 87 (1978), 171–200.

Martinich, A. P. (1975). "Sacraments and Speech Acts," *The Heythrop Journal* 16 (1975), 405–417.
– (1976). "Russell's Theory of Meaning and Descriptions (1905–1920), *Journal of the History of Philosophy* 14 (1976), pp. 183–201.
– (1980). "Infallibility," *Religious Studies* 16 (1980), 15–27.

Meiland, Jack (1970). *Talking About Particulars* (New York: Humanities Press, 1970).

Mill, John Stuart (1881). *Philosophy and Scientific Method*, ed. Ernest Nagel (New York: Hafner Publishing Company, 1950).

Moore, G. E. (1942). "Reply to My Critics," in Schilpp (1942), pp. 533–677.

Morris, Charles (1938). *Foundations of the Theory of Signs, International Encyclopedia of Unified Science* vol. 2, no. 2 (Chicago: University of Chicago Press, 1938).
Munitz, Milton (1974). *Existence and Logic* (New York: New York University Press, 1974).
Munitz Milton and Peter Unger ed. (1974). *Semantics and Philosophy* (New York: New York University Press, 1974).
Nofsinger, Robert E. (1975). "The Demand Ticket: A Conversational Device for Getting the Floor," *Speech Monographs* 45 (1975), 1–9.
Norman, Donald A. and David E. Rumelhart (1975). "Reference and Comprehension," in *Explorations in Cognition*, ed. Donald A. Norman and David E. Rumelhart (San Francisco: W. H. Freeman and Company, 1975), pp. 65–87.

O'Connell, Marvin R. (1974). *The Counter Reformation (1559–1610)* (New York: Harper Row Publishers, 1974).
Ortony, Andrew (1976). "Beyond Literal Similarity," *Psychological Review* 86 (1976), 161–180.
– ed. (1979a), *Metaphor and Thought* (Cambridge:
– (1979b). "The Role of Similarity in Similes and Metaphors," in Ortony (1979a), pp. 186–201. Cambridge University Press, 1979).

Pitcher, George, ed. (1964). *Truth* (Englewood Cliffs: Prentice-Hall, 1964).
Philips, D. Z. (1979). "Philosophy and Commitment," a paper delivered at the University of Texas at Austin, November, 1979.
Platts, Mark (1979), *Ways of Meaning* (London: Routledge and Kegan Paul, 1979).
Putnam, Hilary (1970). "Is Semantics Possible?" in Schwartz, pp. 102–118.
– (1973). "Meaning and Reference," in Schwartz (1977), pp. 119–132.

Quine, W. V. (1960). *Word and Object* (Cambridge: MIT Press, 1960).
– (1972). "Methodological Reflections on Current Linguistic Theory," in Davidson and Harman (1972), pp. 442–454.

Rosenberg, Jay and Charles Travis, eds. (1971). *Readings in the Philosophy of Language* (Englewood Cliffs: Prentice-Hall, 1971).
Russell, Bertrand (1903). *The Principles of Mathematics* 2nd ed. (New York: W. W. Norton & Company Inc., 1937).
– (1905). "On Denoting," in Russell (1956), pp. 41–56.
– (1912). *The Problems of Philosophy* (London: Oxford University Press, 1959).
– (1918). "Philosophy of Logical Atomism," in Russell (1956), pp. 175–281.

- (1919). *"Introduction to Mathematical Philosophy* (London: George Allen and Unwin Ltd., 1919).
- (1956). *Logic and Knowledge: Essays (1901–1950)*, ed. Robert C. Marsh (London: George Allen and Unwin Ltd., 1956).
- (1959). *My Philosophical Development* (London: George Allen and Unwin Ltd., 1959).

Ryle, Gilbert (1932), "Systematically Misleading Expressions," in Flew (1951), pp. 13–40.
- (1953). "Ordinary Language," in Caton (1963), pp. 108–127.
- (1961). "Use, Usage and Meaning," in *Collected Works* vol. 2 (London: Hutchinson, 1971), pp. 407–414.

Schiffer, Stephen (1972). *Meaning* (New York: Oxford University Press, 1972).
Schilpp, P. A., ed. (1942). *The Philosophy of G. E. Moore* (Evanston: Northwestern University Press, 1942).
Schwartz, Stephen P. (1978). "Putnam on Artifacts," *Philosophical Review* 87 (1978), 566–574.
- ed. (1977). *Naming, Necessity and Natural Kinds* (Ithaca: Cornel University Press, 1977).
Searle, John R. (1966). "Assertions and Aberrations," in *British Analytical Philosophy*, ed. Bernard Williams and Alan Montefiore (London: Routledge & Kegan Paul, 1966), pp. 41–54.
- (1968). "Austin on Locutionary and Illocutionary Acts," in Rosenberg and Travis (1971), pp. 262–275.
- (1969). *Speech Acts* (Cambridge: Cambridge University Press, 1969).
- (1971a). "Introduction," in Searle (1971b), pp. 1–12.
- ed. (1971b). *The Philosophy of Language* (London: Oxford University Press, 1971).
- (1972). "Chomsky's Revolution in Linguistics," in Harman (1974), pp. 2–33.
- (1975a). "Indirect Speech Acts," in Searle (1979a), pp. 30–57.
- (1975b). "The Logical Status of Fictional Discourse," in Searle (1979), pp. 58–75.
- (1975c). "A Taxonomy of Illocutionary Acts," in Searle (1979a), pp. 1–29.
- (1979a). *Expression and Meaning* (Cambridge: Cambridge University Press, 1979).
- (1979b). "Metaphor," in Searle (1979a), pp. 76–116.
- (1979c). "Referential and Attributive," in Searle (1979a), pp. 137–161.
Shwayder, David (1972). "Reflections on Kripke," in MacKay and Merrill (1972), pp. 43–78.
Stampe, Dennis (1968). "Toward a Grammar of Meaning," in Harman (1974), pp. 267–302.

- (1974). "Attributives and Interrogatives," in Munitz (1974), pp. 159–196.
Steinberg, Danny D. and Leon Jakobovits, *Semantics: An Interdisciplinary Reader in Philosophy, Linguistics and Psychology* (Cambridge University Press, 1971).
Stevenson, Charles (1944). *Ethics and Language* (New Haven: Yale University Press, 1944).
- (1963). *Facts and Values* (New Haven: Yale University Press, 1963).
Strawson, P. F. (1950a). "On Referring," in Strawson (1971), pp. 1–27.
- (1950b). "Truth," in Strawson (1971), pp. 190–213.
- (1952). *Introduction to Logical Theory* (London: Methuen Company Ltd., 1952).
- (1959). *Individuals* (London: Methuen & Company Ltd., 1959).
- (1961). "Singular Terms and Predication," in Strawson (1971), pp. 53–74.
- (1964a). *The Bounds of Sense* (London: Methuen & Company Ltd., 1964).
- (1964b). "Identifying Reference and Truth-Values," in Strawson (1971), pp. 75–95.
- (1964c). "Intention and Convention in Speech Acts," in Strawson (1971), pp. 149–169.
- (1971). *Logico-Linguistic Papers* (London: Methuen & Company Ltd., 1971).
- (1974). *Subject and Predicate in Logic and Grammar* (London: Methuen & Company Ltd., 1974).
Stroll, Avrum (1961). "Meaning, Referring and the Problem of Universals," *Inquiry* 2 (1961), 107–122.
- (1975). "Russell's 'Proof'," *Canadian Journal of Philosophy* 5 (1975), 653–662.
- (1978). "Four Comments on Russell's Theory of Descriptions," *Canadian Journal of Philosophy* 8 (1978), 147–155.

Tarski, Alfred (1933). "The Concept of Truth in Formalized Languages," in *Logic, Semantics, Metamathematics* (Oxford: Oxford University Press, 1956, pp. 152–278.
- (1944). "The Semantic Conception of Truth and the Foundations of Semantics," *Philosophy and Phenomenological Research* 4 (1943–1944), 341–376.
Taylor, Isaac (n.d.). *Words and Places: Illustrations of History, Ethnology and Geography* (New York: E. P. Dutton & Company, n.d.).

Vendler, Zeno (1972). *Res Cogitans* (Ithaca: Cornell University Press, 1972).

— (1972b). "Illocutionary Suicide," in MacKay and Merrill (1972), pp. 135—145.
— (1976). "Thinking of Individuals," *Nous* 10 (1976), 35—46.

Walker, Ralph C. S. (1975). "Conversational Implicatures," in *Meaning, Reference and Necessity* ed. Simon Blackburn (Cambridge: Cambridge University Press, 1975), pp. 133—181.
Warnock, G. J. (1970). "Words and Sentences," in Wood and Pitcher (1970), pp. 267—282.
Whitehead, Alfred North and Bertrand Russell (1910). *Principia Mathematica to *56* (Cambridge: Cambridge University Press, 1970).
Wood, Oscar P. and George Pitcher, eds. (1970), *Ryle: A Collection of Essays* (Garden City: Doubleday & Company Inc., 1970).
Wittgenstein, Ludwig (1922). *Tractatus Logico-Philosophicus*; republished with a new translation by D. F. Pears and B. F. McGuiness (London: Routledge and Kegan Paul, 1961).
— (1953). *Philosophical Investigations,* ed. G. E. M. Anscombe (Oxford: Basil Blackwell, 1953).
— (1958). *The Blue and Brown Books* (New York: Harper & Row, 1958). Publishers, 1958).

Ziff, Paul (1967). "On H. P. Grice's Account of Meaning," in Rosenberg and Travis (1971), pp. 444—449.
— (1979). "About Reference," *Studies in Language* 3 (1979), 305—311.

Index

Addresse, 98, 122
Adverbial force-words, 71–72
Advoking, 30
Anaxagoras, 5
Apologizing, 54–56
Arguing, 96
Aristotle, 3, 8
Attributive use, chapter ten
Audience, 122
Austin, J. L., 7–9, 11, 45–50, 56, 90, 135
Axiom of existence, 153–58

Behabitives, 56
Bennett, Jonathan, 135
Bergmann, Merrie, 80
Black, Max, 82, 90, 91
Brentano, Franz, 8

Carnap, Rudolf, 12
Causal Theory of Names, 181–2, 188–90
Chomsky, Noam, 9, 72
Circumlocutionary acts, 60
Cohen, L. Jonathan, 90–92
Cohen, Ted, 88–89
Commissives, 56, 57
Communication, 3, 9–10, 17–19
   linguistic, 4, 10–11, 17–19, 124. *See also* Conversation.
   philosophy of, 10, 12–13, 134
Conditionals, 107–09
Conjunction, 105–107, 109
Conversation, 19–21
Conversational implicature, 37–39, 44, 179. *See also* implication
Constatives 46–47
Convoking, 30
Cooperative principle, 20–22, 26, 36, 38, 43, 106, 152, 167

Davidson, Donald, 5, 9, 83, 135, 137
Definite Descriptions, 136–37, 143–48
Dennett, Daniel, 101–2
Descartes, Rene, 8
Descriptions,
   definite, 136–37, 143–48
   indefinite, 141–42

Description Theory of Names, 182–6, 188–90
Disjunction, 109–12
Donnellan, Keith, 161, 163, 169–86, 190
Dretske, Fred, 69–70
Driver, Julia, 87

Entailment, 151–53
Evans, Gareth, 182, 189
Exercitives, 56, 57
Existence, 133, 153–58
Expositives, 56

Fallacies, chapter six
   accent, 97, 101–102
   ad baculum, 97
   ad hominem abusive, 97
   ad hominem circumstantial, 97, 100–101
   ad ignorantiam, 96, 99–100
   ad misericordiam, 97
   ad populum, 96, 99
   ad verecundiam, 96, 99
   amphiboly, 97, 101
   begging the question, 97
   complex question, 96, 98
   composition, 96, 99
   division, 96, 99
   equivocation, 97, 100
   false cause, 96, 99
   hasty generalization, 96
   ignoratio elenchi, 97
   special pleading, 99
   suppressed evidence, 96
   tu quoque, 97
Fodor, Janet Dean, 9
Forgiving, 54–56
Formalists, 105–06
Frege, Gottlob, 70, 182

Geach, Peter, 84
Goodman, Nelson, 9
Grice, H. P, chapters two, four and seven *passim*, 9, 17–18, 20–41, 63–67, 71–74, 79–80, 84, 89–90, 92, 96, 100, 104, 106–9, 111, 135, 179

Hymes, Dell, 9
Hyperbole, 85–86, 103

Identification, 160–66, 174
Illocutionary acts, 48–52, 67
　categories of, 56–61
　declarations, 60
　directives, 60
　commissives, 60
　expressives, 60
　institutional, 59
　operatives, 57
　representatives, 60
　verdictives, 56
Illocutionary force, 52, 67–69, 80
Implication, 112, 151–53
　linguistic, 65
　nonlinguistic, 65
Implicature. See Implication
Indefinite descriptions, 141–42
Indicating, 66–67
Indicative elements, 67–77
Informal Fallacies. See also Fallacies.
　taxonomy, 95–103
Informalists, 105–06
Institutional facts, 58
Interpreter, 18–19, 122, 129
Interrogatives, 57
Invoking, 30
Irony, 86, 103

James, William, 8
John of Salisbury, 6
Joseph, H. W. B., 95

Kahane, Howard, 95
Kant, Immanuel, 6, 21
Kempson, Ruth, 9, 29
Kripke, Saul, 182, 186–91

Language,
　nature of, 3–4, 10
　philosophy of, 1, 10
Leibniz, G. W., 8
Lewis, David, 128, 189
Locutionary acts, 48–50
Lindsay, Peter H., 9
Lying, 103

MacKay, Alfred, 162
Making-as-if-to-say, 80, 81, 82, 85, 86
Maxims of conversation, 11, 21, 43, 163
　manner, 21, 30–32, 97, 101, 105–07

quality, 21, 24–26, 31–32, 34, 35, 36, 80, 81, 86, 89, 96–102, 109
quantity, 21–24, 31–32, 34, 36, 38, 86, 96, 98, 102, 109–12
relation, 21, 23, 26–30, 31–32, 44, 82, 97–98, 100–101, 107–09
Maxims, nonfulfillment of
　being faced with a clash, 32–33, 36
　flouting, 32, 33, 34, 36–37, 80, 81, 102, 109
　opting out of, 32, 36, 102–03
　suspending, 33, 102–03
　violating 23, 32, 33–36, 98–99, 102–03
Meaning
　communicative, 113–25
　interpreter's, 18–19, 129–30
　natural, 113–115
　non-communicative, 114
　occasion, 127–30
　sentence, 106, 134–37, 141
　speaker, 11, 113, 125, 145–46
　timeless, 127–30, 150
　utterance, 127, 130
　utterer's 125
　word, 106, 134–37, 145–46
Meiland, Jack, 162
Meinong, A., 134–37, 154–55
Meiosis, 85–86, 103
Metaphor, chapter five, 103
　nonstandard, 86–89
　standard, 81–85
Mill, J. S., 134
Mood, 72–76
　imperative, 68, 72
　indicative, 41, 68, 72–76, 118
Moore's Paradox, 39–41
Morris, Charles, 12

Names, 137–39, 141, 143, 146–47
　Causal Theory of, 181–2, 188–90
　Description Theory of, 182–6, 188–90
　Olympian Description Theory of, 189–91
Newton, 8
Nonfullfillment of Maxims. See Maxims, nonfulfillment of.
Norman, Donald, 9

Olympian Theory of Names, 189–91
Operatives, 57
Overhearers, 122

Paradox of Reference and Existence, 133
Paskin, Maureen, 119
Performative utterances, 46–47, 67
Performative verbs, 45, 47–48, 51

Index

Perlocutionary acts, 48–49, 52
Phatic acts, 48, 50, 52
Philosophy, nature of, 7–9
Phonetic act, 48, 50, 52
Plato, 5
Predication, 67
Presupposition, 151–53
Promising, 52–54
Propositions, 51–52, 55, 59, 67–69, 70, 139–42, 144, 173

Quine, W. V., 9, 134

Reference, chapters eight through eleven *passim*.
  Speech Act Theory of, 149–67, 181
Rhetic acts, 48, 50, 173
Russell, Bertrand, 4, 7, 134–50, 153–55, 163, 181, 183
Ryle, Gilbert, 5

Sartre, Jean-Paul, 25
Saying-that, 65, 67–69, 71, 80, 81, 83, 85–86

Searle, John R., 9, 51–54, 56–61, 68–69, 70, 83, 90, 92–93, 101–02, 122–24, 153–58, 160–61, 163, 165, 183
Semantics, 10, 12, 111
Socrates, 5–6
Speech acts, 25–26, 43, 45–56, 89, 113, 127, 173
Stampe, Dennis, 170
Starter, 27, 35
Stopper, 27, 35
Strawson, P. F., 6, 28–29, 118–21, 134. 149–55, 159, 163, 181, 183, 188
Stroll, Avrum, 146
Syntax, 10, 12

Tarski, Alfred, 137
Tense, 71
Tone, 70–71

Urmson, J. O., 117

Vendler, Zeno, 6, 47, 56–57, 165–66
Verdictives, 56

Wittgenstein, Ludwig, 4, 6, 103, 134

GRUNDLAGEN DER KOMMUNIKATION
FOUNDATIONS OF COMMUNICATION

Edited by Roland Posner and Georg Meggle

E. M. Barth and E. C. W. Krabbe
From Axiom to Dialogue
A Philosophical Study of Logics and Argumentation

Octavo. XL, 337 pages. 1982. Cloth DM 138,– ISBN 3 11 008489 9 (Library Edition)

Causal Theories of Mind
Action, Knowledge, Memory, Perception, and Reference

Edited by Steven Davis

Octavo. X, 421 pages. 1983. Cloth DM 178,– ISBN 3 11 007730 2 (Library Edition)

Shalom Lappin
Sorts, Ontology, and Metaphor
The Semantics of Sortal Structure

Octavo. X, 177 pages. 1981. Cloth DM 72,– ISBN 3 11 008309 4 (Library Edition)

Meaning and Understanding
Edited by Herman Parret and Jacques Bouveresse

Octavo. X, 442 pages. 1981. Cloth DM 138,– ISBN 3 11 008116 4 (Library Edition)

David Schwarz
Naming and Referring
The Semantics and Pragmatics of Singular Terms

Octavo. XXXVIII, 196 pages. 1979. Cloth DM 72,– ISBN 3 11 007610 1

Meaning, Use, and Interpretation of Language
Edited by R. Bäuerle, Chr. Schwarze, A. v. Stechow

Octavo. X, 490 pages. 1983. Cloth DM 165,– ISBN 3 11 008901 7 (Library Edition)

Prices are subject to change

Walter de Gruyter  Berlin · New York